KORAN, KALASHNIKOV AND LAPTOP

*'the most dangerous moment for a bad government
is that in which it begins to reform'*

Alexis de Toqueville, *L'Ancien Régime et la Révolution*

ANTONIO GIUSTOZZI

Koran, Kalashnikov and Laptop

The Neo-Taliban Insurgency in Afghanistan

OXFORD

UNIVERSITY PRESS

OXFORD

UNIVERSITY PRESS

Oxford University Press, Inc., publishes works that further
Oxford University's objective of excellence
in research, scholarship, and education.

Oxford New York
Auckland Cape Town Dar es Salaam Hong Kong Karachi
Kuala Lumpur Madrid Melbourne Mexico City Nairobi
New Delhi Shanghai Taipei Toronto

With offices in
Argentina Austria Brazil Chile Czech Republic France Greece
Guatemala Hungary Italy Japan Poland Portugal Singapore
South Korea Switzerland Thailand Turkey Ukraine Vietnam

Published by Oxford University Press, Inc
198 Madison Avenue, New York, New York 10016

Published in the United Kingdom in 2009 by C. Hurst & Co. (Publishers) Ltd.

www.oup.com

Library of Congress Cataloging-in-Publication Data is available for this title
Giustozzi, Antonio
Koran, Kalashnikov, Laptop: The Neo-Taliban Insurgency in Afghanistan
ISBN 978-0-19-932-635-8

Printed in India

CONTENTS

PREFACE AND ACKNOWLEDGEMENTS

This book is part of a wider research project in which I engaged in 2003, investigating the sources of the crisis of the Afghan state. As the project started taking shape in early 2003, the Neo-Taliban insurgency was just beginning to manifest itself and at that time I was not planning a specific study to deal with it. By 2006, however, the situation had radically changed and the insurgency was manifesting itself in all its virulence in large parts of Afghanistan. It then appeared to me that a study of the crisis of the Afghan state could not avoid looking at its latest manifestation. Quite the contrary, through the interaction with both Afghans and expatriates I felt now a particular urgency in addressing the ongoing insurgency, despite my natural inclination as an historian to wait for social and political processes to reach a 'conclusion' before producing their analysis.

When I started writing about the Neo-Taliban, I initially planned just a 10,000 words article, but it proved impossible to address the complexity of the topic in such a small piece of work. As I was trying to write my article, I felt greatly constrained by the dearth of scholarly literature on the subject and I had to analyse in depth a much larger number of issues than I had initially planned to. The gap in the existing literature sucked me in and compelled me to write something more ambitious than I had originally intended. Little by little the planned article expanded, turning first into a planned series of articles and finally into the present full-size book. That I felt some urgency in writing the book can be seen from the fact that the whole manuscript, from beginning to end, was written in just three months between the end of 2006 and the beginning of 2007, although it was later revised in several instances between February and May 2007.

Inevitably the present volume cannot pretend to be the definitive book on the Neo-Taliban insurgency, if for no other reason that the insurgency was still going on at the time of signing off. However, by early 2007 certain trends were already sufficiently clear to allow some in-depth analysis, particularly with regard to the weaknesses of the Afghan state, which were exploited by the insurgents. This book is not primarily meant to be an addition to the vast 'counter-insurgency' literature, which tries to identify ways to 'resolve' or defeat insurgencies through a purely technical approach, without dealing with the wider social and political context and the characteristics of the state against which the revolt is taking place. This is a book written by a historian who is trying to understand contemporary developments making use not just of the historical method, but also drawing from other disciplines, such as anthropology, political science and geography. As a result, this book combines an analysis of the development of the insurgency based on available information with my ongoing work, focused on identifying the root causes of the weakness of the Afghan state. Some readers might complain about the absence of a more detailed analysis of specific issues which might be related to the spread of the insurgency, such as the shortcomings of the reconstruction/development effort. In this case I answer that on the one hand several other authors have dealt with such shortcomings in a number of publications, while on the other I am not convinced that there is a direct relationship between the insurgency and the slow reconstruction/development effort. Others might complain about the fact that the book does not engage much with the existing theoretical or policy-oriented literature about insurgencies and counter-insurgency. To all these readers I shall respond that in order to produce an in-depth analysis of the Neo-Taliban in time for contributing to the ongoing debate, certain compromises had to be struck. I could have spent (and may still) years reviewing the literature and trying to integrate the theoretical/policy debate more deeply into my analysis, but then the book could not have been published in 2007. I thought that the best possible contribution to the policy debate would have been to produce the first attempt to analyse the insurgency in depth, hoping that some of the policy makers or those who have influence over them would read it. I also hope that this volume will represent an incentive for other scholars to engage with this topic more deeply.

I started studying Afghanistan in the early 1990s, when my focus was the 'counter-insurgency' policies of the pro-Soviet regime in Kabul. At that time already I tried to go beyond a mere analysis of the security sector and deal with the wider political issue of the social base of the state. From 2003 I have been studying the security sector in its interaction with the central and regional elites, the role of non-state armed groups from the 1990s and the jihad movement of the 1980s. All these streams of research, it seems to me, have great potential for enhancing the understanding of the ongoing insurgency and I have drawn from them for this study, as it appears from the footnotes and the bibliographical references. My research is of course still going on, so that this is not likely to be my final word on the subject.

One note on maps: for technical reasons we had to use old maps which show outdated provincial boundaries and do not show at all recently created provinces such as Nuristan, Sar-i Pul, Daikundi and Panjshir.

It would be impossible to thank all those who contributed in one way or another to this book. The present volume incorporates suggestions and advice from Peter Marsden, LTC Raymond Miller and Amalendu Misra, all of whom read earlier versions of the manuscript. I thank them for taking the trouble of going through it. I wish to thank MIPT for having granted permission to use a graph from their website (http://www.tkb.org). Particular thanks to Mina Moshkiri and others at LSE's cartography department, who redrew my maps professionally. James Putzel, director of the Crisis States Research Centre, made available the funding needed for the research, without which the book would not have happened. Niamatullah Ibrahimi, the Kabul-based research officer of the Centre, accompanied me in most of the trips and contributed decisively in making many of the meetings happen. Wendy Foulds, administrator of the Centre, sorted out the logistical and administrative side of the research. Joost van der Zwan, policy & communications officer of the Centre, helped me stay in touch with media and policy circles and also contributed by giving me access to Dutch-language written material. Special thanks go to Vikram Parekh and David Izadifar for their hospitality in Kabul, to Tom Gregg for hospitality in Gardez, to Talatbek Masadykov and Sonja Bachmann for their hospitality in Kandahar and to Valeri Dotin and Mitko Troanski for their help. Several other individuals also deserve to be thanked for sharing ideas and/or advising me (in alphabetical order): Lal Pacha Azmoon, Bernt Glatzer, Abas Kargar, Akbar Kargar, Massoud Kharokhel, Mervyn Patterson, Thomas Ruttig, Abdul Samad, Eckart Schiewek, Michael Semple, Barbara Stapleton, Noor Ullah, Martine van Bijlert and Abdul Rashid Waziri.

ILLUSTRATIONS

Maps

Graphs

list of illustrations

Tables

GLOSSARY

Al Qaida	a network of Islamist ultra-radical groups, engaged in political violence.
'Alim	Islamic scholar.
AIHRC	Afghan Independent Human Rights Commission
AMF	Afghan Military Forces, the anti-Taliban militias gathered under the Ministry of Defence from the end of 2001.
ANA	Afghan National Army, acronym used to indicate the internationally trained Afghan army (2002–).
ANP	Afghan National Police, acronym used to indicate any Afghan police unit, particularly after 2003.
ANSO	Afghanistan Non-governmental Security Office.
Arbakai	tribal militias in south-eastern Afghanistan.
ASF	Afghan Security Forces, acronym used to indicate militias directly recruited and paid by US forces.
CoP	Chief of Police.
Dawlat-e Enqelabi-ye Islami	'Revolutionary Islamic State', a polity created by a group of Salafis in Nuristan.
DDR	Disarmament, Demobilisation and Reintegration. The standard acronym used to indicate internationally sponsored demobilisation programmes.
Deobandi	Islamic revivalist movement based on strict adherence to Sunna and Shariah.
DIA	Defence Intelligence Agency (Pentagon, United States).

glossary

Harakat-e Enqelab-i Islami	'Islamic Revolutionary Movement', a jihadi group active in the 1978–92 conflict, from whose ranks came many leaders of the Taliban.
Hizb-i Islami	'Islamic Party', an Islamist group based in Afghanistan and one of the protagonists of the conflict started in 1978.
IED	Improvised Explosive Device (mainly roadside bombs).
ISAF	International Security Assistance Force, a multinational contingent deployed in Afghanistan from 2002 to secure and stabilise the country.
ISI	Inter-Services Intelligence directorate (Pakistan).
Jaish al-Mahdi	'The Mahdi's Army', an international jihadist organisation not to be confused with the Iraqi organisation carrying the same denomination.
Jaish-al Muslimeen	'Army of Muslims', a splinter group of the Movement of the Taliban.
Jamaat-i Islami	'Islamic Society', an Islamist party based in Pakistan.
Jami'at-i Islami	'Islamic Society', an Islamist party based in Afghanistan and one of the protagonists of the conflict started in 1978.
Jamaat-al Ulema	'Society of the Islamic Scholars', a political group based in Pakistan.
Jami'at-i Khudam-ul Koran	'Society of the Servants of the Kuran', a splinter group of the Movement of the Taliban.
Jamaat-ud-Da'awa Al-Salafia Wal Qitaab	'Society of the Salafi movement and of the Book', a Salafi group based in Kunar.
Junbesh-i Milli Islami	a military-political group led by Gen. Dostum and based mainly among the Uzbeks of northern Afghanistan.
Khan	rural notable, normally a large landlord.
Layeha	'Book of rules'.
Majlis al-Shura	'Consultative Council'.

glossary

Mawlawi	Islamic religious title.
MoD	Ministry of Defence.
MoI	Ministry of Interior.
NSD	National Security Directorate (Afghanistan's intelligence agency after 2001).
NWFP	North-West Frontier Province, populated by a large majority of Pashtuns.
PRT	Provincial Reconstruction Team, a mix of foreign military personnel (80–150) and civilian elements intended to tie together the military and developmental aspects of security enhancement.
Salafi	followers of a puritanical school of thought based on the example of pious ancestors of the period of early Islam.
Shariah	Islamic religious law.
Shura	'Council'.
Shura-i Nezar	'Coordination Council', a military-political structure created by commander Ahmad Shah Massoud in the early 1980s.
Sunna	the corpus of knowledge of Mohammed's message over which Sunni scholars have reached a consensus.
Rahbari Shura	'Leadership Council' (of the Movement of the Taliban).
Tablighi	Muslim missionary revivalist tendency.
Talib(an)	literally religious student(s), the term is now also largely used to indicate the members of the Movement of the Taliban.
Ulema	pl. of 'alim.
UNAMA	United Nations Assistance Mission to Afghanistan.
UNDSS	United Nations Department of Safety and Security.

INTRODUCTION

'The Taliban is a force in decline.'[1]

'US military estimates suggest there may be only 800 Taliban fighters left.'[2]

'Peaceful elections are a sign that the Taliban are disorganized, weak, and on the run.'[3]

Announcements of an impending victory over the Taliban have been repeated over and over since 2002, particularly after the Presidential elections of 2004, which were said to have been 'a moral and psychological defeat' for the Taliban.[4] In moments of unmitigated triumphalism, some even claimed that 'nation-building' and development work had won over the population,[5] despite much criticism among Afghans and non-Afghans alike regarding the puny results of international aid to Afghanistan and the lack of 'nation-building'.[6] In March 2006, just before the beginning of a series of major clashes, both Afghan and American officials were still saying that 'the Taliban are no longer able to fight large battles'.[7] During 2006 the mood changed significantly and although by the year's end some American, British and Afghan officials were again claiming that the Taliban had been crucially weakened during that year's heavy fighting, the mood in the mass media had turned into one of defeatism and impending doom. In reality, already during 2003–5 a growing body of evidence had gradually become available to cast doubt on the interpretation of the conflict coming from official sources. Rather than being a '2006 surprise', the insurgency had already started developing strong roots inside Afghanistan in 2003 and its spread throughout the southern half of the country took place step by step over four years.

koran, kalashnikov and laptop

To mark the exact beginning of insurgent activities during 2002 is difficult because after the American attack on the Taliban regime in 2001 the background violence never entirely stopped. Throughout the first seven to eight months of 2002 occasional violent incidents occurred in the mountainous border areas of eastern and south-eastern Afghanistan and in a few instances elsewhere too, such as in the case of a rather mysterious attack on Bagrami district (Kabul) in August. Initially these incidents were attributed to remnants of the Taliban and Al Qaida which had been unable or unwilling to flee to Pakistan and were seen as mainly fighting for survival. In most cases this might have been the correct interpretation—although some re-infiltration also seems to have occurred—however, a spate of terrorist attacks in Kabul and an increase in the pace of guerrilla attacks during the late summer highlighted how something new had started. At that time attacks involved only small numbers of fighters and were focused on Afghan 'collaborationists', mainly police and militias attached to the Ministry of Defence. Attacks against US military installations were limited mainly to ineffective sniping and to the isolated firing of rockets, although some American patrols were occasionally ambushed. The areas affected were largely the provinces of Kunar, Paktia, Paktika and Khost, all characterised by mountainous borders with Pakistan and hence easily penetrable. Only a very few incidents were reported from Kandahar and other southern provinces and some of these may even have been the work of simple outlaws (see Map 1).[8]

Better organised efforts to ignite a large scale insurgency seem to have started in September 2002. A recruitment drive was reported to be going on in Pakistan and Afghanistan, while propaganda pamphlets were being distributed in the villages and the first training bases were being established in Pakistani territory. Throughout the autumn the pace of military activities intensified, despite remaining on the whole quite modest. The resurgent Taliban started planting mines on the roads and rocket or mortar attacks on US bases became more frequent. Helicopters were also sometimes targeted and the first IEDs started appearing on Afghanistan's roads, albeit still only occasionally.[9]

Despite the difficulties of operating during the winter in mountainous areas, the insurgency was gathering sufficient momentum to keep the pace up in the following months and indeed expand its operations. The south recorded the first signs of significant anti-government military activity. Afghan security posts on the Pakistani border of the southern provinces of Kandahar and Helmand were repeatedly attacked, while in Zabul the Taliban were already able to penetrate in greater depth, having found a more welcoming environment (see Chapter 2). As increasingly ambitious targets were selected, the size of the insurgent groups grew correspondingly. In January US forces spotted and attacked an eighty-man unit near Spin Boldak (Kandahar Province), seemingly the largest group of insurgents encountered up to that point.[10]

The build-up in Taliban activity continued during the spring of 2003, when US bases started being attacked with whole salvos of rockets and more sophisticated ambushes on road patrols were being organised in conjunction with IED attacks. Groups of fifty insurgents were now regularly seen in several parts of Afghanistan carrying out attacks, splitting into smaller groups of five to ten men and then fleeing. During the summer of 2003 attacks on Afghan security forces started involving even larger groups of insurgents, often 150–200 strong. In mountainous areas close to the border, like southern and eastern Paktika, it was normal for the Taliban to move around in groups of up to 150. The first Taliban stronghold inside Afghanistan was established in the Dai Chopan district of Zabul, where, according to some sources, as many as a thousand Taliban were based. Although the largest number of attacks was still occurring in the south-east and east, the strongest attacks were taking place in Zabul. During the summer the province fell almost entirely under the control of the Taliban, who were also making substantial inroads in the southern districts of Paktika province (see Chapter 2). Although at this stage the south-west was still lagging behind, in

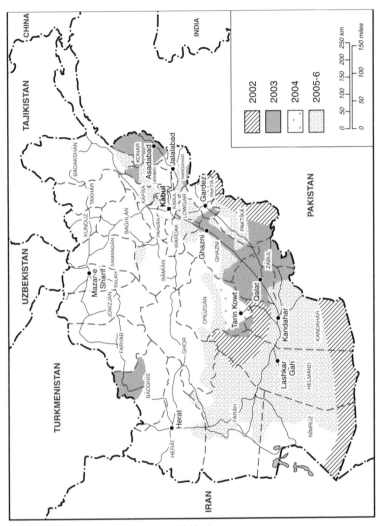

Map 1. Spread of the insurgency, 2002–6.

Note: in 2004 the province of Daikundi was established out of the northern districts of Uruzgan.
Source: press reports; UN sources; AIMS security maps; CENTCOM air operations bulletins.

Kandahar too the presence of the Taliban was growing, with bands of fifty or so active deep into Afghan territory. Throughout Paktika and Zabul they were now moving around during the day and sported satellite phones and new weapons. Even individuals hostile to the Taliban had to admit that much of the population of Zabul was co-operating with them fully.[11]

During 2003 the main achievement of the Taliban was the elimination of government influence in the countryside of Zabul and eastern Paktika. In 2004 they established new strongholds in parts of Uruzgan and Kandahar province. In 2005–6 they infiltrated areas closer to Kandahar city and established strongholds there and in northern Helmand. At the same time they succeeded in virtually eliminating government presence from the countryside of southern Ghazni, much of northern Paktika, some areas of Paktia and Khost and most of southern and central Helmand. Significant Taliban military activities spread to Farah, where districts were being occupied and government officials such as judges murdered. Farah province was easily infiltrated by the Taliban because of its proximity with Helmand, particularly from 2006, once most of Helmand had turned into a stronghold of the insurgents. However, no later than 2005 the Taliban had succeeded in recruiting local commanders in Pur Chaman district, in the mountainous north-eastern part of Farah, despite the presence of only a small minority of Pashtuns there. In 2006 their activities spread to the rest of largely Pashtun eastern Farah (Khak-i Safid, Bala Buluk, Bakwa, Gulistan) and even to the ethnically mixed Farah Rod. Reports by local authorities suggest that at least some local commanders fought on the Taliban's side, while UN sources suggest widespread passive support among the local population. During 2006 the Taliban started infiltrating even Ghor province in central Afghanistan and by early 2007 NATO sources were reporting 'large concentrations' of them there. Infiltration of suspect insurgents in southern Badakhshan was also reported during 2006, with propaganda activity taking place at least in Keran-e Munjan.[12]

In the region of Kabul, which does not share borders with Pakistan, the Taliban did rather well once they had established footholds in the neighbouring provinces. In 2004 they had made their first appearance in Logar and in 2006 they were ready to start escalating their military activities. By that time they had already begun infiltrating the southern district of Kabul province itself, carrying out military activities in Musayi but sending their vanguards towards Sarobi and as close to Kabul as Charasyab. The fact that these areas were once strongholds of Hizb-i Islami might have facilitated the insurgents' infiltration. Towards the end of 2006 NATO had to organise a large-scale sweep operation to clear the area. Although large attacks had occasionally been reported earlier at least in Zabul, during 2006 attacks by as many as three to four hundred Taliban became more common and spread to Helmand and Kandahar. During the battle of Pashmul (Kandahar) NATO estimated that as many as 1,500 Taliban were concentrated in the area. As the end of 2006 approached, NATO sources estimated that the areas affected by the insurgency had more than quadrupled in that year, although this seems to underestimate the spread of the insurgency in 2005 and earlier. The military activities of the insurgents had also increased dramatically. Compared to the previous year, NATO sources reported a six-fold increase in suicide attacks, a three-fold increase in direct fire attacks, a doubling of IED and indirect fire attacks (see also Graph 3).[13]

How and why did this expansion happen? The present work tries to provide an explanation by assessing the sources of the conflict and describing the dynamic of its evolution. The analysis will try to identify which factors were key to the resurgence of the Taliban. The first question to be asked is where the original nucleus of insurgents came from. Chapter 1 describes the 'ideology' of the Taliban and the role of external sponsors. As I argue that the sources of the insurgency are also to be found in the intrinsic weaknesses of the Afghan state, the chapter also looks at its internal fissures, which contributed to breed the rebellion. To fight a war the leadership of an insurgent movement has first to secure renewable sources of recruits, a problem which historically has been difficult to tackle for many rebel groups. Chapter 2 looks at the issue in detail, distinguishing between the original nucleus that decided to start a new war and how that original group developed into something much bigger. The chapter also deals with the different components of the insurgency, which are of great importance in understanding how resilient, amenable to peace negotiations and capable of ultimate victory it might be.

Once an insurgency is underway and starts recruiting successfully, its success is still by no means guaranteed. It needs an appropriately structured organisation to maintain cohesion and to coordinate its activities on the ground. Chapter 3 deals with this aspect and also with the sources of funding which have kept the Neo-Taliban going after 2001. However, even a popular and well organised insurgency might not go very far unless it succeeds in conceiving a winning strategy, pitting its strengths against the enemy's weaknesses. Chapter 4 analyses the strategy of the Taliban in its different aspects: military, psychological and political. Even the strongest strategy will struggle to succeed without at least some tactical proficiency. Chapter 5 addresses the issue, looking at the military technology the insurgents were able to field and at the insurgents' fighting skills.

Finally, no analysis of an insurgency can be complete without a discussion of counter-insurgency efforts, not least because to a large extent they determine the shape of the insurgency itself. Chapter 6 examines the different military actors in the counter-insurgency, as well as the strategies and tactics they adopted. It also looks at the strategies developed by the Afghan government and by international actors to seize political ground from the insurgency and to contain it.

The main argument of this book, as it will emerge from the following chapters, is that despite the role of foreign sponsors, the insurgency would not have succeeded in becoming anything more than a mere annoyance if it had not been able to exploit the intrinsic weaknesses of the Afghan state, both as it was originally conceived and as it was 'rebuilt' from 2001. Without strongholds deep into Afghan territory the leadership of the insurgency would not have been able to spread its influence over much of Afghanistan and would have been left to carry out cross-border raids of little consequence. Strategy, after all, is as much about exploiting an enemy's weaknesses, which the insurgents did. The slow realisation of the sources of the trouble and then the even slower action in addressing these is by contrast the main weakness in the counter-insurgency effort. As of early 2007 the focus was still on finding technical solutions to what is essentially a political problem. The awareness that, as de Tocqueville first pointed out, reforming a 'bad' government creates a particularly dangerous situation is a source of caution. Postponing and delaying reforms, however, is in nobody's interest except in the insurgents' and in that of the Western politicians more concerned with their electoral prospects than with the future of Afghanistan.

NOTES
1   Major General Eric Olson, commander of JCTF 76 in Afghanistan, quoted in Tim McGirk, 'The Taliban on the run', *Time*, 28 March 2005.
2   Scott Baldauf and Ashraf Khan, 'New guns, new drive for Taliban', *Christian Science Monitor*, 26 September 2005.
3   Governor Pathan of Khost province, quoted in Scott Baldauf and Ashraf Khan, 'New guns, new drive for Taliban'.
4   Major General Eric Olson, commander of JCTF 76 in Afghanistan, quoted in Tim McGirk, 'The Taliban on the run'.
5   Tim McGirk, 'The Taliban on the run'.
6   Weinbaum (2004); Rubin (2006).
7   Carlotta Gall, American and Afghan officials quoted in 'Taliban continue to sow fear', *New York Times*, 1 March 2006.
8   '15 killed in attack on Afghan army', *Belfast News Letter*, 8 August 2002; Davis (2002); Jason Burke, 'In the lair of the hunted Taliban', *Observer*, 16 June 2002.
9   Davis (2002); Owais Tohid, 'Taliban regroups – on the road', *Christian Science Monitor*, 27 June 2003; Davis (2003).
10 'Afghan rebels battle US forces', *Reuters*, 28 January 2003.
11 'Montée en puissance de la guérilla des talibans dans le sud-est afghan', *AFP*, 21 September 2003; Françoise Chipaux, 'Les talibans font régner leur loi dans les provinces pachtounes du Sud', *Le Monde*, 7 October 2004.
12 'Un juge afghan abattu dans la province de Farah', *Reuters*, 3 May 2006; 'Over 60 Taliban fighters dead in fierce fighting', *Gulf Times*, 23 June 2005; 'Five Taliban detained in Farah', *Pajhwok Afghan News*, 22 December 2006; Alisa Tang, 'NATO: Taliban set to ramp up attacks', *Associated Press*, 21

February 2007; personal communication with UN official, Kabul, March 2007; interview with Abdul Qadir Emami, MP from Ghor, March 2007.
13 Christian Parenti, 'Taliban rising', *Nation Magazine*, 12 October 2006; personal communication with AREU employee, Kabul, October 2006; Syed Saleem Shahzad, 'Afghanistan's highway to hell', *Asia Times Online*, 25 January 2007; Scott Baldauf, 'Afghan voters face threats', *Christian Science Monitor*, 4 October 2004; Massoud Ansari, 'Almost two years after they were defeated, thousands join the Taliban's new jihad', *Telegraph*, 7 September 2003; Syed Saleem Shahzad, 'Taliban's new commander ready for a fight', *Asia Times Online*, 20 May 2006; 'NATO in Afghanistan', *RFE/RL Afghanistan Report*, vol. 5, no. 20 (1 August 2006); John Cherian, 'Return of Taliban', *Frontline*, vol. 23, no. 13 (1–14 July 2006); McCaffrey (2006); Tom Coghlan, 'British soldier killed by Taliban takes death toll to 20', *Scotsman*, 21 August 2006; Cordesman (2006), p. 5.

1
SOURCES OF THE INSURGENCY

Rumours about attempts by the Taliban to organise an insurgency started circulating in early 2002. Taliban sources at the time confirmed that the leaders of the Movement of the Taliban were in Pakistan trying to reorganise their network and that low rank supporters were regrouping in southern and eastern Afghanistan. However, even members of the Taliban acknowledge that at this stage there was no coordination among the various local groups and no real organisation. Later some members of the Movement would claim that in 2002 a meeting chaired by Mullah Dadullah was held to announce the commencement of hostilities and to distribute tasks and duties to ten top level commanders. The different versions of the beginning of the insurgency agree that the decision to start the insurgency came from a narrow group of Taliban leaders. Why did they do so? Some from within their ranks have stated that in early 2002 they were waiting for some 'offer' from Kabul (presumably for power-sharing), which never came. Hence they were forced to resort to violence.[1] While this might have applied to some of the more moderate figures, who seem to have been working with the Pakistani authorities to put together a viable moderate Taliban party which could then participate in government (see 3.1 *Cohesiveness of the Taliban*), it is doubtful that it ever applied to the whole of the leadership. It is more likely that for 'ideological' reasons they just never accepted defeat and thought it was their duty to fight on. The lull of a few months was probably due to the need to re-adjust, to find secure hideouts, and possibly to recover psychologically from an unexpectedly fast collapse of the regime. Their first attempts to re-mobilise the rank-and-file of the movement were not very successful and few of the 'old Taliban'

11

joined the fight in 2002 (see 2.2 *Early recruitment*). The members of this narrow group of leaders and field commanders were to become the leaders of a much larger movement and they gave to the insurgency its 'ideological' character and defined the direction it was going to take.

1.1 THE 'IDEOLOGY' OF THE TALIBAN

Defining the 'ideology' of the Neo-Taliban is not an easy task, given the lack of transparency of the Movement. However, it can be safely assumed that it is still derived to a large extent from the 'ideology' of the old Taliban. This 'ideology' could be described as a mix of the most conservative village Islam with Deobandi doctrines, with a stress on the importance of ritual and modes of behaviour. Strongly influenced by Deobandi views, the Taliban favoured the reduction of penal and criminal laws to a very narrow interpretation of the Sharia. This was never as evident as in their attitude towards women. Although in principle they were not against women working and studying, their rigidity in enforcing formal dress and gender separation rules effectively led to the complete marginalisation of educated women, at the same time alienating much of the male urban intelligentsia too. Similarly, the Taliban did not favour contacts with the rest of the world, but neither had they objected to them in principle, although from 2000 they became more isolationist in their approach as a result of the influence of their Arab guests. Their rigid application of Shariah just made contacts with the rest of the world difficult and unpractical. Politics, in the realm of the 'old Taliban', was reduced to the demand of an orthodox application of the Shariah, based on a rigid interpretation of the Sunna. As a result, their opposition to the West was based on the rejection of a cultural model, but did not imply a strategic opposition. In this sense, there was no ideology of the Taliban *stricto sensu*, hence the application to the term of quotation marks in this work. It is tempting to see the Taliban as an expression of rural–urban conflict in Afghanistan, but it is important to stress that they were the expression of a specific rural culture, that of village mullahs, and stood in opposition to the tribal codex of Pashtunwali, often ruling against its application (see 2.5 *Taliban, tribes and elders*).[2]

Although much of this applies to the Neo-Taliban too, they also differed from the old Movement on a number of issues. They seem to have absorbed from their foreign jihadist allies a more flexible and less orthodox attitude towards imported technologies and techniques. Not only have they expanded their investment in the production of tapes containing jihadist songs (without musical accompaniment), which they had already been using in the 1990s, but even ventured into the world of video production. A revealing issue is that of the banning of images in any form (television, photography and movies), enforced through to 2001. Already during the years in power the Taliban showed some occasional flexibility in this regard, allowing, for example, foreign journalists to film their fighters (but not the leaders). However, a much more radical departure from the orthodoxy was the large-scale use of documentaries, interviews and footage of speeches in the Neo-Taliban's propaganda VCDs and DVDs, often featuring commanders as well (see 4.7 *Propaganda*). The insurgents carried video cameras with them to the battlefield in order to film the fighting and use the footage for the production of propaganda material. It is telling that at least some Taliban commanders from the ranks of district commander upwards seemed by 2005 to be equipped with laptops even when operating inside Afghanistan, where access to electricity is rare.[3]

More important, the Neo-Taliban became much more integrated in the international jihadist movement after 2001 (see 4.7 *Propaganda*).[4] Their rhetoric featured concepts such as 'global Christian war against Islam' and stressed solidarity with other jihadist movements around the world, which were clearly perceived as part of the same struggle. The internationalisation of the Taliban's 'ideology' might be a key point in the understanding of their strategies (see 4.11 *Mao's epigones, 'Fleas', 'fourth generation' warriors or international jihadists?*), not because of the existence of a serious constituency for pan-Islamism inside Afghanistan, but because it enabled stronger external support. For example, the US-led attack on Iraq in 2003 does not seem to have had a major impact on Afghan opinion and certainly not in the remote rural areas where the Taliban enjoy greater support. However, it is quite possible that it might have contributed to galvanise pan-Islamist sentiment throughout the Muslim world, resulting in greater underground financial support not only for the Iraqi insurgents, but also for the Afghan ones. This, in turn, would have led to the Taliban being increasingly able to fund an expanding insurgency.

One important feature of the 'ideology' of the Taliban was their 'free-market' orientation. There was evidence of this from the beginning of the history of the Movement of the Taliban when in 1994 they accepted financial support from traders to clear up the roads in southern Afghanistan.[5] However, after 2001 they even turned into entrepreneurs. They had no qualms in exploiting the resources of the free market to conduct their war, not only as far as logistics was concerned, but for military operations too. Although the importance of mercenary fighters to the Taliban has probably been overestimated (see 2.2 *Early recruitment*), there is abundant evidence that the Taliban have been paying some fighters by 'piece work', such as carrying out *ad hoc* missions. These could range from firing a rocket at an enemy base to carrying out a targeted assassination (see 4.4 *Establishing structures and a shadow government*). If this reliance on the market was not due mainly to the intervention of foreign services, it would appear to represent an 'original contribution' of the Taliban to the status of the art in 'ideological' insurgency. In the past the free market had been used to run the logistics of rebel movements, such as at least one by the Afghan mujahidin of the 1980s jihad. A number of ideological insurgent movements might have included some recruits motivated by personal gain, but as far as this author knows none ever openly hired fighters for the job.

In any case, the specifics of the 'ideology' of the Neo-Taliban movement matter less than the fact that it had a substantial base of 'true believers'. To all accounts, students of the Deobandi madaras in the NWFP, Afghan village mullahs who had been educated there and the simple villagers who aligned with them were committed and often ready to sacrifice their lives for the cause. US and NATO sources have been claiming heavy Taliban losses since 2002. During 2006 such losses would have more than trebled compared to 2005, to about 3,000 killed. An alternative count suggests that during 2006 about 2,500 insurgents were killed by NATO. The yearly loss rate would therefore be in the range of 12–13 per cent (see 2.1 *How strong are the Taliban?*). Quite possibly NATO estimates of Taliban casualties are overestimated, as was demonstrated in at least a few cases.[6] Whatever the exact numbers, independent sources also indicate that the casualties of the Taliban were heavy indeed, particularly in 2006. A Taliban commander told a journalist in July 2006 that out of eight men who joined the Taliban from his village, three were already dead. What is also evident is their resilience in the face of such heavy losses. In October 2006 NATO sources reported signs of cracking in the Taliban cohesiveness due to the high level of losses, but they had done so at the beginning of 2005 too, citing radio intercepts occasionally showing Taliban commanders complaining about the absence from the battlefield of the leadership. In reality, this interpretation seems to be overstated and despite these losses there was no objective sign by the end of 2006 that the Taliban were cracking. Some friction during an intense conflict is understandable but does not necessarily imply an imminent break-up of the organisation. Those Taliban met by journalists in Pakistan or Afghanistan showed no sign of having lost their determination and faith in final victory, and the reconciliation offers of the government continued to attract little interest among the ranks of the insurgents (see 6.8 *Reconciliation efforts*).[7]

1.2 'REBUILDING' THE AFGHAN STATE: CONTRADICTIONS AND WEAKNESSES

If the beginning of the insurgency was the decision of a small group of men, the choices and activities of another small group of men created a fertile ground for the insurgency to develop. At the end of 2001, as he set out to establish his provisional administration, with the blessing of his American patrons, President Karzai opted to co-opt regional warlords and strongmen into the central government and the subnational administration. The conflict which had started in 1978 had destabilised the provincial environment and created a situation in which the old and well established notable families gradually lost much of their influence as security became the primary concern. This development opened the way to a new generation of 'rougher' local leaders, who were more likely to rely on militias and armed groups to assert their power and influence. At the same time, community affiliations reasserted themselves when the state started collapsing during the 1980s and the centre progressively lost its authority over the periphery. In the southern half of the country people turned to the tribes to provide a modicum of security in the absence of even the traditionally weak central state. Not least because the tribes had lost much of their functionality in many parts of Afghanistan, this in turn favoured the emergence of 'tribal entrepreneurs', who claimed tribal leadership on the basis of a real or alleged unifying role among the different communities in which the tribes had fragmented. In Kandahar, for example, Gul Agha Shirzai had emerged to lead the Barakzais, Mullah Naqib had presented himself as the leader of the Alkozai, Aziz Sarqatib had claimed the leadership of the Ghilzais, Abdul Haleem of the Noorzais, Haji Ahmad of the Achakzais, etc.[8] Temporarily displaced by the Taliban in 1994–2001, most of these figures resurfaced as the regime led by Mullah Omar started collapsing. Of the first group of thirty-two provincial governors appointed in 2002, at least twenty were militia commanders, warlords or strongmen. Smaller militia commanders also populated the ranks of the district governors.[9] In the southern half of the country, the key players were:

- Tribal strongmen Abdul Qadir and his brothers (the Arsalai), allied with Pashai warlord Hazrat Ali in eastern Afghanistan;
- Barakzai strongman Gul Agha Shirzai in Kandahar;

- Popolzai strongman Jan Mohammed in Uruzgan;
- Alizai strongman Sher Mohammed Akhundzada in Helmand.

These, however, were only the tip of the iceberg. In other provinces too and in most districts tens of local strongmen, militia commanders, tribal leaders and local notables who had somehow established a relationship with either Karzai or the Americans were appointed to positions of responsibility, influence and power. This had some important consequences. The most obvious one was that these strongmen were at least in part legitimised through their incorporation in the state structure, despite the fact that for most of them their base of support was quite shaky at best. Another consequence was that the state administration in the provinces was often negatively affected by the need of these strongmen to reward their followers with jobs and positions of influence in order to consolidate their leadership. Strongmen and warlords who became governors and chiefs of police had the legal power to make appointments in the structures they were leading, subject to approval from Kabul. As a result, the provincial administrative departments were soon full of heads of departments who were close associates of the strongmen. The same was true of the local branches of the Ministries of Defence (MoD) and Interior (MoI).[10]

Similar policies adopted with regard to the ministries had deleterious effects on their functionality too. As far as the security of the provinces was concerned, particularly worrying was the case of the Ministry of Interior, which among other functions controlled the police. The need to reform the MoI was recognised at an early stage and a new minister, Taj Mohammed, was appointed in June 2002 with a mandate to undertake sweeping reforms. An elderly man with little support within the ministry, he failed to change anything at the MoI, and in January 2003 yet another minister, Ahmad Jalali, replaced him. He too promised to implement deep reforms, but his achievements during his first year in office were modest. He immediately established human rights offices in each provincial and district police department, and made some efforts to appoint more professionally prepared officers to positions of responsibility, but he never managed to bring the ministry effectively under his control. On paper, he sacked twenty-two out of thirty-two provincial governors and a much larger number of district managers and other officials, but in most cases it was just a matter of shifting them to another province, rather than removing them altogether. Often, when trying to appoint new officials, he faced resistance from the local strongmen, from within his own ministry and from other members of the cabinet. In the early months of his stay in office he sometimes showed a willingness to confront officials reluctant to behave in a disciplined way. For example, in early 2003 he sacked the Gardez chief of police, who was heavily involved in criminal activities. When the latter refused to stand down, Jalali dispatched an armed contingent to accompany the new appointee and even sacked the provincial governor, who had tried to mediate.[11] Despite these undeniable efforts to reassert the central state, towards the end of 2003 and during the first few months of 2004 Jalali's incisiveness appeared to wear off, possibly because he was unable to confront pressures coming from so many sides and to count on the cooperation of the officials of his own ministry. There is plenty of evidence that during 2004 in many cases professionally prepared provincial officials were replaced by unskilled ones, in what could be described as a sort of counter-reform managed by middle-level functionaries of the MoI.[12] Jalali's main political failure was, however, the inability to replace individuals within the ministry itself, which made it difficult to implement any serious policy of new appointments in the provinces. When the time of emergency came and it became essential to strengthen the hand of governors and other administrators in the areas affected by the insurgency, the MoI did not have the capability to do so. As a result Afghanistan's sub-national administration developed after 2001 strong patrimonial traits, looking even less institutionalised than that of the Taliban, of the leftist governments of the 1980s and of the monarchy and republic in the 1960s and 1970s. The system was geared for accommodating strongmen and warlords endowed with their own power base and resources, not for allowing functionaries loyal to the central government to consolidate the influence of Kabul.

In the context of post-2001 Afghanistan, unless they were strongmen governors were not able to exercise strong local leadership even in the rare cases when they might have had the skills for that. The failure of the central government to keep providing sufficient discretionary funds for the governors to interact with elders, clergy and other notables contributed decisively to undermine the administration. If we add that there were few skilled and committed administrators, the consequences in terms of governance become obvious, particularly in the south where state weakness was at its worst. For example, it has been widely recognised that the administration of Helmand was corrupt and ineffective to the point of being effectively 'defunct'. Apart from not delivering much in terms of services, the administration was often behaving arrogantly with the population. The practice of government officials taking goods from the shops and refusing to pay seems, for example, to have been common in Ghazni in 2006. The weakness of the subnational administration contributed to delegitimise the government, paving the way for the insurgency to spread. The autonomous actions of foreign troops, such as house searches and arrests, were not usually communicated to the local authorities, who were thus humiliated and discredited.[13]

The situation was further complicated by the rivalries which crossed the pro-Karzai coalition in southern Afghanistan. A good example of how the effectiveness of this coalition was affected by divisions running within it is provided by the case of Kandahar province. Here the three key players at the end of 2001 were:

- Gul Agha Shirzai, who came out on top initially thanks to American and Pakistani support;
- Mullah Naqibullah, an Alkozai strongman who had supported the Taliban initially and then switched sides in the last days of the regime;
- Ahmad Wali Karzai, the President's brother who rapidly emerged as the leading Popolzai strongman in the province.

This uneasy alliance rested on a precarious equilibrium. In the distribution of the spoils, Gul Agha took control of the administration and customs, Mullah Naqibullah and his associates took the police and much of the MoD-sanctioned militias, while Ahmad Wali initially contented himself with minority shares in the administration and in the militias. The balance of power was bound to shift as the disarmament of the MoD militias got underway, but other changes too contributed to accelerate it. American support for Gul Agha started weakening during 2002, leaving him exposed to the pressure of the two other leading local members of the alliance. Ahmad Wali, able as he was to rely on Kabul's support, was patiently manoeuvring to sideline his rivals and emerge as the expatriates' favourite Kandahari. Mullah Naqibullah, who had long had bad relations with Pakistan and was seen with suspicion by the Americans due to his earlier support for the Taliban, was left without much foreign support and was unable to exploit Gul Agha's decline. In August 2003 Gul Agha was removed from the position of governor and 'promoted' to minister. Although he was able to place a loyalist as governor, this move marked the beginning of a downward trend for his influence in Kandahar. In December 2004 he was reappointed governor of Kandahar for six more months, but never regained the influence he once had, not least because during his absence control of the customs had been transferred to the central government. In March 2005 it was the turn of Mullah Naqibullah to lose control over the police when his deputy Khan Mohammed was removed from the post of chief. Combined with the impact of the disarmament of the MoD militias, this led to the complete marginalisation of Mullah Naqibullah's Alkozais from local power structures. The fight for local control, punctuated by occasional armed clashes between militias and assassinations, ended up with Ahmad Wali Karzai able to control informally local power structures, having 'exiled' rivals to other provinces and replaced them with powerless individuals or with family friends. In the process, however, the old members of the tripartite alliance had been alienated. The departure of the Alkozais from the administration was particularly damaging as they were the main military force within the original alliance and had played an important role in keeping the Taliban away from Kandahar city with their militiamen, many of whom had been incorporated in the police. Only in the context of the rapidly worsening security situation in 2006 had Mullah Naqibullah and Ahmad Wali Karzai renovated their alliance.[14]

The situation in other southern provinces was similar. In Uruzgan, for example, the various strongmen and notables who had supported Karzai's bid to start a movement against the Taliban in late 2001 were rewarded with official positions and then proceeded to face off against each other in a local power struggle, which opened up a space for the Taliban to re-emerge. The most obvious example was Jan Mohammed, a Popolzai personally close to Karzai, who served as governor until early 2006, but the pattern was reproduced at the district level. In Chora district, for example, Haji Dad Mohammed, a Barakzai who had travelled to Uruzgan with Karzai and US Special Forces in 2001, was appointed district governor and was still serving at the end of 2006. Mohammed Gul, a former jihadi fighter who also claimed to have supported Karzai in 2001, was appointed chief of police, but did not get along well with Dad Mohammed and even showed little cooperation with the Dutch after they arrived in 2006. Gul was known as a difficult individual to deal with.[15]

1.3 THE ROLE OF PAKISTAN

The sources of an insurgency are of course not always endogenous, or at least not entirely. Indeed, by 2006 the role of Pakistan in sponsoring the insurgency or at least turning a blind eye to its activities had become a major bone of contention between the Afghan and the Pakistani governments, to the embarrassment of their common ally, the United States. The fact that the Taliban operated from Pakistani territory and used it as a logistical rearguard is no longer controversial, after even the Pakistani authorities admitted to this. However, the issue is whether the Pakistani government was doing enough to prevent or constrain the ability of the insurgents to use

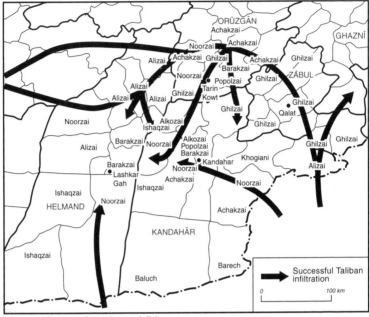

Map 2. Tribes of southern Afghanistan.
Sources: interviews with UN officials and tribal elders, May 2005, January 2006; *Context Analysis Uruzgan Province*, prepared by the Royal Netherlands Embassy in Kabul, Afghanistan, August 2006.

Pakistani territory and to cross the border as they pleased. Afghan frustration at the lack of Pakistani cooperation was shared by some NATO countries, which were by then directly exposed to Taliban attacks in southern Afghanistan. A NATO mission to Pakistan in November 2006 tried to enlist a greater Pakistani cooperation, as did US Secretary of State Condoleeza Rice during her visit to Islamabad at the beginning of the summer. Before that, countless meetings involving the leaderships of either or both the two countries and often US representatives too, including, once, President Bush himself, had taken place in Islamabad, Kabul, Washington and elsewhere.[16]

However, all these efforts achieved the same result, that is very little. In January 2002 the Pakistani authorities arrested some Taliban figures, such as Ambassador to Pakistan Mullah Zaif and a few others, none of whom was known as a military commander or had played a key role in the regime. Again at the end of the summer of 2004 some former Taliban were arrested, including former Deputy Foreign Minister Mullah Jalil, allegedly a close ally of Mullah Omar. In 2005 a new apparent crackdown yielded the capture of Abdul Latif Hakimi, spokesman of the Taliban. However, up to 2006 Pakistan had on the whole arrested just a handful of Taliban, compared to about a thousand 'Al Qaida' activists. As international pressure increased during 2006, the Pakistani authorities tried to appease their Afghan counterparts and NATO with a more substantial gesture, at least in appearance. They rounded up and deported to Afghanistan large numbers of alleged Taliban. The arrests started in July 2006, shortly after Condoleeza Rice's visit to Pakistan. A new wave of arrests took place in November 2006, in correspondence with renewed international pressure. In total 500 alleged Taliban were arrested in Pakistan in 2006, of which about 400 were handed over to Afghanistan. However, the Afghan authorities finally had to release the deportees as they did not appear to be involved with the Taliban, or at least the Pakistani authorities failed to provide any evidence of such. The 'suspects' were handed over to the Afghan authorities apparently on the basis that they could not speak Urdu and were unaware of their whereabouts, although some had been arrested during a raid against a madrasa. In January 2007 another crackdown was announced in Baluchistan, with the arrest of 400 'Taliban suspects'. Only in February 2007 were there signs that Pakistan might finally be beginning to place the leadership of the Taliban under serious pressure, following US Vice-President Cheney's visit and possibly the delivery of precise information concerning the whereabouts of key Taliban commander Mullah Obeidullah, who was then arrested barely hours after Cheney's departure. However, there were strong allegations that another important leader of the insurgency was captured with Obeidullah and then freed, which if true would point to a still less than total commitment of Pakistan in suffocating the insurgency.[17]

In addition to their doubtful cooperation against the Taliban, the Pakistani authorities started to retaliate against Afghan accusations of complicity in the insurgency. In November 2006 they accused the Afghan National Security Directorate (NSD) of involvement in terrorist attacks in the Pakistani NWFP. According to the Pakistanis, a number of Afghan Uzbeks connected with the NSD were arrested after the attacks and a few were even reported to have admitted their contacts with the Afghan intelligence.[18]

The exact role of the Pakistani government in the insurgency is not easy to pin down. Some Pakistani experts believe that some elements in the military and intelligence establishment misled President General Musharraf on Afghanistan and misrepresented the situation. The interpretation that Pakistani agencies might not be acting in a unified way is lent some credibility by the fact that this had already occurred in the 1990s when the victim had been Benazir Bhutto,[19] and is also confirmed by ISAF sources which reported how in some instances the Pakistani army and air force cooperated with US and NATO forces in fighting against cross-border raids. On the other hand, there is evidence that the Pakistan ISI protected Taliban leaders and bases in and around Quetta, including by keeping away journalists and other unwanted presences, and that Pakistani border guards allowed the insurgents to freely cross the border in their presence. A high-ranking Pakistani official, Lt Gen. Safdar Hussein, who was in charge of operations in the NWFP, admitted that the insurgents were operating from Pakistan as early as 27 July 2005. In February 2007 even President Musharraf was forced to admit that in some cases Pakistani border forces had turned a 'blind eye' to the militants crossing the border. Many observers believe that elements within the ISI or former members of that service do help the Taliban directly and some claim to have seen evidence of it.[20] Some observers within the US government even believe the ISI is still providing intelligence and tactical information to the Taliban.[21] Certainly, some former operatives of the ISI and former Pakistani army officers do not hide their strong sympathy for them. There is also some evidence of retired ISI or army officers travelling to locations under Taliban control in Afghanistan to meet leaders of the insurgency. However, evidence is lacking with regard to direct supplies of weapons to the rebels. Some considerations tend to confirm that the Taliban have been receiving some advice from external sources. The main one among them is the adoption of a relatively sophisticated strategy—inspired in part by Mao's theories and in part by the Iraqi experience—by a Taliban leadership which was never known for being well read or sophisticated (see Chapter 4). This would not exclude Arab militants from the potential 'advisors' who could have helped the Taliban develop their strategy and they must certainly have played a role with regard to certain aspects, such as bomb attacks. However, the much stronger stress on traditional guerrilla tactics compared to Iraq and the skills with which the Taliban have targeted different sections of Afghan society suggest the presence of 'cooler' heads and of advisors with long-standing experience of Afghanistan, such as current or former ISI operatives. [22]

If the Taliban receive advice and intelligence from sources like the ISI, this does not imply that they receive hardware from the same sources. Although Gen. Jones of the US Armed Forces stated to the US Senate in September 2006 that the ISI provides aid to the Taliban Shura of Quetta, there is in fact little available evidence that the rebels receive large amounts of weaponry from any single source. Clearly weapons were being purchased on the black market and from several different sources:

- Afghan officials themselves admitted that many of the Taliban's weapons come from or through northern Afghanistan, where they are purchased on the black market;
- in February 2006 a Toyota loaded with weapons was intercepted by the Afghan police on a highway in Baghlan;

- in August 2006 several MoD officers were arrested in Chara-siab for trafficking weapons and ammunition to the Taliban in Logar;
- police sources also confirmed that during Taliban offensives in the south, arms prices peaked in northern Afghanistan: over the summer of 2006 the price of weapons doubled in northern Afghanistan, in part because local commanders were also beginning to rearm; by early 2007 prices of Kalashnikovs were four times as high as in early 2004;
- even greater increases were recorded in the arms markets of the Pakistan North-west Frontier Province, where the price of bullets increased as much as twenty-fold. Hence, if the ISI or the Pakistani army supply the Taliban, they clearly do not give enough to satisfy their requirements fully;
- the involvement of international NGO staff in arms trafficking was also highlighted by the arrest of two foreign nationals in Kabul in December 2006;
- illegal imports of weapons destined to the insurgency are also reported from Iraq via Iran, according to police sources;
- Taliban sources and widespread rumours alleged that ammunition deliveries to the Ghorak district of Kandahar were regularly ending up in the hands of the Taliban, as well as in other districts where administrators traded their supplies for immunity from Taliban attacks.[23]

Whatever the actual role of the Pakistani state in the conflict, the simple fact that most Afghans believe that it is behind the Taliban was a major factor in the conflict. In some cases this played against the Taliban, as the Pashtunistan issue remains alive and well in the consciousness and political culture of Afghan Pashtuns, who often claim the Pashtun lands of Pakistan for the Afghan state. This was particularly the case of the south-east and of Nangarhar province, where Pashtun/Afghan nationalism has deeper roots than in other parts of the country. However, in most other cases the contrary was true and the Taliban might well have benefited from their alleged association with Pakistan. In this sense Kabul's anti-Pakistan propaganda might have been counter-productive. Pakistani influence in southern Afghanistan is paramount, with most economic activity and trade taking place in Pakistani Rupees. The tribes living across the border tend to be attracted more strongly towards the Pakistani side because that is where the economic weight is, while inter-marriage tends to consolidate this influence. In this context, the inability of the Americans to bring sufficient pressure to bear on the Pakistan government to force it to stop the insurgents' activities might have resulted in a belief among Afghans that being on the pro-Pakistan side in the conflict was wiser, as Pakistan was going to be involved in Afghanistan much longer and more effectively than the United States.[24]

However, in a sense the influence of Pakistan in Afghanistan is also a case of attraction exercised by the NWFP, possibly even more than by Pakistan as such. Although the economics of influence worked in favour of Pakistan in the short term, the underlying sentiment might not necessarily be so sympathetic to Pakistan. At least some members of the Taliban seem to have resented the pressure of Pakistani security services, accusing them of forcing the Taliban to attack schools and development projects to prevent Afghanistan from progressing as a country. In this regard there are some indications that the Pakistani authorities might be worried about the simultaneous development of strong Taliban movements in both Afghanistan and the NWFP. Given the obviously strong connection between the two movements, the prospect of a politically unified 'Pashtunistan in being' must be alarming for the Pakistanis, even if that had to happen under an Islamic banner. Some sources allege that the ISI was developing contacts and supporting non-Taliban and non-Hizb insurgent groups in southern and south-eastern Afghanistan, as well as particular individuals and groups within the Afghan Taliban Movement who were seen as more amenable to Pakistani influence and direction. Such sources point out how mainstream Taliban distance themselves from a number of commanders and representatives who are known to be very close to the Pakistanis and rumoured to receive instructions directly from them. If this is true, the insistence of the Pakistani leadership on the need for the Afghan government to negotiate with the Taliban, reiterated several times during 2006, would be easier to understand. In order to prevent the Talibanisation of the two halves of Pashtunistan from continuing and converging, the Pakistanis needed a political deal to set in stone the influence gained so far inside Afghanistan and to freeze the process of radicalisation going on at the grassroots level.[25]

1.4 THE ROLE OF IRAN

There is plenty of evidence that the Islamic Republic of Iran has been actively trying to expand and consolidate its influence in Afghanistan and is carrying out propaganda activities against the US presence. In November 2006 Iranian President Ahmadinejad even stated openly on state television that the foreign troops 'occupying' Afghanistan should leave. However, there is little evidence to substantiate allegations that Teheran has been supporting the Taliban or other insurgent groups. Part of the Afghan press repeatedly published reports concerning alleged Iranian support for insurgent groups in Afghanistan, echoing claims by local administration officials and police officers in western Afghanistan. Some Afghans confirmed such claims to Western journalists, citing anecdotal evidence of direct supplies of weapons and of wounded Taliban being treated in Iran. Some Iranian weapons were found in Panjwai and elsewhere, but Taliban sources claimed to have been purchasing weapons from Iran and not to have received them for free. The fact that the weapons (mortar shells and plastic explosive) were marked as manufactured in Iran militates against Teheran's involvement, as it would likely have been more careful. Even US sources acknowledge that there is no proof of shipments of arms from Iran state agencies to non-state armed groups in Afghanistan. In sum, it does not appear that the Iranians by early 2007 had gone farther than establishing contacts with groups involved in the insurgency, possibly aiming to identify potential tar-

gets to retaliate against in the event of American military intervention in Iran. Transfer of cash to leaders of non-state groups seems to
have occurred, but the insurgents do not seem to have figured among
them. Some diplomats even believe that preventing the Taliban from
regaining power in Afghanistan remains a priority for Teheran. In
fact, due to Afghan-Pakistani tensions, Iran had already plenty of
leverage to influence its eastern neighbour, which increasingly relied
on Iran for its trade. Claims that Iran supported Hizb-i Islami after
2002 are similarly unsupported. Gulbuddin Hekmatyar, the leader
of Hizb-i Islami, resided in Iran until February 2002. Following the
closure of the offices of his party and threats to deport him if he did
not water down his militant rhetoric, the Iranian authorities asked
him to leave the country. While it is certainly possible that Hekmatyar might have maintained contacts with the Iranians after he
left the country, his presumed location in eastern Afghanistan would
clearly prevent large scale Iranian support. Moreover, there was no
sign up to 2006 of a major effort to revitalise Hekmatyar's following
in western Afghanistan.[26]

NOTES

1 Zahid Hussain, 'Taliban's chiefs keep in trim for comeback', *The Times*,
   29 March 2002; Owais Tohid, 'Taliban regroups – on the road', *Christian
   Science Monitor*, 27 June 2003; Elizabeth Rubin, 'In the land of the Taliban',
   New York Times Magazine, 22 October 2006.
2 Maley (1998), p. 15; Dorronsoro (2005), pp. 299-301, 310–11; Rashid
   (1999); Roy (1998), pp. 210–11.
3 Baily (2001), p. 37; Syed Saleem Shahzad, 'How the Taliban prepare for
   battle', *Asia Times Online*, 5 December 2006; Dixit (n.d.); Hamid Mir, 'The
   Taliban's new face', *Rediff* (India), 27 September 2005.
4 See also the interview with a pro-Taliban Mawlawi in Nivat (2006), pp.
   89–91.
5 See Rashid (2000), pp. 22, 190–1.
6 See for example 'Taliban death toll inaccurate', *BBC News*, 10 December
   2006.
7 '2,000 militants killed in special forces operations in Afghanistan since Sept.
   1', *Associated Press*, 13 December 2006; Jason Burke, 'Hunt for the Taliban
   trio intent on destruction', *Observer*, 9 July 2006; Tom Coghlan, 'Taliban

train snipers on British forces', *Daily Telegraph*, 23 July 2006; personal communication with high-ranking British officer, Kabul, October 2006; Tim McGirk, 'The Taliban on the run', *Time*, 28 March 2005.

8   Interview with Ustad Abdul Haleem, Kandahar, January 2006.

9   Assessment carried out during fieldwork in Afghanistan.

10 See Giustozzi (2004) for more details.

11 International Crisis Group (2003b), p. 5; interview with Jalali in *Pak Tribune*, 12 April 2004.

12 Interviews with UN officials in Kunduz, Kabul, Mazar and Herat, October 2003–April 2004.

13 Interview with Massoud Kharokhel, 1 October 2006, Tribal Liaison Office, Kabul; Declan Walsh and Bagarzai Saidan, 'Across the border from Britain's troops, Taliban rises again', *Guardian*, 27 May 2006; Sara Daniel, 'Afghanistan: "Résister aux talibans? A quoi bon!"', *Le Nouvel Observateur*, 10 August 2006. For the opinion of US Ambassador Neumann on the impact of a weak administration see David Rohde and James Risen, 'C.I.A. review highlights Afghan leader's woes', *New York Times*, 5 November 2006.

14 This section is based on Giustozzi (forthcoming) and on a personal communication with UN official, Kabul, March 2007.

15 Harm Ede Botje, 'We zitten darr goed', *Vrij Nederland*, 6 January 2007 courtesy of J. van den Zwan, Crisis States Research Centre, London).

16 Syed Mohsin Naqvi, 'Musharraf: Taliban gaining power', *CNN*, 20 July 2006; Zeeshan Haider, 'Unity, not games on Taliban, Pakistan urges Kabul', *Reuters*, 7 November 2006; Ahmed Rashid, 'Musharraf: stop aiding the Taliban', *Daily Telegraph*, 6 October 2006; 'President Musharaff's visit to Washington', *www.onlinenews.com.pk*, 27 September 2006; Ahmed Rashid, 'Accept defeat by Taliban, Pakistan tells NATO', *Daily Telegraph*, 30 November 2006; Ahmed Rashid, 'NATO commanders demand Pakistan close Taliban sanctuary', *Eurasia Insight*, 6 October 2006; Kristin Roberts, 'Gates seeks Pakistani help for NATO offensive', *Reuters*, 12 February 2007; Declan Walsh, 'Rice puts Musharraf under pressure to rein in Taliban militants', *Guardian*, 19 February 2007.

17 Syed Saleem Shahzad, 'Now Pakistan rounds on the Taliban', *Asia Times Online*, 2 September 2004; Ron Synovitz, 'Afghanistan: Pakistan hails capture of Taliban spokesman as breakthrough', *RFE/RL*, 5 October 2005; Declan Walsh and Bagarzai Saidan, 'Across the border from Britain's troops, Taliban rises again'; 'Pakistan arrests 140 Afghans', *RFE/RL Newsline*, 19 July 2006; 'Afghanistan frees 104 "Talibans" captured by Pakistan', *DPA*, 22 September 2006; 'Pakistan hands over Taliban suspects to Afghanistan', *Reuters*, 24 November 2006; 'Pakistan police arrest dozens of Taliban suspects', *Reuters*, 21 November 2006; 'Pakistan says arrests 500 Taliban this year', *Reuters*, 14 December 2006; Azhar Masood, '400 Taleban suspects held in Balochistan', *Arab News*, 19 January 2007; 'Bush to Musharraf: deal or no deal? White House pressures Pakistani leader to do more on terror', *CBS News*, 26 February 2007; personal communication with UN official,

March 2007.

18 Syed Saleem Shahzad, 'Afghanistan strikes back at Pakistan', *Asia Times Online*, 9 November 2006; 'Afghans among seven held over Quetta bomb blast', *AFP*, 22 December 2006.

19 See Coll (2004).

20 Cordesman (2007); Paul Watson, 'On the trail of the Taliban's support', *Los Angeles Times*, 24 December 2006, who claims to have seen DIA documents according to which ISI operatives were gathering information about US activities in Afghanistan. According to NATO sources, Pakistani volunteers captured in Afghanistan have provided plenty of details on the ISI structure of support for the Taliban (Ahmed Rashid, 'Musharraf: stop aiding the Taliban'); Schiewek (2006), p. 158.

21 Seth Jones, quoted in Declan Walsh, 'As Taliban insurgency gains strength and sophistication, suspicion falls on Pakistan', *Guardian*, 13 November 2006.

22 'Afghan situation a US policy failure, experts tell senators', *Daily Times*, 15 December 2006; David Montero, 'Attacks heat up Afghan-Pakistani border', *Christian Science Monitor*, 12 January 2007; personal communication with Pakistani journalist, Kabul, October 2006; personal communication with Afghan travellers to Quetta, Kabul, May 2006; Laura King, 'Pakistani city serves as a refuge for the Taliban', *Los Angeles Times*, 21 December 2006; Farhan Bokhari, 'Is Quetta Taliban's nerve centre?', *Gulf News Online*, 19 October 2003; Declan Walsh and Bagarzai Saidan, 'Across the border from Britain's troops, Taliban rises again'; Graeme Smith, 'Taliban plot new offensive against NATO', *Globe and Mail*, 18 January 2007; Paul Watson, 'On the trail of the Taliban's support'; David S. Cloud, 'U.S. says attacks are surging in Afghanistan', *New York Times*, 16 January 2007; David Rohde, 'G.I.s in Afghanistan on hunt, but now for hearts and minds', *New York Times*, 30 March 2004; 'Musharraf admits border problems', *BBC News*, 2 February 2007; 'Afghan border: Pakistan's struggle with the Taliban', *CBC News*, 5 December 2006 <http://www.cbc.ca/news/viewpoint/vp_edwards/20061205.html>; Syed Saleem Shahzad, 'Interview: Hamid Gul', *Asia Times Online*, 13 November 2001; Syed Saleem Shahzad, 'Taliban's trail leads to Pakistan', *Asia Times Online*, 13 December 2001; Syed Saleem Shahzad, 'Afghanistan's highway to hell', *Asia Times Online*, 25 January 2007; on the significance of the adoption of more traditional guerrilla tactics see also Jason Burke, 'Taliban plan to fight through winter to throttle Kabul', *Observer*, 29 October 2006; 'No indications Iran supplying weapons to Taliban', *Daily Times*, 12 February 2007.

23 Rubin (2007); Sayed Yaqub Ibrahimi, 'Taliban find unexpected arms source', *Afghan Recovery Report*, no. 206 (12 March 2006); 'Afghan officers arrested for smuggling weapons to Taliban', *Xinhua*, 21 September 2006; Guy Dinmore and Rachel Morarjee, 'To a second front? How Afghanistan could again be engulfed by civil war', *Financial Times*, 22 November 2006; Graeme Smith, 'The Taliban: knowing the enemy', *Globe and Mail*, 27

November 2006; Hamid Mir, 'The Taliban's new face'; 'Weapon smugglers should be arrested', *Hewaad*, 25 December 2006; Zulfiqar Ali, 'Kalashnikov prices shoot up', *Dawn*, 10 February 2007; Fisnik Abrashi, 'Gov't flounders in north Afghanistan', *Associated Press*, 27 February 2007; Senlis Council (2007), p. 32.

24 For a short review of Pakistani influence in Helmand, see Senlis Council (2006d), pp. 7 and 18; Françoise Chipaux, 'Les talibans font régner leur loi dans les provinces pachtounes du Sud', *Le Monde*, 7 October 2004.

25 Elizabeth Rubin, 'In the land of the Taliban'; Syed Saleem Shahzad, 'Pakistan reaches into Afghanistan', *Asia Times Online*, 3 October 2006; Ahmed Rashid, 'Accept defeat by Taliban, Pakistan tells NATO'; report on President Musharaff's visit to Washington, *www.onlinenews.com.pk*, 27 September 2006.

26 David Rohde, 'Iran is seeking more influence in Afghanistan', *New York Times*, 27 December 2006; Tahir (2007); 'Afghan rejects Iran's call to oust occupiers', *AFP*, 27 November 2006; Paul Watson, 'On the trail of the Taliban's support'; Connell and Nader (2006); Pamela Constable, 'Iran said to assist forces opposing Kabul government', *Washington Post*, 24 January 2002; 'Kanadahar official accuses Iran of arming commanders in Afghanistan', *AFP*, 21 January 2002; 'Iran seeking to draw western Afghanistan into its sphere of influence', *Associated Press*, 14 February 2006; Artie McConnell, 'Iranian conservatives seek to influence developments in Afghanistan; *Eurasia Insight*, 14 February 2002; Julian Borger, 'Surprising partners among Tehran's layer of alliances', *Guardian*, 10 February 2007; Graeme Smith, 'Tensions mount over Tehran's Afghan ambitions', *Globe and Mail*, 13 February 2007; Michael R. Gordon, 'U.S. says Iranian arms seized in Afghanistan', *New York Times*, 18 April 2007.

2
HOW AND WHY THE TALIBAN RECRUITED

2.I HOW STRONG ARE THE TALIBAN?

Even sources like the US Armed Forces, NATO and the UN implicitly recognise a marked increase in the fighting force of the Taliban between 2002 and 2006. This is evident when estimates of the strength of the Taliban are compared year-on-year (see Table 1). In this author's opinion though, NATO and US sources tend to release very conservative estimates, often at odds with their own combat casualties assessments. These estimates are likely to reflect the number of insurgents active at any given time, rather than the total number of individuals who joined the insurgency. For analytical purposes an attempt has been made here to break down their estimates into core and local fighters. Note that 'local' does not refer just to the fact that such fighters were recruited locally, but to the predominance of local interests in their motivations (see 2.2 *Early recruitment*); a substantial number of 'hard-core' fighters were also recruited in the villages. Total figures tend to fluctuate a lot because of the seasonal mobilisation of part-time fighters, varying rates of movement across the border and other factors. Estimates of the number of 'hard-core' fighters recruited in the madaras of Pakistan show a greater degree of consistency. In 2004 US estimates were of some 1,000 'hard-core' insurgents inside Afghanistan, a figure which grew to 2–3,000 by 2004 and to 3–4,000 by 2006. UN sources put the estimate for local fighters in the south alone in 2006 at about 6,000. The hard-core combatants recruited away from the villages were doing two- to three-month shifts inside Afghanistan and passing the remaining time resting in Pakistan, spending between a fifth and half of their time at the battlefront, depending on many factors including their agreements with individual commanders. Local recruits would presumably spend most or all the time inside Afghanistan, but would not always be active militarily if the focus of operations was away from their home area. Although these local recruits were not always at the battlefront, they were easier to mobilise than those based in Pakistan. On this basis, the total number of combatants in the ranks of the Taliban and their allies must have reached around 17,000 men by 2006, with 6–10,000 active at any given time. Some Afghan sources were putting the figure as high as 40,000, but this seems to be out of line even with the Taliban's own claims. Of course, these numbers were supplemented by international volunteers and Pakistani Taliban. The numbers of the former appear to have fluctuated between less than a thousand and two thousand, apparently first declining until at least 2004 and then recovering in 2006 and possibly as early as 2005. The pool from which the latter were recruited appears to have numbered in the tens of thousands from 2004, when the conflict in Waziristan started. The importance of the Pakistani Taliban was highlighted when in late 2006 a major upsurge in cross-border attacks took place, following peace deals between militants and Pakistani authorities in Waziristan. According to US intelligence sources, cross-border attacks in Khost and Paktika rose from forty in the two months preceding the agreement to 140 in the two months following it. Pakistani volunteers had, however, been playing an important role in the conflict since at least 2005. A cluster of twenty-five villages in Pakistani Pashtunistan reportedly lost over 100 young men to the jihad in Afghanistan up to the beginning of 2007, while sources from the ranks of the Pakistani Taliban indicated that 175 militants from South Waziristan alone lost their lives fighting in Afghanistan just in 2005–6. During just the first two months of 2007 the bodies of forty-five militants were repatriated to Pakistan. Since an estimated two-thirds of the Waziristan militants are reportedly based in North Waziristan and militants are also based elsewhere in Pakistan, the number of Pakistani martyrs in the new Afghan jihad must be running into several hundreds or more than 20 per cent of total insurgent losses.[1]

Initially foreign volunteers represented a significant share of the ranks of the insurgents. As the ranks of the Taliban expanded, the incidence of the foreign volunteer component lost importance, even if some of them seem to have continued to play advisory roles, accompanying Taliban commanders. When Taliban and foreign insurgents operated together, the commanders were always Afghans, at least according to the Taliban. From the beginning the foreign volunteers were mostly active in the south-east (Khost, Paktika) and in the east (Kunar, Nuristan). At the beginning of 2004, for example, the volunteers still constituted a third of the Taliban's strength in Paktika.[2]

	2002	2003	2004	2005	2006
Estimates by international sources					
Core (active)		1,000		2,000–3,000	3,000–4,000
Non-core				3,000–4,000	4,000–7,000
Estimates by author					
Core	3,000	4,000	4,500	5,500	7,000
core (active)	*500–1,500*	*800–2,000*	*1,200–2,500*	*2,000–3,000*	*3,000–4,000*
core madrasa-recruited	*3,000*	*3,700*	*3,700*	*4,400*	*5,500*
core village-recruited	*0*	*300*	*800*	*1,100*	*1,500*
Non-core village-recruited	1,000	3,000	5,000	7,000	10,000
average active (core + non-core)	*500–2,000*	*1,500–4,000*	*3,000–5,500*	*5,000–7,000*	*6,000–10,000*
Total	4,000	7,000	9,500	12,500	17,000
Foreign volunteers	1,500	1,000	700	1,200	2,000
Pakistani Taliban				40,000	40,000

Table 1. Estimates of the strength of the Taliban.

Sources: press reports, NATO sources, ISAF sources, US military sources, UN sources.

To estimate even roughly what degree of support the Taliban might have at the national level is extremely difficult. To this purpose a few opinion polls were carried out in 2005–6, but using polls to assess the political views of the population in a conflict zone is a quite controversial approach. It is unlikely that villagers in the war zone, aware of the possible fate of supporters of the Taliban, when approached by unknown pollsters would give honest answers to questions such as 'do you support the government?'. It is worth noting that most pollsters declared their inability to carry out polls in some provinces, usually including at least Zabul and Uruzgan, the two main strongholds of the Taliban at the time. When the sample of polled individuals was made available, it seemed very strongly biased towards individuals with at least some education, more likely to be opposed to the Taliban than the rest of the population. In the BBC/ABC poll of October 2006 53 per cent of the sampled interviewees had received at least some education and 59 per cent were literate, a much higher percentage than that usually estimated for the population as a whole (28 per cent). Only 27 per cent of the interviewees with a job were farmers or farm labourers and 7 per cent were unemployed, whereas government figures place unemployment at 33 per cent of the workforce and people employed in the agricultural sector at 56 per cent. Five per cent were police and soldiers (0.6 per cent of the workforce in reality), who would certainly be expected to express support for the government. Fourteen per cent were managers and executives, another category unlikely to sympathise with the Taliban and obviously greatly over-represented. In the World Opinion poll of January 2006 only 36.8 per cent of the sample was Pashtun, as opposed to the obviously overrepresented Tajiks (38.8 per cent), who were much less likely to sympathise with the Taliban; 50 per cent of the sample were literate (as opposed to 28 per cent in the population). Four of thirty-four provinces were not covered, but the poll did not specify which ones.[3]

Still, on the basis of polls like this, NATO sources claimed in 2006 that just 10 per cent of the population in the south supported the insurgents, whereas 20 per cent supported the government and the rest were sitting on the fence. However, local authorities and journalists travelling to the provinces affected by the insurgency had very different views about popular support for the Taliban. In the case of Uruzgan, Dutch sources were estimating that the Taliban controlled

80 per cent of the province, while the Australians claimed that no more than 40 per cent was under the control of government/foreign forces. The former governor of that province, Jan Mohammed, stated that the Taliban could count on the support of the population. The situation was similar in Helmand and Zabul at least (see 2.6 *Recruiting local communities*), and a British official admitted to a Pakistani journalist that the majority of the population in the south-west supported the Taliban.[4]

Clearly, while there is no question that although the insurgency initially had a small constituency, the Taliban successfully expanded their recruitment base from 2003 onwards. Numbers, of course, do not tell the whole story. To understand the expansion of the ranks of the insurgency, we have to examine in detail how the recruitment base widened between 2002 and 2006.

2.2 EARLY RECRUITMENT

The first reports of the Taliban's attempt to create in an organised way a rear support area in the NWFP and in Baluchistan surfaced in December 2001. As early as March 2002 a leader of the Taliban, Mullah Obaidullah Akhund, was reported to have issued a call to arms, while other middle rank leaders were already trying to use nationalist feelings in order to mobilise support against the 'occupiers'. Other sources within the Movement give a somewhat different, although not necessarily inconsistent, account of the start of the insurgency. According to these sources, sometime in the first half of 2002 Mullah Omar would have contacted his old commanders and asked them to carry out a census of their rank-and-file, finding out who was still alive. He then proceeded to launch a recruitment drive among madrasa students in Baluchistan and in Karachi, despatching Mullah Dadullah and Mawlawi Sadiq Hameed to find fresh flesh for the battlefield. A third prominent Talib commander, Hafiz Majeed, was allegedly sent into Afghanistan to seek support among tribal leaders and elders. Whatever the exact timing of the call to arms, a small army of recruiters was soon systematically visiting refugee camps (particularly Girdijangle in the Chagai Hills), madaras, mosques, social gatherings of various types and Pakistani Pashtun villages throughout the region of Quetta, signing up volunteers. Training camps, mostly mobile ones, were then set up around Quetta to train small groups of insurgents. A separate recruitment effort was likely underway in the NWFP. Nonetheless, the appeal was initially not very successful. It appears that relatively few of the 'old Taliban' rushed to join the new jihad. A group of twenty-two fighters interviewed by a journalist in Ghazni at the end of the summer of 2005 included just two veterans of the pre-2002 period, although by the time of the interview some of the 'old Taliban' might also have died in the fighting. In remote areas inside Afghanistan some groups of stray Taliban reactivated themselves towards the end of 2002 or early 2003 (see 4.2 *Rooting out government presence*), but that was about it. As a result, the age of the fighters mostly ranged between twenty to twenty-five years, with commanders being somewhat older at thirty to forty. Only among the top leaders were the 'old Taliban' present in strength, in fact accounting for all of the ten to twelve members of the Leadership Council (see 2.5 *Taliban, tribes and elders* and 3.3 *Command structure*). However, even those 'old Taliban' who did not directly join the insurgency at the beginning might have done so later or in any case contributed to spread pro-Taliban feelings among the population. In Uruzgan in the late summer of 2002, for example, many Taliban were uneasily waiting for further developments in their villages, sometimes continuing to claim their allegiance to the Movement, other times trying to recycle themselves as pro-government and even pro-American. Similarly, the presence of many inactive Taliban was reported in Farah province. In the end, the attitude of the authorities and the changing circumstances of Afghanistan would prove decisive in orienting the decisions of the 'old Taliban'.[5]

Throughout 2002–6 Pakistani madaras continued to provide an inexhaustible flow of new recruits as many Afghan families continued to send their children to study there. The absence of prestigious madaras in Afghan territory and the financially advantageous conditions offered by some Pakistani madaras convinced Afghan families to send their children across the border. However, from 2003 onwards recruitment started following other paths too. An obvious one in the Afghan context was kinship ties, which became a privileged channel of recruitment. It appears, however, that the biggest numbers came through the support of the clergy and through enlisting community support in specific areas (see 2.6 *Recruiting local communities*).[6]

What are the underlying factors of the Taliban's appeal among the Pashtun tribal youth? The interpretation of Imran Gul, programme director of the Sustainable Participation Development Program, an NGO based in Banu, just outside North Waziristan, applies to the NWFP, but appears to have some validity for Afghanistan as well. Gul believes that the tribal system is in crisis and that it can no longer provide 'peace, income, a sense of purpose, a social network' to the local youth, who then turn to radical movements (collectively known as the Pakistani Taliban) as the only outlet where they can express their frustration and earn the prestige once offered by the tribal system. Officials working in the region support this view, claiming that the youth 'oppose the current tribal system because they know that this is not … harnessing their potential'. Military incursions in the tribal areas further undermined the influence of the elders in the NWFP and might have had the same result in Afghanistan. A Pakistani official from South Waziristan expressed similar opinions: 'Military actions and policy have contributed to the anarchical situation that pro-Taliban militants are more than happy to fill. Their demonstrated ability to restore order, prosecute criminals and dispense speedy justice was welcomed by many civilians fed up with violence and insecurity.' The conclusion of an ICG analyst is that 'fear of the militants, combined with resentment against a corrupt administration and draconian laws, has contributed to local acquiescence of Taliban-style governance.' The sidelining of the Waziri tribal elders and the emergence of the clergy in a prominent political role resulted for the first time in the recruitment of members of rival tribes under a common banner for long-term political action. It should be added that the success of the local Taliban was favoured by the implicit complicity of the Pakistani administration of the NWFP, which only allowed pro-Taliban and Islamist political groups to operate in the area, preventing secular groups from competing with them.[7] In Afghanistan the legitimacy of tribal and village elders was weakened by the war and by the emergence of armed strongmen who often tried to replace the elders, without entirely succeeding.[8] Moreover, the youth who grew up in the Pakistani refugee camps were much less likely to be respectful of the tribal elders. Anecdotal evidence suggests that the disruption caused by Afghan militias, police and foreign troops contributed to further weaken tribal and local elders. At the same time the difficulty of the tribal system (where it still existed) or of the rural economy to cope with war, post-war, large scale migration and resettlement, together with the uncertainty about the medium- and long-term future, led many families to seek a diversification of their sources of revenue and influence. Hence an increase in the number of children sent to the Pakistani religious madaras to become mullahs or to the cities to seek employment, both cases contributing to further weaken the influence of the elders over the youth. These alienated youths provided fertile recruitment ground for the Taliban.[9]

2.3 HARD-CORE, MERCENARIES AND OTHERS

Allegations that the Taliban were fielding a largely 'mercenary' force abounded in the press and in the statements of both the Afghan government and the foreign contingents. Reports and estimates suggested that most Taliban guerrillas were little short of mercenaries earning between US$100 and US$350 per month, depending on the region. That would be at least on a par with soldiers of the ANA and possibly as much as three times their income. The Taliban, by contrast, presented their payments as an indemnity for the families of the combatants, who would otherwise be deprived of their source of income. Indeed, the idea that the Taliban are mostly a mercenary force is at odds with strong evidence showing the commitment of Taliban fighters and their readiness to fight to the last man, as well as with the meagre results of the reconciliation programme (see 6.8 *Reconciliation efforts*). Such allegations, therefore, should be treated more as propaganda than anything else. A certain number of 'mercenaries' do indeed seem to have fought on the Taliban side, but their role appears to have been marginal. In line with their free-marketing approach to war (see 1.1 *The 'ideology' of the Taliban*), the Taliban sometimes paid villagers cash (reportedly US$15–55) to harass foreign and government troops with occasional rocket attacks and shooting. This seems a rational attitude considering what the cost would be, both in financial and operational terms, of maintaining teams of trained and committed guerrillas around each enemy military base all the time.[10]

If mercenaries were only a small percentage (10–20 per cent) of the Taliban active at any given time, usually recruited *ad hoc* for short term 'jobs', this does not mean that all the remaining Taliban were hard-core ideological fighters. After 2002 the ranks of the Taliban started filling with local recruits, mobilised by a whole range of different motivations. Table 1 represents a rough attempt to estimate the weight of the two main categories of Taliban, 'hard-core' and 'local'. The ideological hard-core gradually declined in terms of the total strength of the Taliban, even if it was growing in terms of absolute numbers. Some of these local recruits were opportunistic and marginal elements, particularly during the early stages of Taliban penetration in a particular area. Once the insurgency had grown into a significant threat at the regional level, it proved easy for the Taliban to mobilise marginal groups of the population even in areas where they did not yet have significant support. These groups were not politicised and their activities were low-scale, but nonetheless were having an impact. In the Loy Karez area of Kandahar, for example, the Taliban presence was limited in 2006 to just six or seven marginal youth and smugglers who would have benefited from the creation of a lawless environment. Unable to carry out significant military activities, this small group was sufficient to intimidate hostile members of the population in the absence of any state policing of the villages.

As of early 2007 such marginal elements accounted for much of the Taliban's presence outside their core areas. Although it would be inappropriate to describe them as mercenaries, financial incentives likely played an important role among their motivations and they were disinclined to take serious risks.[11]

A larger and qualitatively more important source of recruitment was that element of the population influenced by the clergy (see 2.4 *The role of the clergy*), while the largest contributors of local recruits were communities antagonised by the local authorities and security forces (see 2.6 *Recruiting local communities*). US military sources alleged in 2005 that the Taliban were recruiting under-age fighters (14–16 years old) and forcing families to provide one son for their formations. Later reports from the battlefield did not confirm the presence of large numbers of under-age combatants in the ranks of the Taliban. More or less forced recruitment in the form of requests to families to contribute one son to the cause was, however, alleged by some other sources, although in most cases coercion seems to have been limited to imposing the Taliban's presence in a village and the delivery of food and shelter. Forced recruitment was probably the most extreme form of the involvement of local communities in the war effort of the Taliban, as even in communities which sided with the Movement some families would be reluctant to contribute their sons and had to be forced to. Even when recruitment was endorsed by local notables, the line between voluntary and forced enlistment must have been a thin one.[12]

By 2006 the Taliban had formed a complex opposition alliance comprising:

- at the centre their purely ideologically driven madrasa students (including a significant number from the NWFP);
- a second ring of genuine jihadist recruits provided by village mullahs, mainly driven by xenophobia;
- a third, and by 2006 the largest, ring of local allies (communities and opportunists);
- an outer ring of mercenary elements.[13]

The first two categories can be said to be part of the 'hard-core' Taliban, while the remaining two are both 'non-core' in character (see 2.1 *How strong are the Taliban?*). The exact mix of the various types of insurgents varied greatly from province to province. For example, in areas far from the border, the percentage of madrasa-recruited fighters coming from Pakistan was unsurprisingly lower. Dutch sources estimated that in 2006 only 2 per cent of Taliban fighters in Uruzgan were not originally from that province. The rest of the 300–500 hard-core insurgents estimated to be there (20 per cent of the total) must therefore have been composed of hard-core Taliban recruited in the villages. Similarly in Helmand the total for the hard-core component was estimated at 20 per cent or 250–350 men. In Zabul a source put the hard-core component at 10 per cent, although this appears an underestimate. On average, by 2006 village jihadists might have accounted for perhaps 15–25 per cent of the active fighting strength of the Taliban at any given time, with madrasa recruits accounting for around 25 per cent, local allies for 40–50 per cent and mercenaries for another 10–15 per cent.[14]

2.4 THE ROLE OF THE CLERGY

The clergy as such was not one of the constitutive components of the insurgency in its early days. Most of the leaders of the Movement of the Taliban were indeed mullahs, but there is little evidence that initially a significant number of members of the clergy openly supported the rebels inside Afghanistan. However, the situation changed rather rapidly in many parts of the country, not least because of obvious ideological contiguities between the Taliban and the more conservative components of the Afghan clergy.[15] The Taliban regime had relied on them to control the country and gather information from the villages.[16] There were some sectors of the clergy, such as Sufi Tariqas, which were either politically indifferent or even pro-government and resented the prevarication of the new generation of Deobandi-influenced young mullahs. However, by the early twenty-first century Deobandism influenced probably the majority of the

Afghan clergy, particularly in the areas bordering Pakistan, as most mullahs had been trained in Pakistani madaras aligned with this fundamentalist-leaning school. The old Sufis were in decline. This can be seen as the culmination of a process of politicisation of the Afghan Ulema, which started in the nineteenth century and played to the advantage of the Movement of the Taliban, providing it with a natural constituency within Afghanistan. Whenever surveys of the opinions of the clergy were attempted, they found that regardless of their attitude towards the insurgency, they were hostile to the presence of foreign troops and unfriendly towards the government.[17]

The importance of clerical networks goes beyond the encouragement that they might have given to potential village recruits of the Taliban. In rural Afghanistan, due to the fragmentation of the population in multiple and often rival local communities, the clergy is often the only supra-communitarian network, particularly in remote rural areas. Its role in promoting collective action beyond the community level is therefore crucial.[18] Even the pre-1980s 'fragmented networks' had played an important role in the mobilisation of the jihad movement of the 1978–92 period, bypassing the segmentarity of local communities and allowing it to organise at least alliances at the sub-provincial level. By the 1990s these local networks were showing the tendency to coalesce into wider ones.[19] This was probably a result of the shift which occurred during the 1980s. Madrasa education declined in Afghanistan, where most students would have attended local schools, and moved to Pakistan, where students from different regions would meet and be socialised in each single madrasa.[20] Moreover, many young Afghans growing up in Pakistan were socialised in a non-tribal and more religious environment. It is also likely that the shared Deobandi background played an important role in increasing the homogeneity of the clergy, making political communication and alliances easier.

The first clerical networks to start supporting the Taliban appeared to have been those located in Zabul, where they started supporting the insurgency as early as 2003. At that time the district governor of Shah Joy, one of the districts where government presence was stronger due to the fact that it is crossed by the main highway, esti- mated that the clergy of 25 mosques and madaras were supporting the Taliban within his area of responsibility. By the admission of the provincial governor, by 2006 'Zabul's religious leaders all supported the Taliban. In northern Helmand the first signs that part of the clergy was preaching jihad against the government and Americans emerged in the summer of 2004. A similar pattern was reported at least for Ghazni and Paktika, although the dating is uncertain. In other parts of southern Afghanistan, such as Kandahar province, the mullahs started openly supporting the Taliban later, but by 2006 such support was widespread in the rural districts. Only within Kandahar city did most mullahs remain pro-government. The Afghan security forces were well aware of this and in July 2006 carried out raids in mosques and madaras in several districts, arresting some 150 people, of which twenty-five were then detained. [21]

There were important pockets of resistance to the trend. In Paktia (Paktya) and Khost, the clergy remained hostile to the Taliban well into 2006, due to the strength of local Sufi networks. The conserva- tive Tablighi networks do not appear to have supported the Taliban either. However, the shift of the clergy towards supporting the insur- gency was not limited to the south and parts of the south-east. During 2006 reports emerged that the mullahs of Wardak were beginning to express support for the Taliban. Indeed by 2006 the presence of mul- lahs urging the believers to join the jihad against the government and the foreigners was reported even in Kabul's mosques. The mullahs who railed against the moral corruption dominating Kabul included some who had previously supported members of the government coalition. Mullahs preaching against the government and the for- eigners were reported as far as Takhar and Badakhshan provinces in north-eastern Afghanistan. In Badakhshan, the Taliban seem to have approached mullahs from the southern districts of Jurm, Yam- gan, Keran-e Munjan and Warduj and even to have invited them to Pakistan for discussions.[22]

The Taliban enhanced the role of their allies among the clergy by eliminating or intimidating into silence pro-government mullahs. In Kandahar the killings of mullahs started in the summer of 2003. Between June and July three were killed in the city. The campaign to assassinate pro-government religious figures continued unabated after 2003 and Kandahar remained very much the focus of the assassination campaign. Of twenty clerics assassinated between the summers of 2005 and 2006, twelve were from Kandahar. Another forty were wounded countrywide over the same period, and countless received threats. The focus on Kandahar is probably linked to the concentration in this city of pro-government mullahs, as well as to the fact that in rural areas few mullahs could afford to ignore the death threats. The survivors had three options. They could rely on the protection of armed guards, if they were influential enough to deserve government protection or could afford it. Alternatively, they could live in hiding, which suited the Taliban because it prevented them from preaching. Finally, they could flee to safer places. As a result, the residual influence of pro-government mullahs was almost obliterated in the areas affected by the insurgency.[23]

2.5 TALIBAN, TRIBES AND ELDERS

Some analysts as well as Afghan commentators have seen a tribal dimension in the insurgency, in particular identifying the Ghilzai tribes as the main source of support for the Neo-Taliban. This interpretation of the causes of the insurgency rests on the alleged near-domination of the leadership of the Taliban by Ghilzais, especially the Hotak tribe. This, however, is incorrect, at least as far as the Neo-Taliban movement of 2003–6 was concerned. As Table 2 shows, in 2003–4 the Rahbari Shura (Leadership Council), which includes the main political military leaders of the Neo-Taliban, was not dominated by Ghilzais. If anything, the Durrani tribes were better represented. The 'Ghilzai insurgency' interpretation seems to have been popular within the ranks of US armed forces in Afghanistan, who were reported by some of their NATO allies as seeing the

Rahbari Shura 2003	Rahbari Shura 2004	
Name	*Name*	*Tribal background*
Mullah Omar	Mullah Omar	Hotak (Ghilzai)
Mullah Obaidullah	Mullah Obaidullah	Alkozai (Durrani)
Saifullah Mansoor		Sahak tribe (Ghilzai)
Mullah Dadullah	Mullah Dadullah	Kakar (Ghurghusht)
Akthar Mohammad Osmani	Akthar Mohammad Osmani	Ishaqzai (Durrani)
Jalaluddin Haqqani	Jalaluddin Haqqani	Zadran (Karlanri)
Mullah Baradar	Mullah Baradar	Popolzai (Durrani)
Mullah Rasul		Noorzai(?) (Durrani)
Hafiz Abdul Majid	Hafiz Abdul Majid	Noorzai (Durrani)
Mullah Abdur Razzaq*	Mullah Abdur Razzaq	Achakzai (Durrani)
Akhtar Mohammad Mansoor		Ishaqzai (Durrani)
	Amir Khan Muttaqi	Suleimankhel (Ghilzai)
	Mullah Mohammed Hassan Rehmani	Achakzai (Durrani)
	Qudratullah Jamal	Andar (Ghilzai)
	Mullah Abdul Kabir	Zadran (Karlanri)

Table 2. Composition of the Rahbari Shura and tribal background of its members (all members were Pashtuns by ethnicity).

* It is not clear whether this was Abdur Razzaq Nafiz, who was later killed by the Americans, or Abdur Razzaq Akhundzada, who was member of the Shura in 2004.
Sources: G. Smith, 'The Taliban: Knowing the enemy', *Globe and Mail*, 27 November 2006; 'Taliban Announce Creation of Council to Help "Evict" Leadership in Afghanistan', *RFE/RL Newsline*, 25 June 2003; Tsentral'nyi Bank RF, 'Prilozhenie n. 2, K ukazanniyu operativnogo kharaktera ot 20 avgusta 2002 goda n. 116-T, Obnovlennye spiski lits, imeyushikh otnoshenie k Afganskomy dvizheniyu Taliban'; Sayyid Massoud, *Posht-e purdeh kasi hasht!*, Kabul: Ahmad Printing Press, 2003.

Ghilzai tribe as synonymous with the Taliban, without any attempt to differentiate.[24]

More important, the pattern according to which local communities divided up into pro-government and pro-Taliban did not follow a strict tribal logic. The Taliban were ready to accept anybody who shared their views and accepted their rules, regardless of ethnicity and tribe. Taliban teams were always mixing together individuals with different tribal backgrounds. Clearly, the Taliban did not want to present themselves as aligned with a particular tribe or community. This made it easier for them to move across tribal territories without antagonising the locals, but at the same time was also a way of advertising the Movement as above inter-community rivalry. All those who had supported the Taliban regime and had been marginalised afterwards were prime targets for recruitment, regardless of their tribal background. Even if an estimated 95 per cent of the members were Pashtuns, they did try to recruit members of other ethnic groups as well. In Kahmard district (Bamian) support for the Taliban was reported among a number of small and marginalised Tajik armed groups. In Ghazni by 2006 the Taliban were trying with some success to reactivate groups of Hazara supporters who had cooperated with their regime in 1998–2001. Similarly, the assassination of a German NGO worker in Sar-i Pul in March 2007 is likely to have been carried out by a small gang of former Taliban collaborationists in the north. The presence of pro-Taliban pockets was also reported from 2005–6 in the southern districts of Ghor, where the population is largely Tajik Aimaq. As far as Pashtun tribes are concerned, the 'winner takes all' approach adopted at the end of 2001 ended up creating fissures even within the Popolzais, Karzai's own tribe. In the Shah Wali Kwot district of Kandahar, former collaborators of the Taliban were completely marginalised socially and politically in 2001 and later joined the Taliban to fight. Even among the Achakzais a significant number of Taliban could be found, despite the traditional enmity of many Achakzai communities with the largely pro-Taliban Noorzais. It is true that the tribal distribution of pro-Taliban communities was very uneven. Many were found among the western Ghilzais, who also felt marginalised in terms of spoils distribution. Other southern tribes within which support for the Taliban was widespread included the Kakar and the Tarin, but also many communities belonging to the Durrani tribes were drawn towards the insurgency, first and foremost the Noorzais of Kandahar (see 2.6 *Recruiting local communities*). The uneven participation of the tribes in the insurgency was the result of the tribal politics of the government and local authorities, rather than a conscious targeting by the Taliban (see *2.6 Recruiting local communities* and *1.2 'Rebuilding' the Afghan state*). One good reason for this is that in southern Afghanistan, and much of the south-east too, tribal structures had long disintegrated and tribes had lost their cohesion, if they ever had any.[25]

Some US sources alleged that cooperation between the Taliban and the tribes occurred at the higher level, implying the involvement of tribal leaders. Whether this is correct or not, it cannot be construed to mean that the leaders of the Ghilzais or of any other tribe/confederation supported the Taliban, for the simple reason that such 'grand' tribal leaders do not exist. Outside some tribes of the south-east and east (in any case not the Ghilzais) tribal leadership occurs at the clan and sub-tribe level if at all. There is instead evidence that certainly in at least some areas of Afghanistan elders and secular notables welcomed the Taliban in order to gain support in local struggles against communities connected to the government and old-time rivals (see *2.6 Recruiting local communities*). However, in general relations between elders and Neo-Taliban have not been good. Even in Mullah Omar's native village of Sangisar (Kandahar), the leaders resisted their activities in the area and tried to limit their presence as much as possible. There might be several reasons for this, including the fact that Taliban field commanders were young and elders might have resented their role (or *vice versa*). Moreover, many Taliban fighters and commanders were mullahs or trainee mullahs, a fact which is also unlikely to endear them to the elders, who could easily see them as rivals for influence. Deobandi mullahs and elders refer to alternative systems of legitimisation, one based on residual tribal traditions, control over wealth/land and community management skills, the other based on religion/'ideology' and skills in building bridges among local communities. Indeed, where elders remained strong and in control, they usually actively worked to prevent the infiltration of the Taliban. This is typically the case of the south-eastern provinces of Paktia and Khost, where with a few exceptions as of October 2006 the insurgents were still unable to find hospitality in the villages. In this area the tribal leaders were still able to impose tribal decisions and punish transgressors, particularly among the Mangals (see 2.6 *Recruiting local communities*). A number of anecdotes suggest that often elders have been instrumental in mobilising local opposition to the Taliban. For example, in January 2006 a group of Achakzai villagers in Spin Boldak (Kandahar) forced a group of Taliban out of their village after a gun battle. In another example, the strongman Haji Lalai Mama of Loy Karez village in Kandahar province gathered together a village defence to keep the Taliban away. In Panjwai Haji Lalai tried to do the same by sponsoring an anti-Taliban movement, but was instead forced to flee by the insurgents and had to seek refuge in Kandahar city. Even in Musa Qala, where local authorities tried to portray the elders who signed a truce agreement with the British as indistinguishable from the Taliban, strong contrasts were reported between the latter and the elders once the truce collapsed. Occasionally government authorities seem to have realised the role of elders as potential allies. For example, in the autumn of 2003 the governor of Zabul, Hafizullah Hashem, created a commission to work with the elders of Dai Chopan, a Taliban stronghold. The offer was to trade off government support (provision of services etc.) with allegiance to the Taliban. In order for the tribal elders to play a significant political role, they had to be either incorporated in state-sponsored structures, such as the Peace Strengthening Commission, or mobilised from above to participate in tribal assemblies. However, the inability to provide security at the local level and the general weakness of the subnational administration prevented the government from successfully mobilising potential support among the elders.[26]

Despite the fact that the elders in general showed little enthusiasm for supporting the insurgents, the Taliban would first of all approach the elders in order to be granted the right to enter tribal territory and the villages. If successful, they would establish themselves in the territory and then either work with the elders or gradually marginalise them. In certain areas and on certain issues, such as the opposition to foreign presence or to the eradication of the poppies, the elders were aligned with the Taliban. In areas like these, the Taliban were ready to allow them a say. This seems to have been common in northern Helmand. For example, the elders of Musa Qala were able to negotiate a truce between the British and the Taliban in October 2006. Friction occurred at times between Taliban and elders, but the local commanders of the Taliban most of the time managed to contain it. There and at least in Zabul too, but probably in Uruzgan and parts of Kandahar as well, elders found that the Taliban were the only force which could help express their grudges against the government. Some reports suggested that the widespread use of air power and its side effects contributed to push many elders to side with the insurgents.[27]

If unsuccessful in being allowed into a village's territory or when facing resistance from a section of the elders, the insurgents would start targeting elders in a campaign of intimidation and murder, usually accusing the victims of being US spies. The most famous example of a notable opposing the Taliban and paying the price for it is that of Qari Baba, former governor of Ghazni under Rabbani, who was assassinated in March 2006 after announcing that he was taking over the security of Andar district in order to defeat the insurgency. The elders often found it difficult to oppose the Taliban's onslaught, once the latter became able to concentrate large numbers of their men in a small area. On the whole, it would seem that the Taliban's carrot-and-stick tactics to bring the elders in line were quite successful. During the Presidential elections of 2004, none of the village and tribal elders of the districts of Atghar, Shamulzay, Shinkay, Suri and Nawbahar (Zabul) accepted to take part in the organisation of the electoral process. Three elders from Arghandab district, who agreed to do so, were later executed by the Taliban. Even in Panjwai under the occupation of Canadian and government troops (November 2006), when a delegation including the Minister of Rural Development and the Deputy of the UN Special Representative travelled to Kandahar to meet the elders, several of them refused to attend the meeting. After Operation Baaz Tsuka in December 2006, despite occupying the ground militarily the Canadians could not identify the local elders in order to arrange with them the distribution of aid. In general, the majority of elders appear to have been sensitive to the local balance of force and supported the Taliban whenever the authorities seemed to be unable to control territory. In response to this problem, NATO forces planned the deployment of police forces in the newly freed villages, strengthened by ANA strongholds, to work together as an early warning system against attempts to infiltrate Kandahar.[28]

2.6 RECRUITING LOCAL COMMUNITIES

NATO sources acknowledged a dramatic increase in the number of locally recruited fighters during 2006, even if in September 2006 NATO sources estimated that still 40 per cent of insurgents were coming straight from Pakistan. This was the result of a trend which had started much earlier, during 2003–4 when the Taliban were infiltrating into Afghan territory. Despite having been a mainly southern-based movement since its inception, after 2001 the Taliban did not particularly focus their efforts to infiltrate Afghanistan on any particular region. They started at about the same time all along the Pakistan border, with the south lagging slightly behind the south-east and the east. They met, however, with different degrees of success.[29]

a) *The south-east*
The military effort was initially strongest in the south-east, probably due to the local leadership and charisma of expert guerrilla leaders like Jalaluddin Haqqani, who had played an important role in the jihad of the 1980s. However, much of the south-east turned out to be a not so welcoming place for the insurgents. By 2006 they had only been able to find sufficient sympathy to establish a support infrastructure in Ghazni province, the south-eastern districts of Paktika, like Barmal and Terwah (Gomal), and the Zurmat district of Paktia. Paktia and Khost remained largely hostile to the rebels, mainly due to the strong opposition of the tribal leaders (see 2.5 *Taliban, tribes*

and elders), even if by then there were signs that the support of the tribal leadership for Karzai and the government was waning because of its inability to provide security. The fact that no particular tribe or individual dominated the local authorities suggested the emergence of disgruntled or alienated communities (see 4.6 *Exploiting divisions among communities*). The majority of the few local insurgents seemed to have a Hizb-i Islami background more than a Taliban one. Using his own personal influence among the Zadran tribe and the madrasa network he built in the 1980s, Haqqani was able to maintain a relatively high degree of violence in the districts populated by this tribe. By the end of the summer of 2006 his men were beginning to threaten the road connecting Gardez to Khost, and crossing the mountainous Zadran territory started becoming dangerous. Still, he had not been able to establish real strongholds there. The fact that that road, which had been nearly impassable to Soviet and government troops in the 1980s, was regularly open until at least 2005 and still not closed although somewhat dangerous in 2006 is a clear sign of the weak penetration of the insurgency until then. However, the relentless attacks across the border with Pakistan were by early 2007 beginning to dent local opposition to the Taliban in some districts of Khost province.[30]

By contrast, the areas of the south-east where the influence of the tribal leaderships was weaker and that of the clergy stronger, such as southern Ghazni, much of Paktika and Zurmat of Paktia, saw a much more rapid expansion of Taliban influence. Here the mainstay of Taliban recruitment was the local conservative religious networks, which openly supported the insurgents, but there is evidence that support for the Taliban spread well beyond the clerics and their immediate followers. Unsurprisingly, the Taliban established their influence first where the government was weaker. Central-eastern Paktika, which is also on the border with Pakistan, was one of the first areas to fall under them. Although Paktika was heavily infiltrated by non-Afghan volunteers, according to US officers 'everybody' was fighting against their troops. One explanation might be

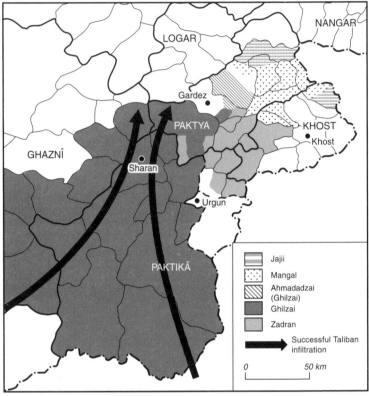

Map 3. Main tribes of south-eastern Afghanistan.
Source: Tribal Liaison Office, Kabul.

that the local population had been turned against the government by the mistreatment inflicted by the local authorities. Southern Ghazni, slightly more remote from the border, followed in 2004. By 2005–6 even eastern Ghazni was falling under the influence of the Taliban. During the summer of 2006 locals were reporting that the population was increasingly sympathising with the Taliban, even if in most cases they did not dare to openly side with them. At about the same time recruitment of locals started. Local support was acquired by such actions as eliminating a notorious local bandit, Bismillah Khan, who had been active on the main highway. In 2006 the government presence had been sufficiently weakened in northern Paktika too (Jajii) and, had it not been for the significant US military presence there, the region appeared well on its way to falling to the insurgents.[31]

b) *The south*

It was, however, in the south, despite the initial military weakness and inexperience of the insurgents, that the Neo-Taliban were most successful. In Kandahar and parts of Helmand and Uruzgan, Karzai's associates and allies with their militias had acted as a bulwark against the penetration of the Taliban (see 1.2 *'Rebuilding' the Afghan state*). However, the same men and their militias drove their local rivals over to the opposition by systematically marginalising them from all positions of power and then harassing them. Communities and individuals who had supported the Taliban, but even some that had not, feared that their tribal enemies might turn the government and the foreign contingents against them. 'Bad tips' by local informers, who were trying to cast their local rivals as Taliban and direct the security agencies or the foreign troops against them, appear to have been given quite frequently. The Taliban then appeared as the only protection available.[32]

This, for example, was the case of many among the Noorzais of Kandahar, who during the Taliban regime had been able to wrest control of the key border post of Spin Boldak from the rival Achakzais. With the fall of the Taliban, rival tribal militias from the two tribes confronted each other in Spin Boldak for some time. By the end of 2001, however, the Achakzais had gained decisive supremacy through their coalition with Gul Agha Shirzai, an ally of President Karzai and key power-broker in Kandahar (see 1.2 *'Rebuilding' the Afghan state*). Control of Spin Boldak was handed over to Achakzai militia leaders.[33] Now in control of the border police and extracting illegal taxes from travellers, they would also use their newly-found power to harass their old rivals and to brand them as Taliban, effectively pushing them over to the opposition. Having started in

Spin Boldak, the conflict spread to Panjwai district in 2006, where much of the population also belongs to the two tribes. The vehicle of the 'contagion' was the Achakzai-controlled border police, which was dispatched from Spin Boldak to contain Taliban infiltration in Panjwai, arousing the hostility of local Noorzais who were aware of its leader Abdul Razik's record in fighting other Noorzais in Spin Boldak. After Razik's border militia was defeated, police and ANA were called in to fight the 'insurgents', pushing Panjwai's Noorzais further into the arms of the Taliban. The Taliban took care to appoint a Noorzai as their field commander in Panjwai, facilitating the incorporation of the disgruntled villagers.[34]

In Zabul the recruitment of locals started no later than 2003. The recruits were Hotak and Tokhi Ghilzais (the two largest local tribes), opposed to the Kabul-sponsored Durrani by a long-running feud. In 2002 President Karzai had dispatched his nephew (a Durrani) to Zabul as chief of police, antagonising the locals. As the situation in Zabul started deteriorating, due to the infiltration of the Taliban and to inter-tribal feuding, Karzai, towards the end of 2003, replaced governor Hamidullah Tokhi, a former local commander and a Ghilzai, with one of his Durrani protégés from Kandahar, Hafizullah Hashem. As a result, Tokhi's men stopped fighting for the government, while Hashem could only bring a limited number of his own men from Kandahar, whose presence moreover was seen by the locals as further antagonism. By the end of 2003 five of Zabul's seven districts were under the control of the Taliban, leaving only the areas around the main highway under the influence of the government.[35]

In Uruzgan, the conflict initially opposed mainly Ghilzai and Noorzai to Popolzais, Barakzais and some Achakzai communities. However, several Achakzai communities in Gezab and in the northern part of Khas Uruzgan also joined the opposition to the Popolzai provincial rulers, who could count on Karzai's support. Some Moghol communities between Khas Uruzgan and Chora, who call themselves Barakzais, were also controlled by the insurgents. Jan Mohammed had a reputation of being an ineffective administra-

Map 4. Activities of the Taliban by area, 2006.
Sources: press reports, AIMS/UN security maps, US situation maps, NATO/ISAF situation maps, UN sources.

tor more concerned with stuffing the provincial headquarters with cronies than with trying to attract development money, but this is not the worst to be said about him. He played divide and rule with the Barakzais and the Achakzais, which if united could have claimed a greater political role in the province by virtue of their numerical superiority. He achieved his aims by appointing members of a clan or sub-tribe to run districts populated by other clans and *vice versa*. He then kept unpopular district governors and chiefs of police in place until a violent conflict exploded. At that point he would side with one of the warring factions against the other. The result was a chaotic war of all against all, with tribes and sub-tribes confronting each other; Jan Mohammed presented himself as the only one able to somehow control this chaos, justifying his lasting occupation of the post of governor, despite the Popolzais being a small minority in Uruzgan. President Karzai repeatedly received delegations from Uruzgan, pleading for him to intervene and restrain Jan Mohammed, but to no avail. Jan's hatred of the Taliban and their alleged supporters derived from having been imprisoned and tortured by them before 2001. The weaker side in the conflict had no other option but to seek the support of the Taliban.[36] Gezab district of Uruzgan is a good example of how the conflict was neither ethnic nor tribal, despite having a tribal component:

- The governor appointed to run the district by Jan Mohammed was an Achakzai, Ahmad Jan, who had formerly been cooperating with the Taliban. By appointing this unpopular character Jan Mohammed achieved two aims: he created a local ruler who was dependent on him for survival and he divided the most influential Achakzai family in the district, of which Ahmad Jan was a junior member.

- The senior members of Ahmad Jan's family, like Ataullah Jan and his father, were so upset with Jan Mohammed that they lobbied to include Gezab district in Daikundi province, a majority Hazara province, rather than in Uruzgan in order to get rid of his influence.

- Jan Mohammed then appointed to the position of chief of police of Gezab a man from neighbouring Khas Uruzgan district, but to the same position in Khas Uruzgan a man from Gezab. Both districts are populated by Achakzais and this move was clearly intended to create animosity between different clans.

- Some of the local authorities had been directly appointed by President Karzai and were not allied with Jan Mohammed, who therefore started manoeuvring to remove them. This was the case of the governor of Khas Uruzgan, Qudus Khan, who had his own following as demonstrated by his election as delegate to the Emergency Loya Jirga of 2002. When the chief of police from Gezab in charge of Khas Uruzgan was assassinated, Jan Mohammed accused Qudus Khan of being responsible and then mobilised tribesmen from Gezab against him. Qudus Khan was killed in the fighting.[37]

Similar conflicts also developed in neighbouring districts, such as Kijran (later to become part of Daikundi province), where in 2003 district governor Abdur Rahman Khan was reportedly harassing local communities with his arbitrary behaviour and tax collection. In Char Chena it was the governor Toren Amanullah who collected taxes and had prisoners complained of ill-treatment. Later the two fought over the control of Kijran. The employment of tribally based militias to fight the Taliban compounded the problem. The Barakzai militia of Nisar Ahmad, for example, had occupied Tarin Kwot at the end of 2001 as the Taliban were fleeing. They proved very useful to Jan Mohammed in securing the surroundings of the provincial capital, but at the price of alienating the population of such places as Balochi Valley, north of Tarin Kwot, which became Taliban strongholds. The farther from Tarin Kwot, the more difficult it proved for Jan Mohammed to control the conflict he himself had started. Some of these districts, like Shahid-i Hassas and Gezab, fell completely into the hands of the Taliban. The power bloc created by Jan Mohammed survived his departure, not least because of the support of US Special Forces and of President Karzai himself. In early 2007 the militiamen of the district governor of Dihrawud clashed with the special reserve police force, losing two men. In revenge the district officials reportedly ordered the killing of the head of the special reserve and one of his men. Special Forces allegedly prevented him from being tried as he was one of their allies. In Tarin Kwot Jan Mohammed's nephew and chief of police, Matiullah, maintained a powerful and well-funded 1,000-strong militia even after his sacking. Within the administration of Tarin Kwot and among US Special Forces Matiullah maintained strong support as the most committed enemy of the Taliban and the most powerful strongman in the area.[38]

The anti-Jan Mohammed factions throughout Uruzgan were soon looking for support and alliances and in many cases found them in the Taliban. Because of the conflict, hundreds of families left their districts for Kandahar and other locations, among them several tribal khans. Their departure allowed the influence of the Taliban to spread further. Once the Taliban had successfully penetrated the villages, they started their own purge of hostile elements, but more effectively than Jan Mohammed or his local allies.[39]

In Helmand the recruitment of locals in the Taliban's ranks was first reported in the summer of 2004. They recruited among communities that suffered harassment at the hands of police and security forces. During the first two to three years of the insurgency, Helmand was not particularly welcoming to the Taliban. In Musa Qala, for example, the Taliban first tried to establish a base in 2004, but did not find much local support and had to leave. By 2006, however, they had become very popular there. The Taliban attributed their success to the abuses of the governor, Sher Mohammed Akhundzada, and his militias, as well as to his refusal or inability to mend his ways or pay compensation despite the mediation of a tribal jirga. Like elsewhere, Karzai's cronies were antagonising many communities, throwing them into the arms of the Taliban. The insurgents did not have to do much, except approach the victims of the pro-Karzai strongmen and promise them protection and support. Attempts by local elders to seek protection in Kabul routinely ended nowhere as the wrongdoers enjoyed either direct US support or Karzai's sympathy. Dad Mohammed Khan, NSD chief of Helmand province, was particularly notorious for his abuses, but retained his position for a long time due to his direct connection with US forces, who thought he was serving them well. Only in 2006 was he removed at the insistence of UNAMA.[40]

A typical case concerned Ishaqzai communities, which had been very influential in Helmand under the Taliban regime, at the expense of the Alizais who had dominated the province until 1994. With the fall of the Taliban, Alizai circles around governor Sher Mohammed Akhundzada were once again elevated to the power they had been holding in 1981–94 and proceeded to marginalise and 'tax' Ishaqzai communities. In 2006 a violent conflict broke out. The Taliban exploited the conflict to consolidate their influence in Sangin district, where the Ishaqzai are the majority of the population, but this did not prevent them from maintaining their pockets of support among Alizai clans hostile to Sher Mohammed, such as in Baghran and in other parts of northern Helmand. Then, when the government and its international sponsors started a half-hearted attempt to eradicate the poppy fields in Helmand, support for the Taliban in the villages was immediately boosted. At that point any expression of support for the government in northern Helmand became impossible. Even the governor, a close ally of president Karzai, and his intelligence chief admitted to that. British troops reported that they could feel the hostility of the locals and that pro-Taliban tapes were openly sold in the bazaar. Stone-throwing by villagers at convoys of foreign troops was not unusual. Villagers appeared to act as informers of the Taliban and seemingly cooperated in setting up ambushes with them. The popularity of the Taliban was not limited to Musa Qala or Sangin. Even a district like Gereshk, not far from Lashkargah, was in 2006 fully infiltrated by the Taliban, who could be spotted in the roads of the district centre without the police daring to intervene. The countryside was *de facto* under Taliban control and even the district governor was admitting that the population was opposed to the government.[41]

The situation in the south was further complicated by the fact that in 2004–5, in part because of the pressure of the international community to clean up his act and in part due to the manipulations of local allies, Karzai and his circle started dropping their local allies one by one. As a result, the old jihadi strongmen stopped acting as a bulwark against the Taliban in 2004–5, as they were being marginalised.[42] This was the case for the Alkozai commander, Mullah Naqibullah, who gradually lost any influence over the provincial authorities and consequently the ability to reward and maintain the loyalty of large numbers of followers (see 1.2 *'Rebuilding' the Afghan state*). The number of Alkozais actively fighting in the insurgency remained relatively low, but the main impact seems to have been that the militarily powerful Alkozai militias were no longer committed to keeping the Taliban away from Kandahar. Because most of Kandahar's police was Alkozai, the development was bound to have a significant impact. The first Taliban teams were spotted in Alkozai-populated Arghandab in 2005, just after the loss of control of the police by the Alkozai. By 2006 the Taliban were talking of courting the sympathy of the population of Arghandab Valley of Kandahar province by mobilising them against the corrupt local police. Mullah Naqibullah continued to maintain his distance from both the government and the Taliban, at least in public: he complained about the behaviour of foreign troops, advocated talking to the insurgents but at the same time invited locals not to join the Taliban. Similarly, in Helmand after the demise of Governor Sher Mohammed Akhundzada in early 2006, his militias stopped actively pursuing the Taliban, allowing a rapid deterioration of security.[43]

c) *The east*

In the east, as in the south-east, the success of the Neo-Taliban was modest. This was due to several factors:

- like in the south-east, tribal structures maintained a high degree of cohesion and of ability to self-rule and self-govern;
- the Taliban always had weak roots in this area, hence the presence of few former members of the Movement to be recruited back into active warfare; Hizb-i Islami members were present in greater numbers, but had often re-integrated in society;
- the presence of a relatively strong intelligentsia, with at least some tribal connections;
- the presence of strong nationalist feelings, which played against an insurgency widely seen as a Pakistani stooge.

Nangarhar province, where all these elements of anti-insurgent resilience were present, proved the toughest nut to crack. An uneasy pro-Kabul alliance between the Arsalai family and warlord Hazrat Ali managed to maintain control over Nangarhar's tribes, combining long-established wealth, connections, influence, tribal management and newly acquired military strength. In Nangarhar educational levels are also significantly higher than the Afghan average. The Nangarhari intelligentsia seems to have maintained strong tribal connections and therefore some influence in the rural areas, correspondingly weakening the role of the clergy. Significantly, the only areas within Nangarhar that the insurgents managed to penetrate to any extent were Hisarak and the Khugyani districts, all characterised by lower educational levels and a greater strength of clerical networks. The comparatively dynamic economy of Nangarhar was more successful than that of other provinces in offering opportunities to the mostly educated cadres of Hizb-i Islami. Finally, Nangarhar is probably the province in Afghanistan where nationalist feelings run highest, due to the prevalence of tribes who live straddling the border with Pakistan and who suffered greatly in the past sixty years whenever Pakistan closed the border to put pressure on Kabul's government.[44]

Hizb-i Islami used to have influence in many villages along the Jalalabad–Torkham road, but it either did not succeed or did not try to reactivate military activities there, although there were allegations that the area was used for planning activities elsewhere. Opportunities were not missing for the Taliban and Hizb-i Islami: Nangarhar was the only province in Afghanistan where in 2005 poppy eradication was implemented effectively, due largely to the cooperation of the governor, Din Mohammed (a member of the Arsalai family). Then the farmers failed to receive the promised compensation, or received only a fraction of it. Rumours abounded of corruption. But the farmers did not turn to the Taliban in significant numbers. Even when Mawlawi Khalis, the old leader of a splinter group of Hizb-i Islami, sided with the insurgency in October 2003, it did not have any appreciable impact outside his home areas in the Khugyani districts. By 2006 some signs of a slow degradation of security in outlying districts were reported. For example, in a single week in the autumn of 2006 twenty-three security-related incidents were recorded in Nangarhar province. Relatively large groups of insurgents were also observed moving around the western districts, a fact which suggests at least some tolerance of their presence by local communities. By early 2007 the insurgents had started attacking local administrators in remote areas, according to a pattern already seen elsewhere. Some incidents related to the behaviour of US forces in the province, such as house searches without accompanying Afghan troops, the killing of a local cleric in a raid against alleged insurgents and the shooting of civilians following a suicide attack, are likely to have contributed to turning the mood of the population increasingly against the foreign troops. Despite all this, by early 2007 Nangarhar was still the most secure province among those bordering Pakistan.[45]

None of the other three eastern provinces was blessed by this combination of factors of resilience. In all three the economy was far from dynamic and former cadres of Hizb-i Islami faced much greater challenges to reintegrate in society. Both the intelligentsia and nationalist feelings were very weak if present at all, especially in Kunar and Nuristan. Although tribal structures were strong in Kunar and Nuristan, tribal governance was suffering the absence of big and established strongmen with good self-governance skills and the consequent political fragmentation. In these two provinces, therefore, government presence and influence was extremely weak, even in terms of alliances with local strongmen. By the 1990s these regions had been largely 'colonised' by Salafi preachers, who were also often organised politically and hostile to the central government. Due to this extreme weakness of the government, in Kunar, in Nuristan and in the northern districts of Laghman, in 2002–3 the insurgents were already able to operate there without much hindrance. Only in the Pashai fiefdom of Hazrat Ali (Nangarhar and Laghman) and in the heavily patrolled southern districts of Laghman was government presence able to keep the insurgents at bay.[46]

Although in Kunar the insurgents seem to have been successful in recruiting a fair number of local former mujahidin of the 1980s and in winning the tolerance or even the passive help of many villagers, they did not score great successes in allying with local communities. This was likely the result of a government presence so weak that it

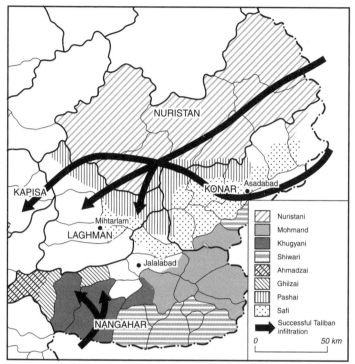

Map 5. Main tribes of eastern Afghanistan.
Source: interviews with local intellectuals and tribal notables, Jalalabad, February 2007.

was not even able to antagonise local communities, which in most cases appeared keen to maintain their autonomy *vis-à-vis* both insurgents and government. A rare exception was Koringal Valley in Pech district, where the local population had a strong tradition of hostility towards the central government. The locals were trying to protect their illegal timber trade from government regulation. The already difficult relationship of the government with the Koringalis was probably made worse by the attitude of district governors such as Mohammed Rehman, who first banned supplies of foods to the valley, then refused to issue identity cards to the valley's residents, and finally threatened to raise a tribal militia to invade the valley and punish the residents. Another area in which the presence of local insurgents had support among the population was Mail valley of Alisheng district (Laghman), where Commander Pashtun seems to have been a popular figure.[47]

d) *The rest of Afghanistan*

In the rest of Afghanistan recruitment among disenfranchised communities had achieved success in some isolated pockets of territory. In Bala-e Murghab and Ghormach of Baghdis, rivalries among local communities created an environment in which the Taliban managed to linger on after 2001, even if the distance from the Pakistan border made logistical support very difficult. During 2003–4 violent incidents in Baghdis were attributed to the Taliban by local authorities, although other sources described the attacks as the result of ethnic strife between the supporters of Governor Ismail Khan and some local Pashtun communities, or as inter-tribal clashes. Baghdis was also allegedly used by the Taliban to infiltrate neighbouring Faryab province. After a lull, in 2006 some insurgent activity was again reported in Baghdis. In northern Afghanistan NATO identified five areas of potential Taliban infiltration, even if there was little sign yet of this occurring.[48]

In Herat the conflict between several Pashtun communities and the Tajiks in control of the central government, as well as within Pashtun communities in Shindand and other districts, offered opportunities for the Taliban to infiltrate. After 2001 Ismail Khan, who had taken control of the western region, maintained only a precarious hold over the predominantly Pashtun districts of the west (Ghuryan, Kohsan and Gulran) and of the south (Adraskan, Shindand). His decision to keep Pashtuns out of positions of power and influence had been a major irritant to their communities, whose leaders also complained of Pashtun tribal leaders being assassinated, allegedly in an organised manner.[49] The abusive behaviour of Ismail Khan's militias against the local Pashtuns seems to have had a unifying effect on the tribes. In July 2002 a group of Pashtun tribal leaders gathered in Herat (presumably clandestinely) and prepared a petition to President Karzai, asking for the removal of Ismail Khan and for an enquiry into the abuses of his 'Tajik militias'. Soon Amanullah Khan, a strongman from Zeerkoh (Shindand), emerged to unify, in part, tribal opposition. Throughout 2002–4 Amanullah Khan survived all attempts by Ismail Khan to overcome him and even launched occasional counterattacks. His mere ability to survive politically and militarily turned out to be a winning card. He began to attract the support of disgruntled Pashtuns throughout the province and beyond. Hundreds of Pashtuns from Ghuryan and other districts joined his ranks. In Farah a former Taliban commander, Mullah Sultan, supported him. At the decisive moment he succeeded in mobilising support from as far afield as the southern provinces, obtaining the help of Gul Agha Shirzai and other strongmen, who sent hundreds of volunteers to fight in his ranks as well as money and weapons. By the summer of 2004 he was able to field a force of a few thousand motivated fighters, many of whom had suffered at the hands of Ismail Khan's men. With some support from Kabul, at least according to Ismail Khan, Amanullah Khan emerged as the leading player in an offensive organised with other disgruntled strongmen and warlords of the region, which in the summer of 2004 weakened Ismail Khan sufficiently for the central government to sack him from the position of governor of Herat. Following Ismail Khan's removal, tension and incidents continued in the region, as the anti-Ismail alliance proved unable to control the situation. The fact that there were no active remnants of the Taliban in the province until 2005 slowed the attempts of the insurgents to exploit the situation, but in that year the first reports of Taliban infiltration emerged with the capture of some emissaries in Herat city. Soon a terrorist campaign started in and around Herat. During 2006 the first manifestations of guerrilla activity emerged in Adraskan and Gulran districts, both populated by the most disenfranchised Pashtun communities. The alliance with Kabul of Amanullah Khan might have contributed to prevent the Taliban from infiltrating the countryside more effectively, but the killing of Amanullah in a tribal conflict in October 2006 removed the last barrier to Taliban penetration and the deteriorating security situation in the district forced the police to deploy new security

	Estimated by Western sources	Claimed by Taliban	Estimated by Afghan government	Author's estimate
Operating from Pakistan	3,000–4,000			5,500
Based in Afghanistan				
Kunar				500
Nangarhar				100
Laghman				200
Nuristan				200
Total east				1,000
Kapisa	200			200
Kabul				200
Wardak				100
Logar				300
Total Kabul region				800
Khost				100
Paktia				400
Paktika				900
Ghazni		900		900
Total south-east				2,300
Zabul	1,000–1,200		1,700	1,200
Helmand	1,500–2,000	2,500		2,000
Uruzgan	2,500			2,500
Kandahar	600–700			1,000
Total south	5,000–6,000	12,000–15,000		6,700
Farah				300
Herat				100
Baghdis				100
Ghor				200
Total west			700	700
Bamian				100
Total based in Afghanistan				11,500
TOTAL	7,000–10,000			17,000

Table 3. Estimates of the strength of the Taliban, 2006.

Sources: press report, UN sources, US military, NATO/ISAF

posts there. Open warfare reached Shindand in April 2007, when following the killing of an American soldier a major operation was mounted, leading to the killing of over a hundred Afghans, including many civilians. Judging from the subsequent wave of protest, it would appear that local opinion was turned decisively against the foreign troops as a result of the violence.[50]

North-east of Kabul the Taliban and Hizb-i Islami maintained strong support among the Pashtun communities of Kapisa and particularly Tagab district, where they represented most of the population there and were divided in rival communities as well as opposed to the Tajik communities of the neighbouring districts. Apart from an estimated two hundred local insurgents, the Taliban were reported to have built up their presence in the area during 2006 to up to five hundred fighters, prompting a NATO offensive to clear the area. Three training centres were found during the offensive, highlighting how the area had already been turned into a stronghold for the insurgency. After the offensive the insurgents withdrew to Kunar and Nuristan, waiting for opportunities to re-infiltrate. In April 2007 they were back in strength and attacked the district centre, blocking the highway for two hours.[51]

Based on the previous discussion of the presence of the Taliban inside Afghanistan, an estimate of their strength province by province is provided in Table 3.

2.7 CHANGES IN RECRUITMENT PATTERNS

As the conflict progressed, victims of abuses by both Afghan and foreign troops and of the side-effects of US reliance on air power began to represent another important source of recruits for the Taliban. They produced large numbers of displaced people, who in many cases sought refuge in camps around the provincial centres, or in Kandahar city itself, where they were often struggling to make a living. These internal refugee camps then turned into recruitment grounds for the insurgents. The Taliban even claimed that at one point the majority of their recruits belonged to this category, although this statement is likely to contain a fair dose of propaganda. However, probably the main boost to the Taliban came not from the bombardment *per se*, but from the revelation that not only the government was weak, but also the foreign contingents supporting it were stretched thin and had a limited capability to control the country. To Afghan villagers, the ability of NATO and the Coalition to win all battles brought little comfort, as the Taliban's ability to roam around in the villages was clearly not going to be challenged, nor their mountain strong-holds eliminated. The expectation that the Taliban would eventually emerge as the winners of the conflict, or at least force for them-selves a favourable compromise, also contributed to push villagers towards them. By the autumn of 2006 wild rumours were circulating among the population, concerning an impending national uprising, negotiations between the Taliban and other groups opposed to the Karzai administration, negotiations between the Americans and the Taliban, and so on. Even where the Taliban had little direct sup-port, the unpopularity of the government and what was perceived as the 'disrespectful' behaviour of the foreign troops, fuelled by lack of understanding for the local culture, had the effect of dividing and demoralising the opposition to the insurgents and creating some nostalgia for the time when the Taliban were in power. A change in the mood of the population seems, for example, to have occurred in Kandahar during the summer of 2006. Taliban elements were openly circulating in the city, claiming to journalists that they were even able to introduce themselves as Taliban to fellow Kandaharis. The gathering of financial and logistical support in Kandahar allegedly accelerated greatly in 2006, with the cooperation of many traders and businessmen, presumably to ingratiate themselves with the po-tential winners of the conflict. The Taliban were also claiming that many government officials were now helping them with supplies and even offering transport services. While these claims might well have been exaggerated for propaganda purposes, independent observers also felt that the mood of the population of Kandahar city was shift-ing. By the beginning of 2007 Taliban teams were beginning to gun down policemen within the city itself, which might be an indication of an enhanced ability to infiltrate the city. Other cities of Afghanistan seemed to some extent affected by the change too. The change in the attitude of the population was not limited to the south, but was detected even in Kabul. Several Afghan MPs, mostly supporting Karzai, expressed to journalists in December 2006 their feelings that the country was again drifting towards a generalised jihad against the foreigners and even implied some sympathy for such a trend.[52]

By 2005 or at the latest by late 2006 the Taliban seemed convinced that the wind was definitely blowing in their favour, a fact which tallies with reports that they were intent on mobilising forces for stepping up military operations. Feeling more confident, the Taliban increasingly focused their efforts at trying to achieve a national mobilisation and trigger a wider jihad movement. This effort consisted of at least three main components. The first, as shown in the Introduction and in this chapter, was aimed at spreading their influence at the village level as wide as possible. The second saw for the first time the Taliban targeting the cities. In the autumn of 2006 reports emerged that the Taliban had launched a big recruitment drive involving even areas outside their control or influence, such as Lashkargah, Kandahar city and refugee camps in central Helmand. Already in 2005 reports emerged that the insurgents were even trying to recruit a more educated constituency, judging from a number of arrests at Khost University in 2005, including students accused of planning terrorist attacks, and in Kabul, including at least one student from Kabul University (Sharia Law). The attempted recruitment of doctors to serve as support staff was also reported.[53]

The third component of this effort targeted the old jihadi commanders, who had mostly been fighting against the Taliban up until 2001. Coalition sources believed that attempts to recruit local strongmen ideologically close to the Taliban cause were going on at least in Kunar as early as 2002, allegedly with the help of some cash. Three such figures, including a relatively prominent one—Emergency Loya Jirga delegate and leader of a Salafi group, Haji Ruhollah—were actually arrested as early as June 2002 on allegation of working with the Taliban, although many critical voices argued against this accusation and the arrest might well have been the result of another 'bad tip'. In late 2003 Mullah Omar was reported to have issued an appeal to independent warlords, militia commanders and strongmen to join the Taliban. Even if this was true, such efforts were quite marginal at that time, both in terms of results and in terms of energy invested in them. By contrast, reports in 2006 suggested that the Taliban had started approaching former jihadi commanders of the 1980s war on a much larger scale, even offering them large one-off payments and monthly contributions of US$500 for joining the insurgency. Although by the end of 2006 it was still too early to see whether these efforts would succeed, it was already obvious that they had created more than a ripple in the Afghan political scene (see 4.9 *Alliances*).[54]

By late 2006–early 2007 the Taliban seemed intent on capitalising on a certain shift of opinion in their favour by relaxing their ideological strictures. At least in some of the areas under their control, such as Musa Qala, they were no longer demanding that men grow a beard, keep their hair short or refrain from watching movies. This appears to have broadened their appeal, particularly in the towns. Taliban commanders were telling journalists that they were not going to impose their convictions so 'harshly' as when they had previously been in power.[55]

NOTES

1   Carlotta Gall and Eric Schmitt, 'Taliban step up Afghan bombings and suicide attacks', *New York Times*, 21 October 2005; 'Interview with President Bush', *CNN*, 20 September 2006; 'Canadian-led offensive may have killed 1,500 Taliban fighters', *CBC News*, 20 September 2006; personal communication with UN official, December 2006; Massoud Ansari, 'Taliban butcher turns baker to fill his men's stomachs for war', *Daily Telegraph*, 15 October 2006; Suzanna Koster, 'Taliban fighters talk tactics – while safe in Pakistan', *Christian Science Monitor*, 9 November 2006; Wright (2006a); Benjamin Sand, 'Afghanistan's Taleban insurgency fueled by drug, terrorist money', *VOA*, 22 August 2006; van der Schriek (2005); Syed Saleem Shahzad,

'Fighting talk from Osama and the Taliban', *Asia Times Online*, 25 April 2006; Robert Burns, 'Commander wants Afghan tours extended', *Associated Press*, 16 January 2007; David S. Cloud, 'U.S. says attacks are surging in Afghanistan', *New York Times*, 16 January 2007; M. Ilyas Khan, 'Taleban in Pakistan commend dead', *BBC News*, 12 January 2007; Riaz Khan and Matthew Pennington, 'Pride, grief and anger at a Taliban recruiting area in Pakistan', *Associated Press*, 28 January 2007; Marzban (2006).

2 David Wood, 'Afghan war needs troops', *Baltimore Sun*, 7 January 2007; 'Menace taliban dans le Sud', *AFP*, 20 February 2004.

3 <http://news.bbc.co.uk/2/shared/bsp/hi/pdfs/07_12_06AfghanistanWhereThingsStand.pdf>; <http://65.109.167.118/pipa/pdf/jan06/Afghanistan_Jan06_quaire.pdf>.

4 Carlotta Gall, 'Peacekeeper commander mired in Afghan combat', *New York Times*, 15 October 2006; 'Macht Taliban in Uruzgan neemt toe', <http://www.rtl.nl//(/actueel/rtlnieuws/)/components/actueel/rtlnieuws/2006/10_oktober/23/binnenland/1023_0020_taliban_rukken_op.xml>; Karimi (2006), pp. 119–23 (courtesy of J. van den Zwan, Crisis States Research Centre, London); Paul McGeough, 'Winning hearts and minds is keeping the Taliban at bay', *Sydney Morning Herald*, 22 February 2007; Shahzad (2007), p. 7.

5 Syed Saleem Shahzad, 'Taliban's trail leads to Pakistan', *Asia Times Online*, 13 December 2001; Michael Ware, 'Encountering the Taliban', *Time*, 23 March 2002; Massoud Ansari, 'Almost two years after they were defeated, thousands join the Taliban's new jihad', *Telegraph*, 7 September 2003; Elizabeth Rubin, 'In the land of the Taliban', *New York Times Magazine*, 22 October 2006; Juliette Terzieff, 'Pakistani tribesmen stay fundamentally faithful to Taliban; Farmers put down plows to take up arms against U.S.', *San Francisco Chronicle*, 11 November 2003; Massoud Ansari, 'On the job with a Taliban recruiter', *Asia Times Online*, 27 November 2003; Wright (2006a); Jason Burke, 'Stronger and more deadly, the terror of the Taliban is back', *Observer*, 16 November 2003; Borhan Younus, 'Taliban hit and run, and come back for more', *Afghan Recovery Report*, no. 185 (10 September 2005); Wright (2006a); Phil Zabriskie and Steve Connors, 'Where are the Taliban now?', *Time*, 24 September 2002; Nivat (2006), pp. 80–93; interview with UN official, Herat, April 2004.

6 Interview with Massoud Kharokhel, 1 October 2006, Tribal Liaison Office, Kabul; Wright (2006a).

7 David Montero, 'Why the Taliban appeal to Pakistani youth', *Christian Science Monitor*, 16 June 2006; International Crisis Group (2006b), p. 22; Syed Saleem Shahzad, 'Revolution in the Pakistani mountains', *Asia Times Online*, 23 March 2006; interview with Abdul Rashid Waziri, former Minister of Tribal Affairs, Kabul, February 2007.

8 On this see Giustozzi (2006).

9 Personal communication with Massoud Karokhel, Tribal Liaison Office, Kabul, February 2007.

10 Benjamin Sand, 'Afghanistan's Taleban insurgency fueled by drug, terrorist money'; Rachel Morarjee, 'Taliban goes for cash over ideology', *Financial Times*, 25 July 2006; Declan Walsh, 'Kandahar under threat, war raging in two provinces and an isolated president. So what went wrong?', *Guardian*, 16 September 2006; Claudio Franco, 'In remote Afghan camp, Taliban explain how and why they fight', *San Francisco Chronicle*, 21 January 2007; Owais Tohid, 'Arid Afghan province proves fertile for Taliban', *Christian Science Monitor*, 14 July 2003; 'A geographical expression in search of a state', *The Economist*, 6 July 2006; Kate Clark, 'Cash rewards for Taliban fighters', *File On 4, BBC Radio 4*, 28 February 2006; Mike Collett-White, 'Les taliban ne manquent pas de recrues', *Reuters*, 23 August 2003; Anthony Loyd, 'It's dawn, and the shelling starts. Time to go into the Taleban maze', *The Times*, 14 February 2007.

11 Wright (2006a); Carlotta Gall, 'Taliban continue to sow fear', *New York Times*, 1 March 2006; personal communication with foreign diplomat, Kabul, March 2007.

12 Daniel Cooney, 'General: hard-hit Taliban recruiting kids', *Associated Press*, 24 July 2005; 'Taliban start recruiting fighters in Ghazni', *Pajhwok Afghan News*, 7 August 2006.

13 For the opinion of a CIA officer in this regard see David Rohde and James Risen, 'C.I.A. review highlights Afghan leader's woes', *New York Times*, 5 November 2006; see also Wright (2006a).

14 Graeme Smith, 'Doing it the Dutch way in Afghanistan', *Globe and Mail*, 2 December 2006; International Crisis Group (2006a); Talatbek Masadykov (UNAMA Kandahar), quoted in Graeme Smith, 'Inspiring tale of triumph over Taliban not all it seems', *Globe and Mail*, 23 September 2006; Hans de Vreij, 'Gevaren in Uruzgan nemen toe', *Radio Nederland*, 2 May 2006, <http://www.wereldomroep.nl/actua/nl/nederlandsepolitiek/dedden060501>; Syed Saleem Shahzad, 'Afghanistan's highway to hell', *Asia Times Online*, 25 January 2007; Elizabeth Rubin, 'In the land of the Taliban'; Kate Clark, 'Cash rewards for Taliban fighters'.

15 Interviews with police officers and UN officials in Takhar and Kunduz, May 2006. See also for example Halima Kazem, 'U.S. thins Taliban's ranks, but their ideological grip remains strong', *Christian Science Monitor*, 18 September 2003.

16 A point made by Barnett Rubin in 'The forgotten war: Afghanistan', interview with Joanne J. Myers, Carnegie Council, 14 March 2006.

17 See Roy (2000), Dorronsoro (2000) and Roy (2002). One survey was carried out by CPAU in Wardak in 2006–7.

18 See Trives (2006) and also Dorronsoro (2000).

19 See Harpviken *et al.* (2002), pp. 7–8.

20 On this shift see Dorronsoro (2000), pp. 11–12.

21 Halima Kazem, 'U.S. thins Taliban's ranks, but their ideological grip remains strong'; Elizabeth Rubin, 'Taking the fight to the Taliban', *New York Times Magazine*, 29 October 2006; Eric Schmitt and David Rohde, 'Afghan rebels

widen attacks', *New York Times*, 1 August 2004; Trives (2006); interview with Afghan journalist returning from the south, Kabul, 9 October 2006; Elizabeth Rubin, 'In the land of the Taliban'; 'Afghan police raid religious institutions in southern Afghanistan', *RFE/RL*, 10 July 2006.

22 Trives (2006); Wahidullah Amani, 'Afghanistan: a long, bloody summer ahead', *Afghan Recovery Report*, no. 219 (15 June 2006); Chris Sands, 'Kabul clerics rally behind Taliban', *Toronto Star*, 22 May 2006; personal communication with police officer, Teluqan, May 2006; personal communication with UN official, Kabul, March 2007.

23 April Witt, 'Afghan political violence on the rise', *Washington Post*, 3 August 2003; 'Taliban targets Muslim clerics in Afghanistan', *CBC News*, 5 August 2003; Declan Walsh, 'Taliban assassins target the clerics faithful to Kabul', *Observer*, 27 August 2006; Wright (2006a); interview with Maulana Obeidullah of the Peace Strengthening Commission, Kandahar, 28 January 2006.

24 Johnson and Mason (2007), pp. 76–9; *Cheragh*, 3 April 2007; Harm Ede Botje, 'We zitten darr goed', *Vrij Nederland*, 6 January 2007 (courtesy of J. van den Zwan, Crisis States Research Centre, London).

25 Interview with security officer, Kandahar, January 2006; Rahimullah Yusufzai, quoted in 'Senate body for launching Pak-Afghan inter-parliaments dialogue', *PakTribune*, 15 December 2006; personal communications with UN officials, Kabul, May 2004 and October 2006; personal communication with Niamatullah Ibrahimi (Crisis States Research Centre), Kabul, October 2006; Syed Saleem Shahzad, 'Taliban line up the heavy artillery', *Asia Times Online*, 21 December 2006; personal communication with UN official, Kabul, May 2005; Elizabeth Rubin, 'In the land of the Taliban'; Syed Saleem Shahzad, 'How the Taliban keep their coffers full', *Asia Times Online*, 10 January 2007; Graeme Smith, 'The Taliban: knowing the enemy', *Globe and Mail*, 27 November 2006. On this topic see also Giustozzi (2006).

26 Wright (2006a); Graeme Smith, 'Taliban are snubbed in their hometown', *Globe and Mail*, 17 April 2006; Jason Burke, 'Stronger and more deadly, the terror of the Taliban is back'; Tim McGirk, 'The Taliban on the run', *Time*, 28 March 2005; interview with Mir Akbar, Tribal Liaison Office, Gardez, 11 October 2006; Trives (2006); interview with security officer, Kandahar, January 2006; Carlotta Gall, 'Taliban continue to sow fear'; Les Perreaux, 'NATO urges Afghans to vacate volatile Panjwaii district', *Canadian Press*, 31 August 2006; Andrew Maykuth, 'An Afghan rebuilding takes shape', *Philadelphia Inquirer*, 6 October 2003; 'Musa Qala braced for NATO assault', *Afghan Recovery Report*, no. 240 (6 February 2007); 'Elders from five provinces demand government to negotiate with the opposition', *Musharekat-e Milli*, 13 February 2007.

27 Syed Saleem Shahzad, 'Taliban deal lights a slow-burning fuse', *Asia Times Online*, 11 February 2006; Alastair Leithead, 'Can change in Afghan tactics bring peace?', *BBC News*, 17 October 2006; Syed Saleem Shahzad, 'Taliban line up the heavy artillery'; 'Civilian casualties trigger anti-govt sentiments',

Pajhwok Afghan News, 21 August 2006; Danish Karokhel, 'Provincial election trouble', *Afghan Recovery Report*, no. 90 (22 December 2003).

28 'Afghanistan: un responsable tribal pendu par des talibans', *Xinhuanet*, 16 July 2005; UNAMA source, 1 October 2006; Elizabeth Rubin, 'In the land of the Taliban'; Les Perreaux, 'NATO urges Afghans to vacate volatile Panjwaii district'; Carlotta Gall, 'Taliban surges as U.S. shifts some tasks to NATO', *New York Times*, 11 June 2006; Françoise Chipaux, 'Les talibans font régner leur loi dans les provinces pachtounes du Sud', *Le Monde*, 7 October 2004; Pamela Constable, 'A NATO bid to regain Afghans' trust', *Washington Post*, 27 November 2006; Brian Hutchinson, 'First foray into Taliban area', *National Post*, 21 December 2006; Paul Watson, 'On the trail of the Taliban's support', *Los Angeles Times*, 24 December 2006; Richard Foot, 'Canada relying on Afghan police in Taliban offensive', *CanWest News Service*, 13 January 2007.

29 Cordesman (2007); Declan Walsh, 'Better paid, better armed, better connected – Taliban rise again', *Guardian*, 16 September 2006.

30 'A geographical expression in search of a state', *The Economist*, 6 July 2006; interview with UNAMA official, October 2006, Gardez; Philip G. Smucker, 'Afghanistan's eastern front', *U.S. News & World Report*, 9 April 2007.

31 Interview with Massoud Kharokhel, 1 October 2006, Tribal Liaison Office, Kabul; interview with Tribal Liaison Office official in Gardez, October 2006. See Trives (2006a) for more details on the insurgency in the southeast up to 2005; 'Sud-est de l'Afghanistan: "Ici, c'est la guerre!"', *AFP*, 20 September 2003; interview with UN official, Gardez, October 2006; Sara Daniel, 'Afghanistan: "Résister aux talibans? A quoi bon!"', *Le Nouvel Observateur*, 10 August 2006; 'Taliban start recruiting fighters in Ghazni', *Pajhwok Afghan News*, 7 August 2006; Mirwais Atal, 'US hearts and minds cash goes to Taliban', *Afghan Recovery Report*, 29 November 2006.

32 Antonio Giustozzi (forthcoming); interview with Afghan security officer, Kandahar, January 2006; Declan Walsh, 'Special deals and raw recruits employed to halt the Taliban in embattled Helmand', *Guardian*, 4 January 2007; David Rohde, 'G.I.s in Afghanistan on hunt, but now for hearts and minds', *New York Times*, 30 March 2004; Carsten Stormer, 'Winning hearts, minds and firefights in Uruzgan', *Asia Times Online*, 6 August 2004; Sara Daniel, 'Afghanistan: "Résister aux talibans? A quoi bon!"'.

33 On the Achakzai militias see Giustozzi (2006).

34 Adrien Jaulmes, 'Les forces spéciales françaises en Afghanistan face aux talibans', *Le Figaro*, 28 June 2006; interview with former Emergency Loya Jirga delegate from Farah, Kandahar, 26 January 2006; Elizabeth Rubin, 'In the land of the Taliban'; Graeme Smith, 'Inspiring tale of triumph over Taliban not all it seems'; Wright (2006a).

35 Owais Tohid, 'Arid Afghan province proves fertile for Taliban'; Elizabeth Rubin, 'Taking the fight to the Taliban'; Mohammed Weekh, 'Provincial tensions ahead of Loya Jirga', *Afghan Recovery Report*, no. 6 (28 May 2002); Françoise Chipaux, 'Dans le plus complet dénuement, la province afghane

de Zabul mène la lutte contre les talibans', *Le Monde*, 24 December 2003.

36 Griff Witte, 'Afghan province's problems underline challenge for U.S.', *Washington Post*, 30 January 2006; Karimi (2006), pp. 119–23 (courtesy of J. van den Zwan, Crisis States Research Centre, London); Harm Ede Botje, 'We zitten darr goed'; interview with tribal notable from Gezab, Kandahar, January 2006.

37 Interview with tribal notable from Gezab, Kandahar, January 2006; interview with tribal notable from Chora, April 2007.

38 Sayed Salahuddin and Mohammed Ismail Sameen, 'Afghan violence erupts, killing at least 61', *Reuters*, 13 August 2003; Afghan Independent Human Rights Commission (2004), pp. 21–2; Graeme Smith, 'Doing it the Dutch way in Afghanistan'; Joeri Boom, 'Tulbanden en Friese vlaggen', *De Groene Amsterdammer*, 12 May 2006; personal communication with foreign diplomat, Kabul, February 2007.

39 See Saeed Zabuli, 'Taliban executes tribal elder in Daikundi', *Pajhwok Afghan News*, 25 December 2006, for the case of an elder hanged by the Taliban for supporting the government.

40 Eric Schmitt and David Rohde, 'Afghan rebels widen attacks'; Syed Saleem Shahzad, 'Rough justice and blooming poppies', *Asia Times Online*, 7 December 2006; Elizabeth Rubin, 'In the land of the Taliban'.

41 Rahmani (2006b); Alastair Leithead, 'Unravelling the Helmand impasse', *BBC News*, 21 December 2006; Syed Saleem Shahzad, 'Taliban line up the heavy artillery'; Carlotta Gall, 'Despite Afghan strictures, the poppy flourishes', *New York Times*, 16 February 2006; Eric Schmitt and David Rohde, 'Afghan rebels widen attacks'; Thomas Coghlan and Justin Huggler, 'A ruthless enemy, a hostile population and 50C heat', *Independent*, 9 July 2006; Raymond Whitaker, 'Blood and guts: at the front with the poor bloody infantry', *Independent*, 1 October 2006; Christina Lamb, 'Have you ever used a pistol?', *Sunday Times*, 2 July 2006; Eric de Lavarène, 'La province de tous les dangers', *RFI*, 19 March 2006.

42 For more details see Giustozzi (forthcoming).

43 Interview with Afghan security officer, Kandahar, January 2006; personal communication with Farouq Azam, London, January 2006; personal communication with UN official, Kandahar, January 2006; see also Graeme Smith, 'The Taliban: knowing the enemy'; Carlotta Gall, 'NATO's Afghan struggle: build, and fight Taliban', *New York Times*, 13 January 2007; Murray Brewster, 'Influential warlord urges Afghan youths to lay down arms, reject Taliban', *Canadian Press*, 24 January 2007; interview with Afghan security officer, Kandahar, January 2006.

44 Interviews with members of the Afghan intelligentsia, Nangarhar University and Pedagogical Institute of Jalalabad, February 2007; interview with the Chief of Police of Nangarhar, February 2007; interview with Afghan journalists, Jalalabad, February 2007.

45 Syed Saleem Shahzad, 'Taliban raise the stakes in Afghanistan', *Asia Times Online*, 30 October 2003; Christian Parenti, 'Taliban rising', *Nation*

Magazine, 12 October 2006; Rahimullah Yusufzai, 'Khalis declares jihad against US', *The News*, 29 October 2003; Senlis Council (2006d), p. 27; 'Afghan district chief escapes assassination attempt', *AFP*, 18 January 2007; 'Nangarhar council on strike over killing', *AFP*, 7 February 2007.

46 Interview with UN official, Jalalabad, February 2006.

47 Personal communication with Massoud Karokhel, Tribal Liaison Office, Kabul, February 2007; Declan Walsh, 'In the heartland of a mysterious enemy, US troops battle to survive', *Guardian*, 5 December 2006; personal communication with UN official, Jalalabad, February 2007; interview with BBC journalist Khpolwak Sapai, Kabul, 5 March 2007.

48 'Seven killed in Afghanistan "Taliban" battle', *AFP*, 26 March 2003; personal communication with UN official, Herat, April 2004; Senlis Council (2006a), ch. 1, p. 61; personal communication with UN official, Maimana, November 2004; 'NATO watchful of Taliban in northern Afghanistan', *AFP*, 20 April 2007.

49 For the case of Yunis Khan in Herat see 'Afghan faction says Herat ruler killed tribal chief', *Reuters*, 4 November 2002. Arbab Nasar was another Pashtun tribal leader assassinated in Ghuryan (interview with former militia commander and tribal notable, Herat, September 2005).

50 *AFP*, 26 July 2002; Interview with former district official and teacher from Shindand, Herat 26 September 2005; Amy Waldman, 'Strife exposes deep and wide ethnic tensions', *New York Times*, 6 September 2004; Anthony Loyd, 'Afghan warlord closes in on prize city', *The Times*, 25 August 2004; personal communication with Herati politician, Herat, October 2006; Ahmad Quraishi, 'Three policemen among four killed in Herat', *Pajhwok Afghan News*, 27 December 2006; *Sada-ye Jawan Radio*, Herat, in Dari 1230 gmt 14 October 2006; Rachel Morarjee, 'Afghan clashes raise concerns', *Financial Times*, 3 May 2007; 'No probe of reported civilian deaths in Afghanistan: US military', *AFP*, 2 May 2007.

51 Jason Motlagh, 'Taming the Afghan badlands', *UPI*, 29 September 2006; 'Operation helps curb Taliban attacks', *Associated Press*, 21 December 2006; Anna K. Perry, 'Operation Al Hasn brings hope to Tagab valley', *Freedom Watch*, 20 November 2006, <www.cfc-a.centcom.mil/Freedom%20Watch/2006/11-November/20nov06.pdf>; Syed Saleem Shahzad, 'Afghanistan's highway to hell'; 'Heavy fighting erupts northeast of Afghan capital', *Reuters*, 17 April 2007; personal communication with military attaché, Kabul, April 2007; *Cheragh*, 19 April 2007.

52 Renata D'Aliesio, 'Hundreds of Taliban die in battle for their training school', *Calgary Herald*, 2 October 2006; Wright (2006a); Senlis Council (2006b), ch. 4; Kathy Gannon, 'Taliban comeback traced to corruption', *Associated Press*, 24 November 2006; 'Civilian casualties trigger anti-govt sentiments', *Pajhwok Afghan News*, 21 August 2006; interview with Afghan journalist returning from the south, Kabul, October 2006; David Rohde and James Risen, 'C.I.A. review highlights Afghan leader's woes'; personal communications with Afghan MPs, tribal leader and notables, Kabul and

Gardez, October 2006; Carsten Stormer, 'Winning hearts, minds and firefights in Uruzgan'; Syed Saleem Shahzad, 'How the Taliban prepare for battle', *Asia Times Online*, 5 December 2006; Pamela Constable, 'Afghan city's rebound cut short. Battles between NATO forces, resurgent Taliban make ghost town of Kandahar', *Washington Post*, 19 August 2006; 'In Kandahar, the Taliban are not a bad memory', *AFP*, 8 December 2006; Ahmad Farzan, 'Two police officers gunned down in Kandahar', *Pajhwok Afghan News*, 26 January 2007; Chris Sands, 'Afghan MPs predict very big war', *Dominion*, 19 December 2006; Jean MacKenzie, 'Bring back the Taleban', Afghan Blog, <http://www.iwpr.net/?o=f-328686&o1=month-2,year-2007&apc_state=hendarr>, 22 January 2007.

53 Syed Saleem Shahzad, 'How the Taliban prepare for battle'; Syed Saleem Shahzad, 'The vultures are circling', *Asia Times Online*, 13 December 2006; Senlis Council (2006b), ch. 4, pp. 13–14; Scott Baldauf and Ashraf Khan, 'New guns, new drive for Taliban', *Christian Science Monitor*, 26 September 2005; Rahmani (2006a).

54 Davis (2002); UNHCR, 'Chronology of Events in Afghanistan', September 2002, p. 3; Pepe Escobar, 'The roving eye part 1: exit Osama, enter Hekmatyar', *Asia Times Online*, 9 October 2002; Jason Burke, 'Stronger and more deadly, the terror of the Taliban is back'; Senlis Council (2006a), p. 18.

55 'Living under the Taleban', *Afghan Recovery Report* (IWPR), no. 249 (4 April 2007); David Loyn, 'On the road with the Taliban', *BBC News*, 21 October 2006.

3
ORGANISATION OF THE TALIBAN

3.1 COHESIVENESS OF THE TALIBAN

The jihad of the 1980s and early 1990s was characterised by a division into a multitude of political parties and groups, of which fifteen were recognised by either Pakistan or Iran. Moreover, the majority of these parties exercised no real control over the armed groups affiliated to them inside Afghanistan. The result was a chaotic jihad with no overall strategy, unity or even coordination, prisoner of the segmentarity of Afghan society. This begs the question of how cohesive the Neo-Taliban and their new jihad movement are. There are obviously disparate groups and components fighting within the insurgency, but there is no consensus on how this affects its cohesiveness. One line of thinking is that because of a lack of 'coherence and cohesion among the different groups ... internal contradictions will likely increase'.[1]

In the early years of the insurgency, the Neo-Taliban did experience a split. Jaish-ul Muslimeen (Army of Muslims) quit the Taliban in September 2003, allegedly over a controversy concerning the need to intensify the insurgency. Led by a Kandahari commander Sayd Akbar Agha, it styled itself after the mainstream Taliban, even appointing a ten-member council as leadership. Mullah Ishaq, deputy military commander of the Taliban in the southern region, was appointed as military commander of the new group. At that time the group claimed to control a third of the Taliban's fighting force, particularly in Zabul and Helmand, where some local commanders had been critical of Mullah Omar's leadership. Whatever its initial success, between the second half of 2004 and the first half of 2005 the Jaish started to rapidly lose support, with its commanders turning back to the mainstream Taliban. By June 2005, when the group merged back into the Taliban, the leadership of the Jaish claimed much more modestly to have 750 fighters. Pakistani sources close to the Taliban expressed the feeling that the Jaish was an attempt by Pakistanis to create a more pliable insurgent movement, which would be more amenable to a political deal once the time was ripe. The fact that the leader of the group, Akbar Agha, was arrested by Pakistan in December 2004 together with another seventeen alleged Taliban middle rank members diminishes the credibility of this interpretation, although his involvement in the kidnapping of three UN workers in 2004 and his rift with other leaders of the group over the alleged US$1.5 million ransom might also be a reason for his elimination from the scene.[2]

The fate of the Jaish suggests that despite the lack of a sophisticated structure of command and control (there is, for example, no report of the existence of anything resembling 'political commissars'), the Neo-Taliban maintained a strong cohesiveness. Another, earlier and allegedly Pakistani-sponsored attempt to promote a group of Taliban independent of Mullah Omar and his circle had fared no better. The son of Nabi Mohammed, the old leader of Harakat-e Enqelab, a party which had once included most of the first generation of Taliban, was apparently involved in the effort to form a party of moderate Taliban, ready to sign a political deal with Kabul. Jamiat-i Khudam-ul Koran was launched in early 2002 by a group of former officials of the Taliban regime and initially attracted a significant number of supporters, but it was largely reabsorbed into the mainstream Taliban within a couple of years. It is not even entirely clear whether Jami'at-i Khudam-ul Koran was a genuinely separate group or just a front of the Taliban, as its members had mostly refused to condemn either Mullah Omar or Osama bin Laden until the very end of 2001. In 2004, when its leader Mohammed Amin Mojaddedi travelled to Kabul to register the group for the parliamentary elections, the rest of the party did not follow. In more recent years local non-state armed groups surfaced, particularly in the south, which do not take orders from the Taliban leadership. A growing participation of former mujahidin commanders in the insurgency was for example reported in some areas like Ghazni, without their apparent incorporation in the Movement of the Taliban. These, however, do not seem to be individual commanders breaking away from the Movement, but appear instead to have entered the jihad autonomously.[3]

The existence of different centres of command and control within the Neo-Taliban themselves can also be seen as a factor militating against the cohesiveness of the Neo-Taliban. The Quetta Shura was generally seen as being more directly under the control of the political leadership of the Movement, which also resided mostly around Quetta. The Peshawar Shura, which was likely based in Waziristan, was sometimes said to have a number of issues with Quetta, relating to the distribution of resources and its own status. The tribal composition of the leadership also differed, with Quetta being predominantly Durrani and Peshawar being largely Ghilzai or of smaller tribes, although there is no evidence that this was ever a source of trouble. Moreover, within the Peshawar Shura there was no such leader with overall legitimacy as Mullah Omar. One example of what could amount to difficult relations between the two Shuras and within the Peshawar Shura was the sometime hesitant commitment of Saifullah Mansoor, a key political figure of the insurgency in Paktia and particularly Zurmat. Having been very active militarily in 2002 and 2003, Mansoor almost stopped his activities in the latter part of 2004 and during 2005, leading to rumours that he might have split from the Taliban or even that he might be negotiating with Kabul. The rumours were strengthened by the fact that he was dropped from the Rahbari Shura (see Table 2). He might have resented the appointment of the other leading figure of the insurgency in the south east, Jalaluddin Haqqani, as regional military commander. However, the impact of these differences, if they ever existed, should not be exaggerated. During 2006 Mansoor became active in the insurgency again, possibly due to better funding coming through the Peshawar Shura. Personal rivalries were also reported to exist even within the

Quetta Shura. The most important one appears to have been one opposing Mullah Dadullah, disliked by many other Taliban commanders because of his extremist attitudes, and Akhtar Osmani, one of the more moderate members of the Taliban leadership. On at least one occasion the contrast between the two appears to have ended in a physical confrontation, in which Osmani was allegedly beaten by Dadullah. The rivalry was in any case terminated by the killing of Osmani by NATO forces in December 2006, but some sources from within the Taliban claimed that Dadullah had tipped the enemy off about Osmani's location.[4]

The fluidity of the Neo-Taliban, its lack of rigid structures and its *modus operandi* all contribute to prevent small cracks and fissures from having much impact on its functionality. The Taliban maintain a sufficient degree of cohesion in the field through the strong ideological commitment of their 'cadres' and the accepted legitimacy of its leadership. The killing of Osmani inside Afghanistan in December 2006 and of Dadullah in May 2007 suggest that contrary to what alleged by sources opposed to the Taliban, the leadership travels often to the zone of operations, which helps to maintain such legitimacy. The leadership established at an unknown date some simple but clear rules to help maintain discipline in the field, the Layeha (Rulebook) of the Taliban. The salient points are:

- fighters are only allowed to move to another district with the permission of their commander;
- any prisoners have to be handed over to the commanders;
- selling equipment is forbidden;
- captured weaponry is to be distributed fairly;
- the harassment of 'innocent people' is forbidden;
- searching houses and confiscating weaponry without permission of a senior commander is forbidden;
- old jihadis with a bad reputation are not allowed into the Movement;
- fighters sacked for bad behaviour may not be recruited by other groups;

- suspected spies should be properly tried before being punished;
- disputes with the population have to be resolved by senior commanders or the Council of Ulema or elders.[5]

As far as can be judged from available information, Taliban throughout Afghanistan tend to respect these rules, a fact which suggests the continuing functionality of a unified chain of command (see 3.3 *Command structure* and 5.2 *Manoeuvrability and coordination*).

A potential factor of medium and long-term fragmentation of the Taliban is represented by the extensive recruitment of local communities, which could one day quit the Movement once their interests start diverging. Not much is known about the specifics of the deals worked out between such communities and the Taliban themselves, but whatever little evidence is available suggests that the Taliban have been taking care of integrating local causes as solidly as possible. Intermarriages and the training of local youth in the madaras have reportedly been used to consolidate the alliances. Eventually, such practices might succeed in merging the core with its peripheral components, even if in the short term the latter maintained their pre-eminent local interests. The Taliban's micromanagement of local communities, with their ability to rely on village mullahs to identify friends and potential foes and subsequently ruthlessly eliminate the latter, is likely to be playing a key role in the consolidation of the Movement (see 2.4 *The role of the clergy* and 2.5 *Taliban, tribes and elders*). Tactics such as 'clear and sweep' operations and air bombardment (see Chapter 6) might also have helped bring the different components of the insurgency together in the common hatred of the 'foreigners'.

3.2 FUNDING

If ideology is certainly an important source of cohesiveness not only for the Neo-Taliban but also for any insurgent movement, the way in which funding is channelled to the insurgency is also potentially very important. Localised sources of revenue inside the area of operations, for example, might contribute to make field commanders more

koran, kalashnikov and laptop

independent of the political leadership. Diversified external sources of funding might contribute to a political split within the leadership if they are managed by different individuals or factions within the insurgent movement. Judging from the absence of successful challenges to the leadership, it would appear that the leadership of the Taliban largely managed to maintain a unified control over revenue.

According to sources inside the Taliban, in 2002 Mullah Omar started raising funds for the new jihad within his network of contacts in Pakistan and the Gulf, composed of 'Karachi businessmen, Peshawar goldsmiths, Saudi oil men, Kuwaiti traders and jihadi sympathisers within the Pakistani military and intelligence ranks', as well as presumably of sympathetic Pakistani Islamic militants. Support by Afghan traders was also claimed, as far as the Gulf. In early 2006 Mullah Dadullah reportedly travelled to the UAE to raise funds. As the population perceived a growth in the insurgency's chances of success, support from local traders also seemed to grow (see also *2.7 Changes in recruitment patterns*). Some reports suggest that the Taliban were awash with cash. Reportedly, a raid against one of their safehouses netted US$900,000. However much the Neo-Taliban were able to raise inside Afghanistan, the Taliban's fund gathering does not seem to have been done directly by field commanders. The leadership appointed 'officials' in charge of logistics, who were presumably reporting back to the Pakistani-based Shuras. This way, the leadership prevented field commanders from establishing their own independent sources of revenue.[6]

The role of the narcotics economy in the funding of the Taliban remains a matter of controversy. Certainly the unpopularity of eradication policies, when they were finally re-implemented at least in some measure in 2005, offered an opportunity to the insurgents to gain a foothold in a number of communities, not least because of the alleged unfairness in the implementation of eradication. Already the first eradication effort in 2002 was characterised by bias in favour of the large growers and by corruption in the management of the compensation funds. When in 2005–6 eradication was attempted again, similar problems surfaced, and again in 2007. In Uruzgan, the wheat seeds sent by the Americans to be distributed to the farmers as an alternative to the poppies were sold by government officials rather than distributed to the farmers. There are clear signs that the Taliban did not hesitate to exploit this opportunity, despite their earlier opposition to the growing of poppies (2000–1). In Helmand they appear to have offered protection to the farmers targeted by eradication. Certainly the poppy harvest area started growing exponentially after the Taliban firmly established themselves in the province. UNODC estimated that during 2006 the harvested area grew by 250 per cent, while in early 2007 local authorities estimated a near doubling of the area under cultivation over 2006. In Kandahar, they were even reported to have offered financial assistance to farmers whose fields were being eradicated, in exchange for support in fighting against the government. The decision in late 2006 not to pay compensation to farmers any more for the eradication of their fields is also unlikely to have been welcomed. This, however, fits into a more general pattern of the Taliban exploiting any differences between local communities and central government (see 2.6 *Recruiting local communities*) and should not be construed to imply necessarily that the Taliban were specifically targeting poppy-growing communities for support. In any case, once the Taliban established themselves in poppy-growing areas, they did cooperate with both poppy-growing farmers and the traffickers. Despite the Taliban's claims that they only support the farmers but not the traffickers, there is evidence that apart from taxing the poppy harvest, the Taliban might sometimes have provided protection to drug convoys. It is not clear, however, whether this happened in exchange for cash or whether it was an 'exchange of favours', such as the provision of shelter and food. Clearly the traffickers enjoy safe passage in Taliban-controlled areas. It is also believed that on some occasions traffickers' militias and Taliban have fought together against the intrusion of foreign forces in the strongholds. Drug traffickers might be helping the Taliban in order to create a situation of insecurity which makes poppy eradication and more general counter-narcotics impractical. Some sources even suggest that the relationship between the traffickers and growers and the Taliban might with time have become more organic and have ended in marriage alliances, in line with Taliban practice in dealing with local communities.[7]

Does this evidence amount to a proof that the insurgency is funded by drug revenue? A more accurate analysis suggests that such a claim is somewhat off the mark. Much of what is described as the Taliban's cosiness with traffickers and growers reflects the Movement's readiness to exploit any opportunity offered by free trade (see 1.1 *The 'Ideology' of the Taliban* and 2.2 *Early recruitment*). This is, for example, the case when donkeys transporting drugs out of Afghanistan are used to take weapons and ammunition to Afghanistan for the Taliban, as suggested in some reports. How important the revenue from the narcotics trade is to the Taliban is not clear. Some Afghan and international officials suggest that the Taliban make more money than other external partners involved in the trade, such as government functionaries. Others, including most foreign diplomats, maintain that drugs remain a secondary source of revenue for the Taliban and that there is little evidence of them encouraging the farmers to grow poppies and of their involvement in the trade. This author tends to side with the second group, for three reasons. First, the traffickers are unlikely to be willing to give up a major share of their profits to the Taliban, particularly in the presence of overproduction and of competition from corrupt police officers and increasingly even ANA officers in courting their favours (see 6.3 *Afghan police* and 6.4 *Afghan National Army*).[8] Second, if substantial amounts of money were turned to field commanders, this would likely have resulted in a fragmentation of the Taliban chain of command, as commanders would become more autonomous. There is, however, no sign of that (see 3.1 *Cohesiveness of the Taliban*). To the extent that traffickers pay money to the insurgents, they are more likely to hand it over to field commanders, both because they are probably more approachable and because the traffickers have no interest in strengthening the leadership of a movement which might one day turn against them, as it did already in 2000. Third and last, the Taliban do not really control Afghanistan's borders and, as claimed by US and NATO sources, have to cross it in small groups or even as individuals (see 4.1 *Infiltration*). Therefore, it is not clear to what extent they would be of much help to traffickers in crossing the border with Pakistan, compared to the help which would derive from purchasing the collaboration of Afghanistan's border police and other security forces.

The issue of external sources of funding is for obvious reasons a difficult one to address. The Taliban have no qualms in admitting that they receive money from Arab sympathisers, while at the same time claiming that such financial support is not sufficient to acquire sophisticated anti-aircraft and other weaponry. Pakistani Islamic parties and groups like Jamaat-i Islami and Jamaat-ul Ulema are very vocal supporters of the Taliban insurgency and rank-and-file Taliban have admitted to journalists to have in the past received direct support from them, even if the Pakistan government has banned raising funds for jihadi activities.[9] As mentioned earlier, the question of whether the Pakistani authorities provide material help remains open (see 1.3 *The role of Pakistan*). What matters most from our perspective, however, is how external funding is channelled to the Taliban. Although no information is available in this regard, the fact that such disparate sources of funding did not lead to the permanent splitting of the Movement suggests that support must be channelled directly to the top leadership. How this can happen when jihadist movements worldwide have the tendency to be very fragmented organisationally is not clear, unless the Pakistani authorities imposed a degree of control over revenue as a pre-condition for letting the Taliban operate from their country and then channel it directly to the top leaders.

3.3 COMMAND STRUCTURE

The organisational structures of the Movement of the Taliban were far from very sophisticated. The function of political direction belonged to supreme leader Mullah Omar and to a leadership council (Rahbari Shura), appointed by Mullah Omar in March 2003 and composed initially of ten members but later expanded to twelve, then eighteen and finally to thirty-three (see Table 2 for the membership of the Rahbari Shura when it counted ten and twelve members [2003–4]). The expansion of the Shura reflected the need to balance its composition as the Movement expanded and tried to attract support throughout an ever greater part of Afghanistan. In addition to the Rahbari Shura, the Taliban seem to have established also a sort of Shadow Cabinet, with positions such as 'defence minister' (Haji Obeidullah) and 'minister responsible for religious questions' (Mullah Abdul Ali), but little information is available about the workings of this 'cabinet'. By the time the Rahbari Shura had expanded to twelve members, there had already been changes in its composition, possibly because of the changing correlation of forces within the Movement, but also because of combat losses. The most important development was the removal of Saifullah Mansoor (see 3.1 *Cohesiveness of the Taliban*). In October 2006 the formation of another council (Majlis al-Shura) was announced by Mullah Omar, but little was known of its functions except that it was composed of thirteen members, mostly well known commanders already members of the Rahbari Shura.[10]

The Taliban's military organisation was based on five operational zones (see Map 6), each led by an old guard Taliban commander (see Table 4). Two more commanders were in charge of the logistical areas of Quetta and Peshawar. The regional military command structure also saw many changes. In September 2003, a few months after its establishment, it was already necessary to replace Hafiz Abdur Rahim, military commander of the southern zone, killed in combat. Dangar was assassinated in November 2004 in Pakistan, but it is not clear who replaced him in the Kabul region. The largest of these regions, the south, appears to have been run initially by a triumvirate composed of Dadullah, Abdur Razzaq Akhund and Osmani, but Hafiz Abdur Rahman seems to have taken over at some point in

2003, until he was killed. Razzaq disappeared from the scene after allegedly developing some problems with the leadership on 'organisational and procedural matters', while Osmani and Dadullah did not get along well. As a result, when Dadullah was reappointed in 2004, Osmani apparently switched the military role with that of 'facilitator' in developing alliances with the southern tribes. According to Taliban sources there were headquarters in Baghran from where operations in the south were run, which did not play much of a role in the war up to early 2007, but was supposed to become of key importance once the 'final offensive' started. The most significant development appears to have been the appointment of Haqqani as overall military commander in 2006, a role earlier played somehow by the badly matched Dadullah/Osmani couple. The appointment seemed to have stemmed from Mullah Omar's dissatisfaction with the military performance of the southern fighters, which Haqqani, the most experienced of the Taliban commanders in terms of guerrilla operations, was supposed to improve. Haqqani had previously been in charge of military operations in the south-east. Although sources in NATO sometimes see Haqqani as the leader of a separate insurgency element, most sources agree that he remained loyal to Mullah Omar even if the relationship between the two went through a period of crisis in the last few years of the Taliban regime.[11]

Below the regional commanders the Taliban command structure included provincial and district commanders. The latter might have been appointed only in mid-2005, when Mullah Dadullah announced the establishment of provincial leadership councils. At the lowest level were tactical commanders, leading groups and teams of five to fifty men. There was not much formal organisation, but a considerable degree of flexibility in the number of men each commander was allowed to have, another 'free market' attitude aimed at maximising the incentives for local recruitment and motivating the commanders. However, a number of measures were taken to guarantee a minimal degree of discipline and balance. The rotation of commanders at the various levels seems to have been frequent and might

	2003	2006
Military commanders		
Kabul region	Anwar Dangar	?
East	Mullah Kabir	Mullah Kabir
South-east	Mullah Saifullah Mansoor	Sirajuddin Haqqani
	Hafiz Abdur Rahim? Or	
	Dadullah Razzaq and Osmani	
South	jointly	Mullah Dadullah
General commander	Baradar	Jalaluddin Haqqani

Table 4. Military leadership of the Taliban, 2003
Sources: press reports, interviews with locals in Kandahar.

Map 6. The Taliban's military commands.
Sources: press reports.

have been a deliberate attempt to maintain control and prevent the development of personal fiefdoms. The insistence on forming mixed groups of combatants, including mixing people from different tribes and provinces with the locals, might in part too have answered a similar concern. According to the Layeha of the Taliban, commanders were not allowed to take in fighters from other groups, a measure presumably aimed both at preventing rifts among commanders and at preventing the emergence of big commanders who could turn into semi-independent warlords. In the end, much rested on the appointment of trusted and ideologically committed field commanders, even more than it would to most guerrilla movements. Although sometimes direct orders to mount operations were received, most of the time the local commanders acted autonomously, based on their understanding of the strategic and political aims of the Movement. Commitment was privileged over skills and often madrasa-educated young men wielded an unusual amount of power by the standards of a society like Afghanistan's, where age and experience are considered to be major sources of social status. Tactical mistakes were often forgiven as long as ideological purity was demonstrated. This was due to the difficulty of carrying out command and control from the top most of the time. The use of satellite phones as a means of strategic coordination and operational control of the insurgency had to be abandoned relatively early in the conflict, due to US monitoring of communications (see also 5.1 *Military technology of the insurgency*). It was replaced by old fashioned messengers, of course a much slower (but secure) system.[12]

NOTES

1   International Crisis Group (2006a), p. 8.
2   Syed Saleem Shahzad, 'Pakistan reaches into Afghanistan', *Asia Times Online*, 3 October 2006; Janullah Hashemzada, 'Jaishul Muslimeen returns to Taliban fold', *Pajhwok Afghan News*, 23 June 2005; Syed Saleem Shahzad, 'Another Taliban song and dance', *Asia Times Online*, 10 September 2004; Tim McGirk, 'The Taliban on the run', *Time*, 28 March 2005; 'Afghan hostage-takers disband after ransom dispute', *AFP*, 1 December 2004; 'Pak arrests UN workers' abductor', *PTI*, 11 December 2004.
3   Syed Saleem Shahzad, 'Time to talk: US engages the Taliban', *Asia Times Online*, 24 November 2005; Syed Saleem Shahzad, 'Taliban's trail leads to Pakistan', *Asia Times Online*, 13 December 2001; *Afghan Islamic Press*, Peshawar, in Pashto, 1621 gmt 9 June 2004; Syed Saleem Shahzad, 'Pakistan reaches into Afghanistan'; interview with former mujahidin commander from Ghazni, Kabul, October 2006.

4   Cordesman (2007); interview with Farouq Azam, London, January 2006; Syed Saleem Shahzad, 'Taliban's new commander ready for a fight', *Asia Times Online*, 23 May 2006; Graeme Smith, 'The Taliban: knowing the enemy', *Globe and Mail*, 27 November 2006; 'Afghanistan: captured spokesman reveals rifts within Taliban', *ADN Kronos*, 19 January 2007; 'Deep differences between Taliban leaders', *Anis*, 25 December 2006.

5   Sami Yousafzai and Urs Gehriger, 'A new layeha for the Mujahideen', *Die Weltwoche*, 29 November 2006, <http://www.signandsight.com/features/1071.html>; Christopher Dickey, 'Afghanistan: the Taliban's book of rules', *Newsweek*, 12 December 2006.

6   Elizabeth Rubin, 'In the land of the Taliban', *New York Times Magazine*, 22 October 2006; Syed Saleem Shahzad, 'How the Taliban keep their coffers full', *Asia Times Online*, 10 January 2007; Graeme Smith, 'Inspiring tale of triumph over Taliban not all it seems', *Globe and Mail*, 23 September 2006; Syed Saleem Shahzad, 'How the Taliban prepare for battle', *Asia Times Online*, 5 December 2006; Peter Bergen, 'Afghanistan 2007: problems, opportunities and possible solutions, testimony to the House Committee on Foreign Affairs', 15 February 2007.

7   Raymond Whitaker, 'Opium war revealed: major new offensive in Afghanistan', *Independent*, 21 January 2007; Griff Witte, 'Afghan province's problems underline challenge for U.S. resilient insurgency', *Washington Post*, 30 January 2006; Wright (2006b); Senlis Council (2006d), p. 21; Syed Saleem Shahzad, 'Afghanistan's highway to hell', *Asia Times Online*, 25 January 2007; 'Helmand heads for record poppy harvest', *Afghan Recovery Report*, no. 241 (9 February 2007); Tom Coghlan, 'Bribery wrecks drive to root out opium', *Daily Telegraph*, 27 February 2007.

8   Wright (2006b); Declan Walsh, 'Better paid, better armed, better connected —Taliban rise again', *Guardian*, 16 September 2006; Alastair Leithead, 'Unravelling the Helmand impasse', *BBC News*, 21 December 2006; Jelsma *et al.* (2006), p. 7.

9   'Menace taliban dans le Sud', *AFP*, 20 February 2004; Scott Baldauf and Owais Tohid, 'Taliban appears to be regrouped and well-funded', *Christian Science Monitor*, 8 May 2003.

10 'Jalaluddine Haqqani: une légende moudjahidine devenue figure des talibans', *AFP*, 20 February 2004; Sami Yousafzai and Urs Gehriger, 'A new layeha for the Mujahideen'; 'Mullah Omar names a new Majlis Shura', *MEMRI Special Dispatch Series*, no. 1310 (5 October 2006), <http://memri.org/bin/articles.cgi?Page=subjects&Area=jihad&ID=SP131006>.

11 *Reuters*, 17 March 2004; 'Afghan commander shot dead in Pakistan', *BBC Monitoring International Reports*, 12 November 2004; Rahimullah Yusufzai, 'Pakistan: Taliban chief forms body to organize jihad against foreign troops', *The News*, 24 June 2003; Paul Watson, 'Widespread U.S. intelligence leaks in Afghanistan', *Los Angeles Times*, 12 April 2006; Syed Saleem Shahzad, 'Taliban line up the heavy artillery', *Asia Times Online*, 21 December 2006; 'Taliban military commander Mullah Dadallah: we are in contact with Iraqi

mujahideen, Osama bin Laden and Al-Zawahiri', *MEMRI Special Dispatch Series*, no. 1180 (2 June 2006); Syed Saleem Shahzad, 'Taliban's new commander ready for a fight'; Cordesman (2007); 'Jalaluddine Haqqani: une légende moudjahidine devenue figure des talibans', *AFP*, 20 February 2004.

12 Schiewek (2006), pp. 158-9; interview with Afghan security officer, Kandahar, January 2006; Sami Yousafzai and Urs Gehriger, 'A new layeha for the Mujahideen'; Christopher Dickey, 'Afghanistan: the Taliban's book of rules'; Syed Saleem Shahzad, 'Time out from a siege', *Asia Times Online*, 9 December 2006; Syed Saleem Shahzad, 'Taliban line up the heavy artillery'; Syed Saleem Shahzad, 'Another Taliban song and dance'.

4
THE TALIBAN'S STRATEGY

Chapters 2 and 3 explained how the core group of Taliban which started the insurgency in 2002 was relatively successful in recruiting a large following and in maintaining a sufficient degree of cohesiveness. Their next task towards mounting a significant challenge to Kabul was to produce a well crafted strategy and implement it effectively. This had to be done from scratch since the Taliban had little experience in fighting an insurgency. The main exception was Jalaluddin Haqqani, but initially his role was limited to the south-east. Allies like Hizb-i Islami never cooperated closely with the Neo-Taliban at the top level (see 4.9 *Alliances*). Whether the rigidity of the Taliban's leadership is interpreted as a principled stand or as mere stupidity, the intellectual resources and flexibility to conceive a fully-fledged strategy were clearly absent.[1] Hence there is reason to believe that a major contribution in putting together a strategy for the insurgency came from the Pakistani ISI (see 1.3 *The role of Pakistan*), as well as from Arab fellow jihadists.

The most common description of the post-2001 Taliban insurgency is as a typical case of asymmetric conflict, defined as 'a weaker adversary using unconventional means, stratagems, or niche capabilities to overcome a stronger power'.[2] Undoubtedly, the disparity of strength and resources between the Neo-Taliban and the ISAF/ Coalition was enormous. Given the amount of cash they paid to their fighters and the type and quantity of equipment they used, the Taliban may have spent anywhere between US$25 to 40 million in 2006 to fund the conflict. According to one of Bin Laden's aides, his organisation received US$200 million in financial support from non-state Arab sources during ten years of anti-Soviet jihad.[3] Since some funding is likely to have reached other sources too during those 10 years, it is not unrealistic to estimate that the ongoing insurgency in Afghanistan might have been receiving in excess of US$20 million per year. By contrast the US were spending about US$15–16 million per Talib killed in 2005 and about half that amount in 2006, mainly due to the attempts of the Taliban to fight pitched battles. The monthly US military expenditure in Afghanistan was running at US$1.3 billion in 2006.[4] Thus the tactics and technologies used by the Taliban and the foreign continents are fully consistent with asymmetric warfare (see Chapter 5). This asymmetry is well illustrated in an incident that occurred in Kajaki of Helmand in February 2007: in response to a single round fired by the Taliban, British troops responded with 'dozens of mortar rounds, bursts of red tracers from a 50-calibre machinegun, illumination flares, the flaming rush of a Javelin missile and the juddering explosion of a 1,000kg guided bomb dropped from a Harrier jet'.[5]

However, while asymmetric warfare is certainly part of the Taliban's strategy, it does not cover many aspects of it. Lieutenant General Barno, who commanded the US contingent in Afghanistan in 2003–5, sees Afghanistan as a typical example of Fourth Generation Warfare, borrowing Hammes' development of the asymmetric warfare concept. Fourth Generation Warfare 'uses all available networks—political, economic, social, and military—to convince the enemy's political decision makers that their strategic goals are either unachievable or too costly for the perceived benefit. It is an evolved form of insurgency.'[6] In Barno's words 'Fourth Generation Warfare argues that the enemy's target becomes the political establishment and the policymakers of his adversary, not the adversary's armed forces or tactical formations. The enemy achieves victory by putting intense, unremitting pressure on adversary decision makers, causing them to eventually capitulate, independent of military success or failure on the battlefield.' Barno's is the view from the top, that is the view of a general well aware of the impact of the enemy's strategy on policy makers and public opinions.[7]

The predominant view from the field, that is the view of US officers directly involved in fighting in the districts, is that the military strategy of the Taliban seems to be loosely based on the mimicking of Mao's theories. In part, this might well be due to US Special Forces officers superimposing what they have learnt in Fort Bragg on to a rather messy reality on the ground. There are, however, some obvious resemblances. The first phase of infiltrating the population and gaining influence over it was completed in parts of Afghanistan as early as 2003, although in other parts it was still going on in 2006. The second phase, of consolidation of 'base areas', organised guerrilla warfare and the creation of political structures in safe areas, started in some areas in 2003 and was still in process throughout 2004–6. By late 2005 or early 2006 the Taliban might have judged that they had established secure bases in parts of Uruzgan and Helmand at least, as little counter-insurgency effort was at that time being focused on such areas. As a result, they might have decided to take steps towards kicking off (somewhat prematurely) the third phase or 'final offensive' in 2006, as discussed in section 4.8 below. In any case, the Taliban would have had only second or third hand access to Maoist theories and are likely to have only absorbed certain elements of those.[8]

Another interpretation is that the Taliban's is the typical 'war of the flea'[9] and is similar to the war fought by the Afghan mujahidin against the Soviet army in the 1980s: 'fighting in villages to deliberately provoke air strikes and collateral damage' and getting American forces to 'chase illiterate teenage boys with guns around the countryside like the dog chasing its tail and gnawing at each flea bite until it drops from exhaustion'. What follows is a detailed analysis of the strategy adopted by the Neo-Taliban against the background of these different interpretations and of the different influences which might have contributed to shape it.

4.1 INFILTRATION

Due to the Neo-Taliban's initial poor organisational state, in 2002 their military activities were limited to cross-border raids and the harassment of US garrisons, mainly through launching long-distance rockets. However, small teams of ten to twenty insurgents were already infiltrating the Afghan countryside with the purpose of identifying villages that could provide hospitality and support. Without that support, the ability of the Taliban to penetrate Afghan territory would in most cases have been limited to the distance covered in one or two days' walk, particularly in flat areas which did not offer much in terms of cover or hideouts. Even at that limited depth, carrying out attacks would have been difficult without a place to hide afterwards: the attackers would have needed to walk all the way back to Pakistan, exposing themselves to the risk of being intercepted.

In order to penetrate deep into the territory, they needed to build up some support among the villagers and this was clearly the priority at that stage. In the future too the appearance of this 'vanguard' of the Taliban would herald the news that a particular region had been cho-

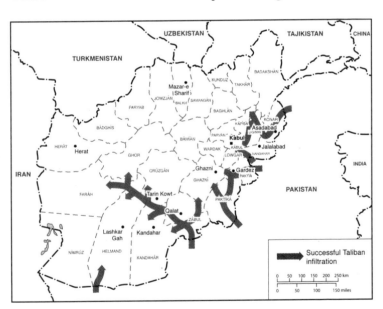

Map 7. Main infiltration routes of the insurgents, 2002–6.
Sources: press reports, US military.

sen for infiltration by the insurgents. These groups were able to cross the Pakistani border undetected throughout 2002–6, although they had to downsize from 60–100 members in 2003 to five or less in 2005 as interdiction efforts by the Coalition strengthened. As of January 2007 ANA sources were reporting the presence of 135 such teams, of three to fifteen men each, in the central-eastern region alone (Kabul, Panjshir, Parwan, Kapisa, Bamyan, Wardak, Logar, Laghman, Kunar, Nangarhar, Nuristan), belonging to Taliban, Hizb-i Islami and 'Al Qaida'. The strategic task of these 'vanguard' teams was to prepare the ground for a later escalation of the insurgency. The teams would visit the villages and carry out propaganda exercises, as well as threaten elements of the local population deemed hostile. Local notables would be asked to allow the movement of the Taliban in their areas and warned of the consequences in case they failed to comply. Occasionally these teams would carry out terrorist or guerrilla actions, mostly aimed at reinforcing the threats against anti-Taliban elements and at destroying whatever little presence the Afghan state had in the countryside. 'Night letters' were circulated as a way to threaten anti-Taliban elements in areas where open propaganda or direct visits were not possible, such as in the administrative centres, which were also home to police and army garrisons. By establishing contact with individuals formerly close to the Taliban regime and by challenging the villagers with their propaganda, the 'vanguard' teams elicited responses from the local population which allowed them to identify people and communities who could be trusted and who could provide shelter, supplies and intelligence. Suitable locations for ammunition and weaponry stockpiles would also be identified, so as to allow the insurgents to infiltrate the region later without carrying weapons and using the main roads. Even more than the mujahidin of the 1980s, the Taliban relied on the development of a thick network of small bases, where heavier weaponry such as 12.7mm machine guns, recoilless guns and mortars as well as ammunition would be stored, allowing the fighters to move around without cumbersome equipment and maintain a high degree of mobility. As a result, the insurgents were able to amass large numbers of fighters over short periods of time in any of their strongholds, like Uruzgan. In sparsely populated and desert areas, the insurgents relied on hundreds of small huts used by nomads as well, which could for some time allow them to survive even away from the villages.[10]

In its simplicity and effectiveness, the reliance on small teams of insurgents to infiltrate the villages and weed out pro-Kabul elements was to prove one of the strongest aspects of the Taliban's strategy. It pitted Taliban strength (abundance of committed, ideologically indoctrinated young fighters, able to achieve basic tasks even without supervision by field commanders) against government/Coalition weaknesses (shortage of manpower, little presence in the villages, inability to patrol extensively away from the main roads, lack of effective intelligence network).

4.2 ROOTING OUT GOVERNMENT PRESENCE

As important to the Taliban as identifying sympathisers and potential supporters was identifying and eliminating or rendering inoffensive government workers and collaborators. The assassination campaign targeted at 'collaborationists' started in 2003 and affected from the beginning even those areas that were not, or not yet, the object of intense Taliban military activities. For example, the southern districts of Ghazni had seen the incubation of the insurgency during 2005, and by 2006 the stage of wiping out those who were the 'collaborationists' was fully underway. In the district of Andar (Ghazni) alone as many as twenty-eight officials were assassinated in just six months between 2005 and 2006. Most assassinations in practice took place in the administrative centres, where government officials and other pro-government elements tended to be more resilient and often refused to comply with the Taliban's demands. The targets included senior clerics, doctors, teachers, judges, policemen, National Security Directorate officials, NGO workers and anybody cooperating with the government. The largest execution was reported in December 2006, when twenty-six villagers in Panjwai district were killed for having passed on information to NATO and government agencies. There were even allegations that the Taliban were willing to offer bounty payments of as much as $250 for the killing of Afghan government officials and civilians working with the foreign contingents. Losses were heavy among district governors and chiefs of police operating in the areas most affected by the insurgency, such as the remote districts of Kandahar, the northern and southern districts of Helmand, most of Zabul and Uruzgan. There were also attempts on the lives of key figures in the region, such as two governors of Helmand, Sher Mohammed Akhundzada and his successor Eng. Daoud. Governor of Paktia Taniwal fell victim to one such attack, while a plot to assassinate Paktia MP Padshah Khan Zadran was also reported. In some cases the insurgents were even reported to have kidnapped relatives of government officials to force them to quit their post or cooperate with the Taliban.[11]

The weakness of the state administration as a key factor in the deligitimisation of government in the eyes of sections of the population has already been identified (see 1.2 *'Rebuilding' the Afghan state*), but the Taliban were quick to target and cause the final collapse of whatever state administration was left. In many districts the threats of the Taliban easily succeeded in driving government officials away to seek refuge in the cities. Most districts in Helmand, Uruzgan and Zabul were either completely abandoned or not functional because of a lack of staff. As early as December 2003 the Taliban were starting to circulate night letters even in the core of the Afghan administrative system in the south, in Kandahar city.[12]

Subnational administrations were not the only form of government presence in the rural areas. In fact, the educational system was in a sense even more important because it was the only service provided by the state at the village level. It is therefore unsurprising that the Taliban immediately started targeting schools. In Kandahar province threats to teachers were already being delivered in late 2002 or early 2003 in some remote areas like Ghorak on the border with Helmand and Uruzgan. Gradually teachers started being threatened in other parts of the province too: Panjwai from October 2005, Dand from May 2006 etc. In other provinces the pattern was similar: threats to the teachers heralded the arrival of the insurgents. In Wardak they started in 2005, in some parts of Logar and Laghman in 2004.[13]

Threats and selective attacks succeeded in closing down schools in many areas (see Table 5). Not only were teachers threatened, but students, schoolgirls and their parents too (see 4.5 *Seeking popular support*). First the insurgents would deliver night letters and oral warnings threatening teachers and students. In these threats they accused schools of being centres for the propagation of Christianity and Judaism and used changes in the school curricula as a demonstration of the de-Islamisation of the schools. At a second stage, often after many months of repeated threats, actual violence followed. During 2005 and the first half of 2006 at least seventeen teachers and education officials were assassinated throughout Afghanistan, sometimes in gruesome attacks including decapitation. Eighty-five teachers and students were killed during March 2006–March 2007, while 187 schools were attacked. Although the Taliban leadership has denied having ordered attacks on schools and teachers, Taliban militants interviewed by Western journalists have confirmed the use of threats or worse to force schools to close. Moreover, this practice was in line with the rules contained in the Taliban's Layeha, as reported in the press. It is true, however, that, conscious that the villagers often appreciated state education, the Taliban stayed clear of opposing education as such and always declared that what they opposed was mixed male–female classes and the attendance of non-veiled girls, as well as the new curricula and the 'propagandist role' of teachers against the mujahidin. Interestingly, the Taliban did not object to the re-opening of a school in Musa Qala once the British troops had been withdrawn. In January 2007 the Taliban went as far as announcing that they would open their own schools in the areas under their control from March, initially only for boys and later for girls too. The Taliban claimed to be already printing textbooks and to have planned the investment of US$1 million in the opera-

Schools		Total	Open	Closed
Zabul province				
	2006	181		165
Uruzgan province				50
Kandahar				
	2005			49
	2006	335		218
Maaruf district	2004	40		40
Ghorak district	2003	9	3	6
Helmand				
	Jan-06	224	41	183
All south	Nov-06	748		380

Table 5. Impact of the Taliban campaign against schools.
Sources: UN official, Kandahar, January 2006; press reports.

tion. Of course the schools would teach an 'Islamic' curriculum and no maths or sciences would be taught. The announcement suggests that the Taliban must have been considering such a move for some time, given the amount of resources that it would be necessary to mobilise. It is not clear how satisfied parents would be with purely religious curricula in the 'new' schools, but the move might be related to the widespread formation of self-defence units among villagers to protect state schools, which could have affected as many as half of Afghanistan's 9,000 educational institutions.[14]

Doctors too were sometimes targeted by the Taliban. After four doctors were killed in southern Afghanistan, most of those remaining fled the countryside. NGOs, most of which the Taliban viewed as vehicles of moral 'corruption' and as objective allies of international intervention in Afghanistan as well as of the Kabul government, were also extensively targeted (see Graph 3) and not just in southern Afghanistan. In fact, according to an Afghan source, by 2006 the focus of anti-NGO activity had already moved away from southern Afghanistan. In that year the total number of NGO workers killed in the south was just two, if for no other reason than the drastic reduction in NGO activities in the area. By contrast, nine workers were killed in the north, thirteen in the west and four in the Kabul area, although it was not always clear who the attackers

105

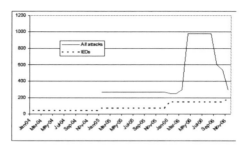

Graph 1. Military attacks carried out by all insurgents in Afghanistan, 2004–6: total and IED attacks.

Sources: press reports, US military, NATO/ISAF.

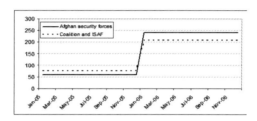

Graph 2. Military attacks carried out by all insurgents in Afghanistan against Afghan security forces and foreign troops.

Sources: press reports, US military, NATO/ISAF.

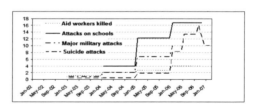

Graph 3. Attacks carried out by all insurgents in Afghanistan: aid workers killed, attacks against schools, major military attacks and suicide bombings.

Sources: press reports, US military, NATO/ISAF.

were. The Taliban were certainly successful in driving NGOs away or forcing them to cooperate. Already during 2003 NGOs started reducing their activities in Zabul and Uruzgan, following the killing of an international Red Cross worker. In Kandahar, already in 2003 the number of NGOs deploying foreign workers had dropped from twenty-two in 2002 to seven or eight and even those were not venturing to the outlying districts. US NGO Mercy Corps, for example, by October 2003 had already downscaled its activities in southern Afghanistan from forty-two districts in early 2003 to six. In Zabul eighteen NGOs were active in 2002, but just two were left by the end of 2003. Some of the few NGOs still operating in the south after 2003 were allegedly buying the tolerance of the Taliban with cash. By 2006 even UN agencies, which had been attacked only rarely, were operating in just six of the fifty southern districts. In the east twenty-one of forty-five districts were closed by 2007, with another five only partially accessible.[15]

4.3 DEMORALISATION OF THE ENEMY

Despite the apparent influence of Maoism in the Taliban's strategic elaboration, there was more to it than just mimicking the Chinese master. A key aspect of their strategy was a focus on psychological more than military achievements, probably intended, in part at least, to make up for the limited military skills of their guerrilla army. Mullah Dadullah outlined in an interview how this attitude was a deliberate strategy to scare state officials away from serving in the districts. Thus the Taliban deliberately tried to demoralise their enemies through relentless attacks, often against the same targets, and regardless of their own casualties.[16] The attempt was clearly to convince their opponents that the Taliban were in for the long run and that their determination was unshakable. Hence the war was unwinnable for their enemies.[17]

The strategy of repeatedly attacking enemy posts was quite successful and undoubtedly the Taliban achieved the demoralisation of the pro-government militias (AMF) relatively early. Between

2003 and 2004 the AMF *de facto* stopped patrolling the countryside and confined their activities to the barracks and the administrative centres (see 6.2 *Afghan Militias*). By 2005–6 there were clear signs that most of the police force too was utterly demoralised and rapidly losing any combat effectiveness, except for some tribally-based units motivated by intra-community rivalries and for some more professional units, such as those of Zabul province. By the summer of 2006 the ANA had also come under considerable pressure, as had, though to a lesser extent, British and Canadian troops (see 6.3 *Afghan police* and 6.4 *Afghan National Army*). Possibly sensing an opportunity to deal the final blow to the 'collaborationists', during 2006 the Taliban increased further the focus of their military activities against Afghan forces, against which attacks multiplied fourfold. There was also a heavy increase in attacks against foreign troops, up 250 per cent, but while in 2005 there were 1.28 attacks against foreign forces for each one against Afghan government forces, in 2006 the ratio was down to 0.88. Early indications for 2007 showed a further strengthening of the focus on Afghan forces; the ratio for February was 0.1, according to ANSO.[18]

This strategy of demoralisation also included the beheading of prisoners, which was seen with awe by ordinary Pashtuns for whom the respect of corpses is a major concern, although this might have caused outrage as well. Occasionally bodies of executed 'collaborationists' would be displayed as a warning to others. Interpreters working for the foreign troops were also reserved a special treatment consisting of body mutilations. Another aspect of the strategy of demoralisation, suicide attacks, was adopted relatively early, apparently in May 2003, but its effective implementation was slowed by the difficulty of finding sufficient recruits. With the help of large numbers of foreign volunteers, suicide bombings picked up in 2005 and most of all in 2006, when they reached an average of around ten per month (see Graph 3). Although most of the victims were civilians (in 2006: 206 Afghan civilians, 54 Afghan security personnel and 18 foreign soldiers), it seems that the Taliban were not targeting them, contrary to what their Arab partners in Iraq were clearly doing. With 117/139 (depending on the source) suicide bombings in twelve months, they could easily have slaughtered many more. The high number of civilian casualties compared to military ones is likely to derive from the technical shortcomings of bombers and bomb-makers, resulting in premature explosions. Hence the purpose of the suicide attacks was not to terrorise the population, but to show the Taliban's commitment and determination in the struggle, as well as to inflict casualties on the military and turn every civilian into a potential bomber in the eyes of the enemy. This was to result in a wider gap forming between foreign troops and Afghan civilians, an aim that was achieved at least to some extent. Occasional shootings of Afghan drivers by foreign troops often caused protests from the public, as did the ever increasing security measures taken to protect buildings and convoys. However, the suicide bombing tactics also caused an upsurge of hostility against the Taliban, who were sometimes forced to deny the responsibility of certain attacks that had resulted in heavy civilian casualties. Such was the case of an attack in Spin Boldak in January 2006, one of the few in which no intended military target was identified.[19]

The final success of any strategy of demoralisation through repeated and relentless attacks in the end depends on the ability to sustain the high casualty rates that it implies. At the end of 2005 the leadership of the Taliban clearly believed that it could afford a faster tempo of operations. Until then the conflict had maintained a strongly cyclic character, with violence abating during the winter and then recovering in spring. For example, during the spring of 2004 Coalition forces were being attacked ten to fifteen times per week, but only five times per week during the following winter.[20] This was likely due to the difficulty of moving supplies and reinforcements from Pakistan, more than to any direct impact of the weather on the combatants, as evidenced by the delay of the cycle on the actual weather conditions. Attacks by the Taliban would normally peak in December–January and then decline until March–April. However, the winter of 2005–6 signalled much more sustained Taliban activity than usual, which might have resulted from a decision·of the leadership to strengthen the impact of the demoralisation strategy by not giving the adversary any rest.

The determination to pursue strategic goals regardless of casualties is also evident from the attitude of the leadership towards US air power. This was certainly feared by the Taliban and they kept trying to avoid it, but with little success (see 5.3 *Tactical skills*). Members of the Taliban admitted to Western journalists to be suffering heavy casualties from air strikes. During 2005–6, as the need to upgrade the scale of their operations became more pressing, the Taliban were reported to have debated how aggressive they could afford to be in the face of overwhelming US air power. In June 2006 contrasts within the Taliban were once again reported, concerning the wisdom of maintaining an aggressive posture in the face of the heavy casualties inflicted by air power. Given that the summer of 2006 was characterised by the heaviest intervention of US air power thus far, clearly the debate was resolved in terms of carrying out further attacks and ignoring the cost of human casualties.[21]

4.4 ESTABLISHING STRUCTURES AND A SHADOW GOVERNMENT

Once a support structure had been put in place by the 'vanguard' teams, the Taliban would be ready to move in greater numbers and upgrade the level of their military activities, from the occasional roadside bomb and sniping to full-fledged ambushes and attacks on government roadblocks and posts. The next stage would then be to establish large strongholds deep into Afghan territory, which could include training centres and other facilities created to allow the carrying out of large scale sustained operations far from the Pakistani border. In order to make the creation of these rear bases possible, a rugged geography was essential but not sufficient. A degree of popular support of a different order from what the 'vanguard' teams might have enjoyed was also necessary (see 4.5 *Seeking popular support*).

In order to develop such a base of popular support, and as the state foundered under Taliban attacks or because of its own inherent contradictions, the Taliban started setting up their own 'no-frills' administration. It was centred on the judiciary, whose services were in high demand in the countryside because of the total failure of the central government to establish a reasonably reliable judicial system. Many villagers were also attracted by the Taliban's courts because they were exclusively based on the Sharia, a fact that also earned them the active endorsement of the clergy. The Taliban's judicial system was quite rough and had the tendency to quickly dispatch individuals accused of being informers of the enemy, a common allegation for any stranger found in areas under Taliban control. Nonetheless, the system offered a greater degree of predictability and reliability than the arbitrary behaviour of government security forces. Judges and 'police' were paid through tolls collected from travellers and transport vehicles, while donations were gathered to fund works of public utility, such as maintaining water canals.[22]

The Taliban's judiciary did not extend very wide. In fact, as of mid-2006 it still covered only eighteen districts (see Map 8). In part because of this, field commanders too were actively involved in mediating local disputes and administering justice, including ordering executions.[23] Otherwise the administration of the Taliban was very lean to say the least. It appears that the Taliban established some sort of subnational administration as early as 2003, as shown by passing references to the existence of 'shadow governors' or 'governatorates' at least in Ghazni, Zabul, Paktia, Kunar, Nangarhar and Paktika. In early 2006 Mullah Dadullah announced the appointment of representatives to all districts, while before that the military leader assigned to each district seemed to have played a political/administrative role too, however rudimentary. Some attempt was made to establish a parallel health service, offering jobs to health staff (with little apparent success) or kidnapping doctors and nurses. By early 2007 the Taliban were actually claiming to have established clinics at least in Helmand.[24]

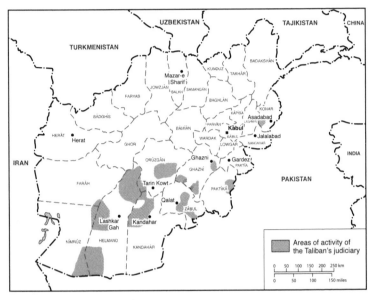

Map 8. Areas where the Taliban claimed to be operating their judicial system, 2006.

Sources: press reports.

A key aspect of the Taliban's efforts to establish a sort of shadow government in their strongholds was the attempt to project an image of authority stronger than Kabul's. For example, in a number of districts, such as Andar and Zurmat, the government authorities ordered a ban on motorbikes to prevent the Taliban from moving easily around the territory. The Taliban responded with a ban on all vehicles, communicated it effectively by visiting village after village, and then enforced it by shooting the tyres of the few vehicles that still ventured onto the roads. At least in Andar the Taliban clearly won the confrontation, as ten days into the ban many motorbikes started reappearing on the roads, but only very few cars. Another common method employed to intimidate opponents and demonstrate how weak the government's hold was consisted of setting up road blocks and forcing travellers to go through identity checks. Buses and trucks, especially if government-owned, would often be burnt. Taliban fighters manning the road blocks would routinely warn travellers to grow beards and stop listening to 'unauthorised' music, but would otherwise behave kindly to those not working for the government or the foreigners; another way to create a gap between 'collaborationists' and the bulk of the population. At least in Logar, where reception of Kabul-based television stations is good, the Taliban would also warn villagers to remove the aerials, clearly aiming at isolating the villages from government propaganda. Afghans working for the government or for some NGO risked execution, particularly if they were soldiers or policemen on leave. This was common on secondary roads, but in some areas it even happened on the highways. In order to prevent the Taliban from stopping the traffic, the government had to establish surveillance posts along the highways, immobilising valuable manpower resources. For example, in October 2006 there were nine police and one ANA posts along the Kabul–Gardez highway alone. Sometimes Taliban patrols and checkpoints could also be found in small district towns nominally under government control, while individuals known as members of the Taliban would openly wear the typical black turban as a reminder of the widespread presence of the Movement. The white flag of the Taliban would also be displayed wherever possible.[25]

4.5 SEEKING POPULAR SUPPORT

A degree of popular backing was needed by the Taliban in order to establish a structure to support the insurgency inside Afghanistan, but seeking popular support was also part of a wider strategy to split the state from the population and create a gap as wide as possible between them. To achieve this the Taliban showed a remarkable readiness to engage local communities and appropriate their grievances against the central government or the foreign troops (see Introduction, 2.6 *Recruiting local communities* and Chapter 6). At the same time, the Taliban had to avoid antagonising potential constituencies and the effort in this direction was made evident on several occasions.

In the Presidential and Parliamentary elections of 2004 and 2005 respectively, the expectation on the side of the government and its external supporters was that the Taliban would do all they could to sabotage the process. Instead, the Taliban showed their readiness to defer to the desire of local communities to vote and avoided any major effort to sabotage the electoral process, despite having declared their opposition to the elections. In both cases the Taliban effectively implemented a near-truce at the beginning of the electoral campaign, although they continued threatening to kill candidates who did not have an agreement with them. Coalition sources initially claimed that the Taliban had simply failed to disrupt the elections because of their military weakness, which is a very unconvincing explanation. Although the pace of their major military operations dramatically abated at the beginning of the electoral campaign in September 2004, small-scale attacks multiplied (see Graph 5). Moreover, they had been carrying out large attacks until well into the summer and restarted doing so soon after the elections. October also marked one of the lowest ebbs in the number of casualties inflicted by terrorist attacks, after a very violent summer, and was immediately followed by a rapid increase in November (see Graph 4). UN electoral workers with experience of the south acknowledged that truces were being established at the local level with Taliban commanders, in order to allow the registration of the voters and subsequent holding of the elections. Not a single polling station was seriously attacked anywhere in the country, despite the fact that they were distributed in the rural areas too. It is hard to believe that the Taliban, who could take districts and police stations, would not be able to take a polling station defended by a few policemen, had they wanted to.[26]

Other factors might more reasonably have motivated the Taliban to avoid sabotaging the presidential elections, namely the desire for a strong showing in the elections for Hamid Karzai, in order to strengthen his legitimacy as the future underwriter of a potential political deal to end the insurgency (see 4.10 *Negotiations*). At the time, Karzai had not yet publicly emerged as a bitter antagonist of

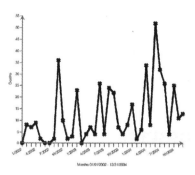

Graph 4. Deaths caused by terrorist attacks in Afghanistan, 2002–4. Courtesy of MIPT terrorism knowledge database.

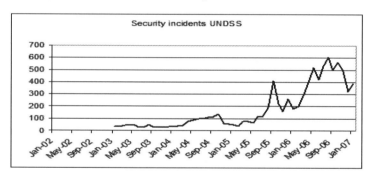

Graph 5: Security incidents 2003–7 according to UNDSS. Source: UNDSS.

Pakistan, and Islamabad might also have encouraged the Neo-Taliban to strengthen him as a counter-balance to strongly anti-Pakistan northern factions such as Shura-i Nezar. In the case of the Parliamentary elections of September 2005, the desire not to antagonise the population seems an even stronger explanation for the Taliban's mansuetude during election time. Again no significant attacks were carried out against the polling stations.[27] After the elections US officers in the field claimed that the Taliban were deliberately lying low in order to speed up the withdrawal of Coalition forces so that they could then proceed to overthrow the Karzai regime, but this explanation fails to account for the fact that in the summer of 2005, including up to the elections (18 September), the military activity of the insurgents had been reaching new peaks (see Graph 5).[28] In September UNDSS registered over 400 attacks, by far the highest number recorded thus far. An alternative explanation, also coming from US officers, but accepted by some analysts too, is that the Taliban were hoping to bring a substantial number of sympathisers to the parliament. The Taliban indeed claimed to have their own men among the candidates, but several of the candidates with a Taliban background do not appear to have maintained a good relationship with the Movement and issued statements critical of the insurgency or stated their fear of being assassinated by their former comrades. In any case, the number of candidates with a Taliban past was modest and only four were actually elected. It is unlikely that the Taliban would have determined their attitude towards the elections on the basis of the large number of candidates with a past in Hizb-i Islami,[29] given the rather loose alliance between the two organisations (see 4.9 *Alliances*). The desire to avoid alienating local communities, which wanted to send representatives to the parliament and to the provincial councils, remains the most likely explanation.[30]

Another aspect of the Taliban's effort to secure popular support was their (often clumsy) attempt to manage violence and to target it carefully. Although there are many examples of atrocities carried out by the insurgents, there seems to have been a clear effort to focus the violence on whomever the Taliban considered a collaborator of the government and of the 'occupiers'. There might have been some latitude exercised in the application of the rules issued by the leadership, but in general they appear to have been respected. It is true, for example, that the Taliban did not resort to easy ways of creating havoc such as the large-scale rocketing of cities, which, by contrast, the mujahidin of the 1980s had used widely.[31] 'Collaborationists' were first warned to quit their job and/or stop cooperating with the government and the foreigners. In some cases the Taliban were reported to have walked down the roads of villages with loudspeakers, threatening death to the 'collaborationists', but the recourse to 'night letters' or face-to-face warnings seems to have been more common. After several warnings, the resilient 'collaborationists' would be beaten up or their property damaged. Finally, in case even this tactic failed, the Taliban would proceed to eliminate the 'collaborationist' physically. Of course, in the case of IEDs and suicide bombings unwanted civilian casualties were unavoidable, not least because of the weak technical proficiency of the insurgents (see 4.3 *Demoralisation of the enemy*). However, even in these cases the Taliban sometimes presented their excuses for their mistakes, confirming the existence of a serious concern for their image among the population. According to a DIA document viewed by a journalist, a split occurred within the Taliban leadership concerning the use of suicide bombing, with Mullah Omar and others opposing an increase in its use due to concern with civilian casualties.[32]

Yet another indication of the Taliban's desire to win the 'hearts and minds' of the rural population is the fact that they used to warn rural communities (including small district towns) of planned attacks, giving them the chance to evacuate or at least take shelter. Even if this was presented by NATO as harassment of the population, it was clearly to their benefit. The Taliban paid a price for this, since it often also signalled to the enemy that an ambush was forthcoming. By contrast, attacks in urban areas were never preceded by warnings, leading to high civilian casualties. The Taliban also stayed clear of interfering too much with the life of the inhabitants of the areas under their control. Finally, they would stop depredations and impose law and order, attacking the criminal gangs who had earlier often worked under the protection of the police (see also 2.6 *Recruiting local communities* and 6.3 *Afghan police*). The Taliban's Layeha explicitly forbade practices such as harassing 'innocent people' and searching houses and confiscating weaponry without permission of senior commanders. It also banned recruiting old 1980s jihadis with a bad reputation and fighters sacked by other groups for bad behaviour. If disputes with the population still arose, they had to be resolved by senior commanders or the Council of Ulema or elders, another attempt to prevent arbitrariness in dealing with the villagers (see 3.1 *Cohesiveness of the Taliban*). Reports from the field show that the Taliban were not taxing travellers at the checkpoints, contrary to what the government militias, police and army were doing. They were also not looting farmers' harvests when crossing fields. As a result, many villagers did not perceive the Taliban as a threat, even when they did not directly support them.[33]

4.6 EXPLOITING DIVISIONS AMONG COMMUNITIES

Avoiding ill behaviour towards the villagers could have helped create a generally positive disposition towards the Taliban, but would not have itself sufficed to turn large areas into their strongholds. The next step in the Taliban's strategy was the targeting of rural communities as a source of support in areas where such communities were divided and at odds (see 2.6 *Recruiting local communities*). The Taliban displayed considerable skill in identifying local rivalries and siding with communities opposed to Kabul and its local allies. Where such opposition had not taken root, the Taliban would actively try to create the conditions for this to change. The south-eastern region provides a good example. During 2002–5 the Taliban failed, despite constant attempts, to penetrate Paktia and Khost provinces in the south-east, where the local tribes were on good terms with each other and continued supporting the central government despite numerous grievances.[34] Until the end of 2006 the Taliban had only been able to create a base of support among sectors of the population in Zurmat district, the most tribally mixed districts of Paktia/Khost and one which the tribal élites were unable to control effectively. The assassination of Governor Taniwal in September 2006 was clearly an attempt to destabilise the region. They seemed to have calculated, with some reason, that the need to appoint a new governor would likely lead to competing demands by the various tribes, each claiming the position for itself. Similarly, their attacks on elders and senior clergy were intended to foster social disorder and create cracks which they could then infiltrate. In this case, President Karzai avoided playing the Taliban's game and appointed as a replacement a UN official with extensive experience of the region, but originally from Nangarhar province, presumably in an attempt to avoid upsetting the delicate tribal balance.[35]

By the second half of 2006 the Taliban were experiencing problems with this strategy, as it relied on siding with some communities and against others. The problem is intrinsic to this mode of support-building: while it is relatively easy to pit one community against another and hence build a base of support, to move beyond that and form a wider and more solid alliance is very difficult because many communities have been antagonised in the process. Towards the end of 2006 prominent commanders of the Taliban like Haqqani and Dadullah were reportedly trying to win over the tribes by pledging to share power and resources with them. Exporting the model of mobilisation to areas where the Taliban had weak roots or none at all proved even more problematic. In 2006 Tajik, Hazara and Shi'a commanders were approached to join the jihad, sometimes with success. For example, sources allege that at least two Shi'a commanders from Bamyan and northern Afghanistan agreed to cooperate with the Taliban in the event of a large-scale offensive of the Taliban. However, mobilising such scattered pockets of support among non-Pashtuns was contingent on reaching the critical mass needed to launch a countrywide movement, which proved to be a vicious cycle. In the south, the critical mass had been provided by the madrasa recruits. As of early 2007 no similar groups had yet emerged to play the same role in other regions.[36]

4.7 PROPAGANDA

Gen. David Richards, commander of NATO forces in Afghanistan, reportedly said that he never saw 'a more sophisticated propaganda machine' than the one put together by the Taliban. The propaganda effort was rumoured to be under the responsibility of Qudratullah Jamal (aka Hamid Agha), former Information Minister of the Taliban regime. If he was indeed in charge, he had certainly improved his skills. Compared to the weak, naïve and clumsy public relations displayed by the Taliban of 1996–2001, the Neo-Taliban demonstrated after 2001 a much greater ability to manipulate the press and their interlocutors. Between 2002 and 2005 they already showed an unprecedented readiness to talk with journalists over the satellite phone or sometimes to arrange meetings, although they were still quite reluctant compared to fellow insurgents in other countries. During 2006, however, their availability to the press increased dramatically and Taliban commanders appeared more confident and eager to invite journalists to visit 'liberated' areas. During 2006, for example, they were leaking information to the international press, with the apparent intention of confusing their enemies with regard to where they would strike next and what strategy they would adopt during the coming spring. In one case in November 2006 they announced an impending offensive against Arghandab valley north of Kandahar city, first step towards taking Kandahar city itself. Then they claimed that the plan was to cut off both the Kandahar–Herat road and the Kandahar–Kabul road. They also claimed that a widespread tribal insurrection was in the making and would start in the spring, explaining the relative slow-down in fighting from November with the need to finalise agreements, improve coordination and restock arms dumps inside Afghanistan (see also 4.9 *Alliances*). They also tried to play divide and rule with members of the state administration, hinting that only former communists were cooperating with the government, while former jihadis were helping the Taliban. Similarly, they would leak information to journalists, alleging that a number of non-Islamic countries had offered help to the Taliban, a clear attempt to sow distrust between the US-led coalition on one side and Russia-led front on the other.[37]

There was much more to the Neo-Taliban's propaganda campaign than manipulation of the press. Some aspects of their propaganda and psychological warfare effort were not innovative at all and reproduced practices which had already been used during the 1980s jihad. For example the use of 'night letters', usually handwritten tracts which were widely distributed to villagers or nailed to the doors of houses, mosques and other public buildings. More innovative, though still not a first, was the enlistment of singers to support the cause. Their tape cassettes and CDs (hundreds of titles) were widely and cheaply available for sale in the bazaars of Afghan towns and villages, apparently manufactured by the Taliban and sympathising entrepreneurs. The number and availability of these products increased sharply during 2006. Sales too, despite a government ban, were reportedly increasing during 2006. The Taliban also produced magazines, although their impact must have been more modest given the low levels of literacy, and established both a radio (Voice of Sharia) with mobile transmitters in at least two provinces and a web site (www.alemarah. org) for the delivery of news and propaganda.[38] Where the Taliban were real innovators (together with the Arab jihadis in Iraq) was the introduction of VCDs and DVDs containing explicit propaganda commentary and preaching, featuring topics, ideas and arguments such as:

- heroic and successful episodes of their guerrilla campaign;
- episodes from other 'jihads' elsewhere in the world, primarily Iraq but also Lebanon, Waziristan and Palestine;
- the US invaded Afghanistan like the Soviet Union did and that therefore jihad is justified;
- the conflict is part of a global Christian war against Islam;
- the Kabul government is therefore a mere puppet and the only legitimate authority are the Ulema;
- in the ANA soldiers are not allowed to pray;
- confessions of 'spies' and their execution;
- our low-tech techniques can hold the ground against sophisticated US weaponry;
- success will eventually be achieved and martyrs will win heaven;
- interviews with successful commanders;
- footage showing the effects of US bombings in Afghanistan and Iraq;

- 'Christian' atrocities against Muslims in Poso (Indonesia);
- appeals by prospective suicide bombers for more volunteers;
- US soldiers desecrate bodies of Taliban fighters by burning them;
- the Koran is desecrated in Guantánamo toilets;
- Prophet Muhammad is desecrated in Danish cartoons;
- the convert to Christianity Abdul Rahman is helped by foreigners in getting away with the crime of apostasy.[39]

Like the music tapes, these VCDs and DVDs seem to be commercially manufactured by sympathetic entrepreneurs, probably based in Pakistan, such as:

- Omat productions;
- Manbaul-Jihad;
- Abdullah videos;
- As-sahab.[40]

Initially these products were sold (however cheaply), but were later also distributed for free, which together with their increasing availability in the bazaars suggests that more funding was being channelled into these types of activities. Clearly the Taliban gradually strengthened the role of propaganda in their war effort. Their task was facilitated by the weakness of the psyops effort on the NATO/US side.[41] The importance of propaganda in the Taliban's effort seems to support to some extent Gen. Barno's thesis that the insurgency was an example of 'fourth generation warfare', except that the bulk of the propaganda was not aimed at Western public and governments, but at Afghan and Muslim public opinion. The actual impact of these propaganda efforts on the Afghan population was far from clear at the time of writing, except for the fact that sales of CDs and DVDs seemed to be doing well. The build-up in anti-foreigner sentiment from 2006 onwards (see 2.7 *Changes in recruitment patterns*) might well at one point lead to an enhanced role for pan-Islamic sentiment as a factor of increased recruitment, but there was little evidence of that having been the case up to early 2007.

The reliance on pan-Islamic themes for propaganda purposes might, however, have contributed to mollify the attitude of some sections of the population towards the insurgents, even without leading to much direct recruitment.

4.8 THE THIRD PHASE: 'FINAL OFFENSIVE'?

Until 2006 there was little that could be even remotely described as an attempt of the Taliban to launch a coordinated offensive. The view of US officers is that the Taliban did not mount a coordinated offensive in 2004 because they had been weakened by US counter-insurgency, but it is more likely that they never planned to or were incapable of doing so at that stage. Even if at the beginning of 2004 they had announced their intention to attack and take a major city and to attack US military bases, they were in reality largely busy infiltrating the territory and establishing infrastructures. By 2006 the situation had changed and they were ready to pursue the ambitious plans stated as early as 2004. Whether the 2006 fighting can effectively be described as an 'offensive' is a matter of debate. It is possible to speculate that the Taliban might have been under pressure from their Arab, Pakistani and other 'donors' to deliver a steady pace of advancement and some high profile victories. It is also possible that the leadership of the Taliban might in any case have planned to escalate its military operations well in advance as a move towards a new stage of the insurgency, taking on US and allied military forces in larger scale engagements. A fourth hypothesis is that the replacement of US troops with Canadian troops in Kandahar in the spring of 2006 might have been seen by the insurgents as an indication of the intention of the US to withdraw from the country and as a golden opportunity to score easy victories, boosting the morale of the insurgents and possibly forcing a hasty retreat of the Canadians from Kandahar.[42] Whatever the immediate reason for this decision to escalate and whatever term is used to describe the escalation, there is no question that the Taliban for the first time—at least since what the US military calls Operation Anaconda in March 2002—openly challenged the foreign contingents in a large battle.[43]

In part, the escalation of 2006 was due to special circumstances, beyond the will of the Taliban leadership. In particular, the clashes with the British in Helmand province were likely motivated by the attempt of the British to penetrate the northern strongholds of the Taliban. In fact, the fighting subsided once the British adopted a less aggressive posture at the beginning of the autumn and the Taliban never tried to approach Lashkargah, the provincial capital of Helmand. By contrast, in Kandahar throughout the spring and summer of 2006 the Taliban had moved the focus of their operations very close to the city and the highway, possibly in an attempt to drag the Canadians out of Kandahar and hurt them. The Taliban attempted a single attack on fortified positions at the end of March and then relied on ambushes, roadside bombs and suicide attacks to wear the Canadians out.[44] Although attacks on outposts manned by foreign troops were rare even in 2006, they might have been sufficient for the Taliban to conclude that concentrations of 300–400 Taliban were short of the critical mass needed to overwhelm even company- or platoon-size detachments. Moreover, such attacks were particularly costly in terms of casualties, as the fighters had to expose themselves and face airstrikes both during the attack and when withdrawing. The Taliban leadership and its advisors seem to have concluded that it needed to mobilise larger concentrations in order to achieve the critical mass necessary to inflict serious casualties. This would of course have greatly compounded the problem of manoeuvring and coordinating in the field, a problem of difficult solution given the near absence of educated cadres within the ranks of the Taliban. Together with the desire to limit casualties in its own ranks, this consideration probably reinforced the necessity of drawing the enemy out to fight on the Taliban's ground of choice.

Based on the experience of anti-Soviet jihadis and on their own interpretations of the strategy and tactics of the Soviet army, the leaders of the Taliban seem to have identified the solution to their dilemmas in the vineyards of the area of Pashmul, between the districts of Panjwai and Zhare, a mere 20 km from Kandahar city. The local mujahidin were convinced that the Soviet army could never take Panjwai because its grapevines, drainage ditches, high walled compounds and 'scores of escape tunnels and trenches' built during the 1980s offered good protection from air bombardment as well as shelter from air reconnaissance. Why should the ruse not work against the US Air Force? Moreover, the deployment of Taliban among the villagers of Panjwai and Zhare was probably seen as a deterrent against large-scale air bombardment. During March–July Pashmul had been the staging area of most attacks against Canadian troops, but in August the Taliban tried to make their presence as obvious and as provocative as possible, turning up in large numbers in full daylight, establishing training centres and giving out every signal that they intended to turn the area into a stronghold that could be used to scale up activities in central Kandahar province, including Kandahar city itself. They moved into Pashmul from Maywand district, where they already enjoyed a 'free rein'. Some sources even alleged that the Taliban were planning to infiltrate Arghandab district north of Kandahar, which is contiguous with Panjwai. NATO estimated in the end that as many as 1,500–2,000 Taliban might have been concentrated in the area, although many of them appear to have been local tribesmen allied to the insurgents. In any case, this was certainly by far the largest concentration of insurgents of the whole conflict to date. The build-up lasted several weeks and caused considerable edginess in both Kandahar and Kabul. Eventually the trap set by the Taliban worked, with NATO becoming convinced that a major threat to Kandahar was imminent, the more so since Pashmul is well positioned to threaten the highway connecting Kandahar to Herat. Some signs of infiltration of Taliban fighters into Kandahar were already reported during the summer. However, the offensive mounted by NATO forces was probably bigger and more sophisticated than the Taliban had expected, with US Special Forces trying to cut off the retreat to the insurgents while the Canadians were staging a frontal attack. The Taliban moreover miscalculated NATO's and specifically the Canadians' reluctance to approve the large-scale bombing of populated areas, particularly when accurate targeting was difficult because of the vineyards. NATO instead invited the villagers to leave the area and then launched massive air attacks, which included 2,000lb bombs, despite the fact that substantial numbers of civilians had opted to stay.[45]

The other miscalculation committed by the Taliban leadership concerned the strength of the Soviet Army's determination to take Pashmul, on which assumption the theory of the impregnability of Pashmul was based. It is indeed much more likely that the Soviets were not excessively interested in the area and therefore never invested large resources in taking it. They could certainly have bombed it heavily, had they wished to do so, as the Americans did in September 2006. The final result of the Taliban's miscalculations was hundreds of casualties on their side, although NATO had to pay a political price for the significant civilian losses.[46] Moreover, forced to withdraw by their inability to fight effectively under constant bombardment, the Taliban were subjected to raids by US Special Forces, which inflicted more casualties. The final toll of 1,100 killed, as estimated by NATO, might be an exaggeration or not, but undoubtedly the battle of Pashmul was a serious tactical defeat for the Taliban.[47]

In the immediate aftermath of Pashmul the Taliban did not mount any other major operations and went back to their usual tactic of avoiding direct confrontations with superior NATO forces, as highlighted by operation Baaz Tsuka in the area around Pashmul in December 2006, when the Taliban withdrew without fighting despite having sizeable forces there. However, once the stakes had been raised, it was no simple task for the leadership of the Taliban to fall back on low-scale insurgency tactics. The fact that the Taliban claimed that the withdrawal was contingent on pro-Taliban elders being handed local control by NATO forces might be a sign of how having raised the stakes in the conflict possibly created a problem of image for the Taliban, who had now to live up to its claims of being about to launch a 'final offensive' or 'national uprising'. At the beginning of the autumn of 2006 the Taliban leadership even announced the continuation of large-scale operations throughout the forthcoming winter, in what was seen at the time as an act of defiance. However, as the end of November approached, Mullah Dadullah, military commander of the southern region, announced that the offensive would be postponed to the following spring due to cold weather. Was Dadullah's excuse conceived to mask the weakening of the insurgency after having suffered very heavy losses? Insurgent attacks in November 2006 were 28 per cent fewer than in October, as reported by NATO, then picked up again in December and January. The winter of 2006–7 was not a particularly cold one, but heavy rains in March might have made travel more difficult. It is true that Afghanistan appeared set for a cold winter as November was colder than expected, but the Taliban are also likely to have been buying time while trying to come up with new strategies to upgrade their activities, as well as redeploying fighters. Reports that Mullah Omar was intensifying his efforts to communicate with field commanders and to encourage them also suggest that a further strengthening of military activities was being planned. In particular, the Taliban were reportedly planning to move the focus of their military activities closer to Kabul. Their build-up in Tagab and the infiltration of Kabul's southern surroundings, including an old Hizb-i Islami stronghold like Sarobi valley, the control of which would have allowed cutting the road to Jalalabad, suggest that their intentions were serious (see 2.6 *Recruiting local communities*). By the end of the autumn the situation in a couple of districts in the southern part of Kabul province was showing signs of deterioration and Afghan security forces were not patrolling any more at night. NATO sources were worried that these districts could be used as a 'gateway' to Kabul city. It is possible that in the minds of the Taliban's leaders, combining an offensive in the south with scaled-up operations around Kabul would stretch NATO thin and hamper its ability to fight effectively. The discovery of logistical bases and a field hospital capable of catering for as many as 900 men near Lashkargah, as well as news of a large-scale movement of fighters across the border, suggest serious Taliban planning towards a major effort to cut off the provincial capital of Helmand as well. However, their objectives were confounded by the fact that the adversaries were now aware of the importance of the mountain strongholds and during the winter NATO forces and in particular the British increased the pace of their activities against these areas, in order to disrupt the Talibans' capability to organise a spring offensive. Having enjoyed years of relatively undisturbed control over the logistical redoubts of Helmand, the Taliban were for the first time put under serious pressure, even if most British military activity was concentrated in Garmser and Gereshk, trying to prevent supplies from reaching the Taliban from the shorter route, that is the Pakistani border of Helmand. The Taliban had to start developing alternative routes, for example they tried to pressure the Hazara population of Kijran district (Daikundi) towards allowing the movement of Taliban's caravans between Zabul and Helmand. Indeed, the penetration of Taliban in the southern districts of Daikundi was reported by local Afghan authorities in April 2007. However, even if successfully developing alternative routes, the Taliban's plans for future offensives might have been seriously disrupted in the short term by the British raids.[48]

The fighting around Kandahar in 2006 could be seen as a confirmation that some Maoist concepts of guerrilla warfare seem to have made it in to the mindset of Taliban commanders. Until then their commitment to the 'third phase' had been mostly rhetorical. Some of them had openly talked of 'closing in' on Kandahar, Khost, Jalalabad, Asadabad and Gardez as early as 2003. Bringing the war to the cities of Afghanistan, after having surrounded them, was allegedly part of the Taliban's planning in early 2004, when they claimed to be about to start the 'war of the cities' by the summer. In December of that year the Taliban actually circulated information that the insurgents were infiltrating the cities in the hundreds and indeed a small-scale terrorist campaign started later in Kabul, Mazar-i Sharif, Kandahar and Herat,[49] but this soon petered out. In any case, if the fighting around Kandahar in 2006 was meant to be the beginning of the Taliban's 'third phase', it was clearly a premature move. As of March 2007 they were somewhat toning down their claims to be about to launch a countrywide offensive, shifting the focus once again towards the southern part of the country.

4.9 ALLIANCES

Until 2006 the Taliban did not achieve much success in the formation of alliances with other groups that shared grievances against the central government. The agreement with Hizb-i Islami in 2002 appears to have been more a matter of Gulbuddin Hekmatyar's willingness to emerge from obscurity than the result of a genuine interest on the part of the Taliban leadership. Hizb-i Islami never effectively integrated its forces with the Taliban's, or even successfully coordinated the military effort, although some coordination occurred at the local level. There were also persistent rumours that Hekmatyar might have different strategic aims too, due to his having declared jihad against the foreign forces but not against the government. This was construed by some observers to imply that he might be trying to manoeuvre for a deal with the government, after having infiltrated the state administration with 'former' members of his party, although he explained in one interview that his failure to mention the Afghan government was due to the fact that it was not even worth mentioning. Later again a misquoted interview in March 2007 was interpreted as Hekmatyar offering negotiations without conditions to Kabul, whereas he was just repeating his usual line (and the Taliban's) that foreign troops had to be withdrawn before any negotiations could take place. In any case, towards the end of 2006 Hizb-i Islami seemed intent on strengthening its identity of an insurgent group as separate from the Taliban, appointing for the first time a spokesman (Haroon Zargoun) and beginning to claim military operations for themselves. Hekmatyar admitted to the press the existence of problems in co-ordinating and integrating his forces with the Taliban's, but attributed the failure to the lack of willingness among the ranks of his allies. The fact that he mentioned the lack of resources as an explanation for the low level of Hizb-i Islami's military activities suggests that the lack of cooperation might imply an unwillingness to share resources on the Taliban's side.[50]

Paradoxically, the potential value of Hizb-i Islami to the Taliban might have increased exactly as Hekmatyar was trying to distance himself. As during 2006 the Taliban were rapidly reaching the limits of the area where their activists could reasonably hope to infiltrate (that is their old strongholds in the south and south-east), Hizb-i Islami's old constituencies in the east, north-east, around Kabul and maybe even in the west must have looked attractive to them. Hekmatyar's residual resources were modest but not insignificant. After 2001 his party had been mainly active in eastern Afghanistan (Kunar, Nuristan, Laghman, Nangarhar). Another significant pocket was active in Kapisa (Tagab district) and parts of Kabul province, while some residual capability appeared to exist also in Wardak, Logar, Parwan, Kabul, Paktia, Paktika, Khost, Kandahar, Baghlan, Balkh and Badakhshan, where military activities were, however, very small in scale or non-existent. NATO sources put the strength of Hizb-i Islami very low, at 300–400 fighters in 2006, which looks like an underestimate given the geographical spread of the party's activity. Again, this should be interpreted as an average for active fighters. A total figure of around 1,500 appears more realistic. Hekmatyar's efforts to re-establish contact with his former commanders added to his value to the Taliban. His emissaries were already reported in Kunduz during 2004 and police sources suggested in May 2006 that such networks were being re-activated in Takhar too. In his efforts Hekmatyar scored at least a few successes, particularly in Kapisa province, where his men were reported to have spread their activities beyond Tagab, in Nejab, Kohistan and Kohband districts. Propaganda activities were reported at least in Herat city too. In November 2006 official sources reported the distribution of weapons to local commanders in Kunduz, apparently by pro-Taliban elements. On

December 23 suspected insurgents were arrested in that province and said to be part of a network extending to Baghlan province too. The network included 250 activists of the Taliban, according to security officials, but many of them are likely to have been former Hizbis.[51]

A number of other groups ideologically close to the Taliban are known to operate in Afghanistan (see Table 6), but they are all small and largely insignificant, although a few (like Jamaat-ud-Da'awa Al-Salafia Wal Qitaab, the Bara Bin Malek Front of Mullah Ismail in Kunar and the Nuristani Dawlat-e Enqelabi-ye Islami) might have some influence at the local level, wherever Salafi groups have long had strong roots. It should also be considered that despite ideological contiguities the Salafis do not maintain good relations with the Taliban due to the mistreatment of their leadership by the Taliban regime. The largest insurgent group after the Taliban and Hizb-i Islami, Jaish ul-Muslimeen, was a Taliban offshoot and was reabsorbed in 2005. The Jaish ul-Mahdi was also formed by a former Talib in 2002 and actively cooperates with international jihadi volunteers inside Afghanistan.[52]

As for the international volunteers, 'Al Qaida' or whatever they might be called, their impact on the military capabilities of the insurgency was much greater (see 2.1 *How strong are the Taliban?*), but the relationship with the Taliban appears to have been often uneasy. In early 2007 some press sources reported a disagreement between the two concerning relations with the Pakistani government, to which 'Al Qaida' was reportedly very hostile. In the east at least, the foreign jihadis had their own network of support, separate from that of Hizb-i Islami and the Taliban. In some cases, for example parts of Paktia, local commanders had to ask the foreign volunteers, particularly Arabs, to leave in order not to alienate the population. In Kunar too the Arabs were reported not to be on good terms with Afghan insurgents, who considered them undisciplined and extreme in their behaviour. As a result, the contribution of the volunteers to the advancement of the cause of the insurgency was at best a mixed one.[53]

In order to have some impact on the dynamic of the conflict, the Taliban would have to make alliances with some influential organisation. In fact, from 2005 the leadership showed a new interest for talking to its old northern enemies, possibly a result of their growing self-confidence and of the belief that the Movement had developed into a valuable partner for a countrywide revolt. Taliban sources claimed to have established contacts with personalities of the old Jami'at-i Islami as early as the spring of 2005, confirming rumours circulating in Kabul at that time. According to these sources, the Jami'atis stated their shared hatred for the presence of foreign troops in the country

	2002	2003	2004	2005	2006
Taliban	4,000	7,000	9,500	12,500	17,000
Of which Jaish al Muslimeen			*1000*	*750*	*Re-absorbed into Taliban?*
Hizb-i Islami	800	1,000	1,000	1,250	1,500
Al Qaida			700	1,000	2,000
Jamaat-ud-Da'awa Al-Salafia Wal Qitaab					90
Council of the Secret Army				very small	joins Hizb-i Islami in summer 2006
Islamic Revolutionary State of Afghanistan	150	150	150	150	100
Jaish al-Mahdi					low hundreds

Table 6. Insurgent groups operating in Afghanistan, strength estimates. Sources: press reports, interviews with locals and with former members of Hizb-i Islami, UN sources.

and promised to join the fight at a later stage. Taliban sources even claimed that Professor Rabbani, leader of Jami'at, admitted to the Afghan press that his associates were talking to the Taliban. The contacts were reportedly continuing in 2006. UN sources reported that in Badakhshan the rise of Karzai's appointee and former head of the NSD unit in charge of protecting the President (10th Directorate), Zalmay Mojaddedi, contributed to local commanders such as Nazir Mohammed and Sardar Khan, once at odds, forming an opposition alliance. Zalmay Mojaddedi, a minor commander until his appointment to the NSD, won a parliamentary seat in Badakhshan in part at least due to massive support from the security and administrative machinery of the state. Nazir and Sardar had already been alienated by the failure of the central government to reward their loyalty with appointments to positions of power after the demobilisation of the militias they had been commanding. According to some UN sources, approaches between Taliban, conservative mullahs and former jihadi commanders were taking place between the end of 2006 and the beginning of 2007.[54]

These claims of course could just be an attempt to sow discord within the anti-Taliban front. However, sources close to the government and old Jami'atis agreed that northern militias, strongmen and warlords were turning increasingly hostile to the Kabul government during 2006, which they felt had been increasingly marginalising them. NATO sources believed that local conflicts in the north could allow the Taliban to infiltrate the region. The Taliban maintained some influence in Baghdis province after 2001 (see 2.6 *Recruiting local communities*) and from there, in 2006, they were believed to be infiltrating the southern districts of Faryab province, where conflicts among Uzbek warlords, between factions like Junbesh and Jami'at and between Uzbek warlords and Pashtun tribal strongmen created a favourable environment. In December 2006 a rocket attack was reported against Maimana, the provincial capital of Faryab. Between 2005 and 2006 the clear demonstration of government weakness and of the inability of the foreign contingents to control the territory, as well as their obvious overstretching, contributed to lower the threshold beyond which various groups holding grievances against the central government would find it convenient to join the armed opposition. The May 2006 riots in Kabul were widely seen as a demonstration of the government's inability to control even a modest crowd of rioters.[55]

4.10 NEGOTIATIONS

If elements derived from Mao's classical theory were present in the Taliban's strategy, the question remains open of whether this genuinely reflected the determination to conquer political power or whether it was used as a tool of political pressure on the Karzai administration to force it to the negotiating table. For all their image of an extremist movement, there are some indications that the Taliban might have always been aiming for a negotiated settlement. Talks with Karzai had been going on at least since 2003, although it is not clear how far up the Taliban leadership Karzai's contacts were. It appears that the Taliban contacted Kabul through UNAMA and that Kabul agreed to negotiate one month later, after receiving the green light from the US embassy. US military authorities officially endorsed the possibility of talks with 'moderate members' of the Taliban in December of that year. The actual content of the negotiations, however, is not known, nor is it clear whether the 'moderate Taliban' were testing the ground for the leadership of the Movement or were acting on their own initiative and autonomously. After a period of apparent suspension, negotiations were resumed, as admitted by President Karzai himself in 2007.[56]

One possibility is that there might have been different attitudes towards negotiations with Kabul among the Taliban. Even as late as December 2006, after President Karzai launched the idea of parallel 'Peace Jirgas' to be held in both Afghanistan and Pakistan at the beginning of 2007, with the aim of improving the cooperation of the Pakistani side in containing the insurgency, Qari Mohammed Yousuf, who claimed to be a representative of the Taliban in Pakistan but is sometimes dismissed as something short of a genuine spokesman of the Movement, stated that the Taliban might attend the jirgas if they were invited, with some conditions. However, a few days later another Taliban spokesman, Sayed Tayeb Agha, said that the rebels would never participate in such exercises as long as foreign troops were still in Afghanistan. The Taliban might of course have also been indulging in a tactical attempt to sow divisions within the Kabul ruling coalition, between elements favourable to negotiations and others opposing them. However, some facts seem to show that negotiations might indeed have been on the agenda of the leadership of the Taliban. The unofficial truce during the Presidential electoral campaign of 2004 would have made sense particularly if the Taliban were trying to build up Karzai as a legitimate negotiating partner (see 4.5 *Seeking popular support*). Furthermore, the fact that the Taliban until Sping 2007 had never targeted the UN in their terrorist attacks and ambushes is likely to have been due to the fact that they needed this organisation as a broker in negotiations with the government. Otherwise it would have been easy for them to throw the government and its international sponsors into a deep crisis by forcing the departure of the UN mission. This could easily be achieved by assassinating a few international members of staff. Despite many limitations, the UN mission played a key role in shoring up an often incompetent government and in some cases helped in preventing the explosion of local civil wars, for example in the northern half of Afghanistan. If a political deal was ever an organic part of the strategy of the Taliban, it is obvious they would not want to divulge it. Most diplomats would agree that successful negotiations in conflict resolution must always be conducted in secret. In the case of the Taliban, moreover, it would have been difficult to ask the rank-and-file to risk their lives on the battlefield if the leadership had admitted that it was negotiating with Kabul. Given the initial weakness of the Movement, mustering together a credible military threat must have been a priority in order to achieve a strong negotiating position.[57]

Given their rigid ideological background, why would the Taliban have wanted to negotiate? Given available evidence, a definite answer is impossible to give. One might speculate that until 2005 or 2006 the Taliban were not so confident of their ultimate victory and thought that their only chance was to find an accommodation with Kabul. It is also possible that they were forced to include negotiations in their agenda by the Pakistani authorities. These might have sponsored the insurgency as a last resort after attempts to create a legal political party based on the old Taliban (Jami'at-i Khudam-ul Koran, see 3.1 *Cohesiveness of the Taliban*) failed to achieve the aim of guaranteeing Pakistan's influence in Kabul. The Pakistanis might also have feared that a prolonged conflict would have led to the convergence of the two Taliban movements (Pakistani and Afghan) into a single entity (see 1.3 *The role of Pakistan*). Taliban sources repeatedly stated that the departure of foreign troops from Afghanistan was a *conditio sine qua non* for any agreement, which could be interpreted both as a sign of availability to negotiations and as an attempt to avoid negotiations by imposing an unacceptable condition. The former Taliban ambassador to Pakistan, Zaif, seemed to believe that some flexibility in this regard might have been possible and negotiations could have started before a withdrawal of the foreign troops, although such withdrawal would still need to be part of any agreement. The introduction of 'Islamic elements' in the legislation and in the system of government would also be required.[58]

It has also to be considered that there seems to be widespread support for negotiations leading to peace among the Afghan population, a fact which gives a strong incentive to both sides in the conflict to voice support for negotiations even when unwilling to offer reasonable conditions to the adversary. The propaganda purpose of some statements of the Taliban and of the Kabul government appears obvious. For example, while the Taliban made the withdrawal of foreign troops a key demand, in December 2006 President Karzai threw the ball back in their field when he announced that he was prepared to negotiate even with Mullah Omar, as long as he freed himself from 'foreign slavery' (i.e. Pakistan). Another example is that of the Peace Jirgas launched by Karzai in September 2006. Both Karzai and Musharraf tried to create the conditions for better manipulating the jirgas. For example, Karzai appointed three of his close supporters and collaborators among the four members the Afghan Peace Jirga Commission.[59]

4.11 MAO'S EPIGONES, 'FLEAS', 'FOURTH GENERATION' WARRIORS OR INTERNATIONAL JIHADISTS?

As shown in the previous paragraphs, there are valid elements in all three interpretations of the Neo-Taliban's strategy outlined at the beginning of the chapter. Up to 2005 the 'war of the flea' theory seemed to apply well to the Taliban, but the fighting around Kandahar in 2006 represents a departure from that model. At first sight at least, the developments of 2006 strengthen the interpretation of the Taliban insurgency as inspired by Maoist concepts. The idea that some second- or third-hand inspiration was taken from aspects of Mao's theories, purged of their People's War content, received some confirmation already in the form of the phases of infiltration and of stronghold build-up, but until 2005 the third phase had only existed in the shape of some claimed intention of surrounding and taking cities. The 2006 fighting around Kandahar seemed intended to be a first attempt at implementing this third phase and as such lends new credibility to this interpretation. Elements of Mao's theories could have made it to the leadership of the Taliban through some external advisor, or through some old Islamist mujahidin of Hizb-i Islami, some of whom were familiar with these concepts having read Mao.

Mao, however, was not fighting a power much superior in terms of both resources and technology (Japan was not that superior technologically, although it did have superior doctrine, training, resources and organisation). In the context of Afghanistan in 2002–6, like in that of Vietnam, taking a major city was not a realistic enterprise. Compared to Giap, the leadership of the Taliban (or their advisors) could have had the hindsight that militarily a Tet-like offensive was bound to fail. There is no evidence that this was the case and that the Kandahar offensive was not meant to succeed militarily, but on the other hand no military commander could ask his men to sacrifice their lives in a battle without hope. Hence even if the aim was just to create a psychological effect, the leaders of the Taliban would not want to divulge the notion. If this was the case, the theory of 'fourth generation warfare' would seem to fit well with the case of the Taliban, although whether this is really something new in historical terms is open to debate. The Taliban's improving skills in manipulating the press also point in this direction.

Nonetheless, some elements of the strategy of the Taliban do not fit well with any of these theories. Although the Neo-Taliban paid some attention to the manipulation of Western government and public opinion, the bulk of their effort was directed at winning over the Afghan public, as well as a wider Islamic one. It is also not clear whether they really tried to target public opinion and those governments perceived as not fully committed to intervention in Afghanistan. The offensive against Kandahar could be read as an attempt to throw the Canadians off-balance, given that Canadian public opinion was rather cool towards the Afghan mission and that the Conservative government did not have a majority in parliament. However, the Dutch in Uruzgan would have been an easier target, given that their government had already fallen and that elections were forthcoming. According to opinion polls, the Dutch public was even more sceptical of the mission than the Canadian one and the ground in Uruzgan was more favourable to insurgency operations than in central Kandahar province. Still, the summer was relatively quiet in Uruzgan.

This author supports an alternative interpretation, according to which the Neo-Taliban had become much more integrated in a supra-national jihadist movement than the 'old Taliban' ever were and that they increasingly believed that the decisive factor in winning the war would not be Western public opinion, but the support of their Muslim brethren. Hence their priority increasingly became the mobilisation of Muslim opinion worldwide as a source of funding and moral support, as well as of volunteers.[60] Other aspects of their strategy were becoming either subordinated to this, or confined to a secondary role. Ultimately, the belief was that victory would come with the overstretching of the enemy through the creation of 'one, ten, a hundred Iraqs', rather than with country-specific strategies. Since there is little evidence that the leadership of the Neo-Taliban already held this view when they started the insurgency in 2002, it is likely that this strategic view emerged gradually, under the influence of external advisors, financial contributors and allies. The jihadist perspective, moreover, was not necessarily incompatible with most of the characteristics of the 'war of the flea', of Maoist warfare or of 'fourth generation warfare' and the transition from any of them could take place almost seamlessly. Tactics and strategies could be pragmatically picked from the market of ideas and concepts as long as they fit in with the jihadist grand strategy. Given the current status of knowledge, it is impossible to say whether the conversion to a global jihadist strategy is permanent or not. It might have been dictated by the need to secure more funding from particular sources, rather than by a genuine belief in its intrinsic value.

NOTES

1 See Sami Yousafzai and Ron Moreau, 'The mysterious Mullah Omar', *Newsweek*, 5 March 2007.
2 See Jandora (2005). See also Cassidy (2003).
3 Gerges (2006), p. 174.
4 Belasco (2006).
5 'A double spring offensive', *The Economist*, 22 February 2007.
6 For a summary of Hammes' argument see Hammes (2005).
7 Hammes (2006), p. 2, also quoted in Barno; Barno (2006), pp. 16–17.
8 Naylor (2006).
9 The term is borrowed from Taber (1965). See also Johnson and Mason (2007), p. 87.
10 'NATO in Afghanistan', *RFE/RL Afghanistan Report*, vol. 5, no. 20 (1 August 2006); Tim McGirk, 'The Taliban on the run', *Time*, 28 March 2005; personal communication with Niamatullah Ibrahimi, Crisis States Research Centre, Kabul, 24 January 2007; Carlotta Gall, 'Despite years of U.S. pressure, Taliban fight on in jagged hills', *New York Times*, 4 June 2005; Claudio Franco, 'In remote Afghan camp, Taliban explain how and why they fight', *San Francisco Chronicle*, 21 January 2007; 'Socaust media briefing post Op Slipper', 27 September 2006, <http://www.defence.gov.au/media/SpeechTpl.cfm?CurrentId=6034>; Bill Graveland, 'Les talibans: un ennemi difficilement saisissable', *Associated Press*, 27 December 2006; ANA sources, January 2007.
11 Wright (2006a); Borhan Younus, 'Taliban call the shots in Ghazni', *Afghanistan Recovery Report*, no. 213 (25 April 2006); Andrew Maykuth, 'Taliban rampage in Ghazni', *Philadelphia Inquirer*, 10 September 2006; David Rohde, 'Afghan symbol for change becomes a symbol of failure', *New York Times*, 5 September 2006; Brian Hutchinson, 'Taliban execute 26

male Afghans', *CanWest News Service*, 19 December 2006; Claudio Franco, 'Islamic militant insurgency in Afghanistan experiencing "Iraqization"', *Eurasianet*, 8 November 2005; April Witt, 'Afghan political violence on the rise', *Washington Post*, 3 August 2003; Rahmani (2006b); Senlis Council (2006e), pp. 18–19; Declan Walsh, 'Better paid, better armed, better connected – Taliban rise again', *Guardian*, 16 September 2006; Syed Saleem Shahzad, 'Taliban line up the heavy artillery', *Asia Times Online*, 21 December 2006; Kim Sengupta, 'Helmand governor escapes blast as he battles for job', *Independent*, 13 December 2006; 'Man who wanted to assassinate Padshah Khan Zadran is arrested', *Hewaad*, 19 December 2006; Declan Walsh, 'Kandahar under threat, war raging in two provinces and an isolated president. So what went wrong?', *Guardian*, 16 September 2006.

12 Human Rights Watch (2006), pp. 39–41; interview with Afghan security officer, Kandahar, January 2006; Jason Burke, 'Taliban rising', *India Today*, 1 December 2003; 'Taliban issues warning to people of southern Afghan province', *RFE/RL*, 6 March 2007.

13 Human Rights Watch (2006).

14 Tom Coghlan, 'Taliban use beheadings and beatings to keep Afghanistan's schools closed', *Independent*, 11 July 2006; Human Rights Watch (2006), pp. 39–41, 50–1; interview with Afghan journalist returning from the south, Kabul, October 2006; Jason Straziuso, 'New Taliban rules target Afghan teachers', *Associated Press*, 9 December 2006; Suzanna Koster, 'Taliban fighters talk tactics – while safe in Pakistan', *Christian Science Monitor*, 9 November 2006; Michael Evans *et al.*, 'Aid effort fails to impress war-weary Afghans', *The Times*, 27 January 2007; Noor Khan, 'Taliban to open schools in Afghanistan', *Associated Press*, 21 January 2007; Javid Hamim, Saeed Zabuli and Samad Rohani, 'A turn from burning to learning', *Pajhwok Afghan News*, 21 January 2007; 'Schools face murderous challenge', *Afghan Recovery Report*, no. 241 (9 February 2007); personal communication with UNICEF official, Jalalabad, February 2007; Laura King, 'Afghans try to stop attacks on their schools', *Los Angeles Times*, 11 February 2007; 'Militant attacks at Afghan schools killed 85 students, teachers last year, minister says', *Associated Press*, 29 April 2007.

15 Geoffrey York, 'Taliban rising', *Globe and Mail*, 29 May 2006; Guy Dinmore and Rachel Morarjee, 'To a second front? How Afghanistan could again be engulfed by civil war', *Financial Times*, 22 November 2006; Victoria Burnett, 'Afghan officials see Taliban resurgence', *Boston Globe*, 25 September 2003; Talatbek Masadykov of UNAMA, quoted in April Witt, 'Afghan political violence on the rise'; Ahmed Rashid, 'Afghanistan and Pakistan, safe haven for the Taliban', *Far Eastern Economic Review*, 16 October 2003; Françoise Chipaux, 'Dans le plus complet dénuement, la province afghane de Zabul mène la lutte contre les talibans', *Le Monde*, 24 December 2003; interview with Maulana Obeidullah, Peace Strengthening Commission, Kandahar, January 2006; Talatbek Masadykov, quoted in James Rupert, 'Corruption and coalition failures spur Taliban resurgence in Afghanistan', *Newsday*, 17

June 2006; personal communication with UN official, Jalalabad, February 2007.

16 See the example of Lizha (Khost) in Paul Watson, 'On the trail of the Taliban's support', *Los Angeles Times*, 24 December 2006.

17 David Rohde and James Risen, 'C.I.A. review highlights Afghan leader's woes', *New York Times*, 5 November 2006; Schiewek (2006), p. 161.

18 Syed Saleem Shahzad, 'Taliban raise the stakes in Afghanistan', *Asia Times Online*, 30 October 2003; personal communication with UN official, Kabul, October 2006; Cordesman (2007); UNDSS weekly reports, February 2007.

19 Scott Peterson, 'Taliban adopting Iraq-style jihad', *Christian Science Monitor*, 13 September 2006; Senlis Council (2006a), p. 9; Lee Greenberg, 'Renewed Afghan fighting comes amid signs of Taliban buildup', *Ottawa Citizen*, 30 October 2006; Owais Tohid, 'Taliban regroups – on the road', *Christian Science Monitor*, 27 June 2003; Syed Saleem Shahzad, 'Taliban raise the stakes in Afghanistan'; Jason Straziuso, 'Outgoing Gen. sees more Afghan battles', *Associated Press*, 30 December 2006; Ron Synovitz, 'Afghanistan: are militants copying Iraqi insurgents' suicide tactics?', *RFE/RL*, 17 January 2006; 'Afghanistan blames blasts on Taliban and al-Qaeda', *AFP*, 21 January 2006; 'New U.S. commander in Afghanistan predicts more suicide attacks this year', *Associated Press*, 30 January 2007.

20 'L'activisme recule en Afghanistan (général américain)', *Xinhuanet*, 7 March 2005.

21 Tom Coghlan, 'Taliban train snipers on British forces', *Daily Telegraph*, 23 July 2006; Scott Baldauf and Ashraf Khan, 'New guns, new drive for Taliban', *Christian Science Monitor*, 26 September 2005; 'Canadian troops cite evidence of rift among Afghan insurgents', *RFE/RL Newsline*, 29 June 2006.

22 Rubin (2007); International Crisis Group (2003a); Mirwais Atal, 'US hearts and minds cash goes to Taliban', *Afghan Recovery Report*, no. 236 (28 November 2006); *Pajhwok Afghan News*, 6 June 2006; Syed Saleem Shahzad, 'Rough justice and blooming poppies', *Asia Times Online*, 7 December 2006; Syed Saleem Shahzad, 'Taliban line up the heavy artillery'.

23 One execution in Daikundi province is mentioned in 'A geographical expression in search of a state', *The Economist*, 6 July 2006.

24 Elizabeth Rubin, 'In the land of the Taliban', *New York Times Magazine*, 22 October 2006; Syed Saleem Shahzad, 'Taliban raise the stakes in Afghanistan'; 'Taliban makes gains against Afghan government', *Stratfor*, 7 August 2003; Sami Yousafzai and Urs Gehriger, 'A new layeha for the Mujahideen', *Die Weltwoche*, 29 November 2006, <http://www.signandsight.com/features/1071.html>; Declan Walsh, 'Beaten, robbed and exiled: life on the frontline of someone else's war', *Guardian*, 20 June 2006; Senlis Council (2006a), p. 11; 'Armed men abduct doctor, driver in S Afghanistan', *Xinhua*, 25 February 2007; James Bays, 'Taliban "in control" in Helmand', *Al Jazeera*, 25 February 2007; Schiewek (2006), p. 161.

25 *Pajhwok Afghan News*, 21 April 2006; interview with Massoud Kharokhel, Tribal Liaison Office, Kabul, October 2006; Borhan Younus, 'Taliban call the shots in Ghazni'; Elizabeth Rubin, 'Taking the fight to the Taliban', *New York Times Magazine*, 29 October 2006; David Rohde, 'Afghan symbol for change becomes a symbol of failure'; Victoria Burnett, 'Afghan officials see Taliban resurgence'; interview with UN official, October 2006, Gardez; personal communication with UN official, Gardez, October 2006; Senlis Council (2006a), p. 9.

26 Eric Schmitt and David Rohde, 'Taliban fighters increase attacks', *New York Times*, 1 August 2004 (interview with General Barno); Daniel Cooney, 'General: hard-hit Taliban recruiting kids', *Associated Press*, 24 July 2005 (interview with General Kamiya); 'Neo-Taliban says it won't attack polling stations, but will disrupt elections', *RFE/RL Newsline*, 23 August 2005; Borhan Younus, 'Taliban hit and run, and come back for more', *Afghan Recovery Report*, no. 185 (10 September 2005); personal communication with British diplomat, Kabul, February 2005; personal communication with Joint Election Management Body logistical officer, May 2004; *BBC News* reporters' log – Afghan vote, 9 October 2004.

27 Erben (n.d.). Although there were as many as two dozen attacks on election day, they do not seem to have been targeted at voters: see Akram Gizabi, 'Landmark Afghan parliamentary election goes smoothly', *Eurasia Daily Monitor* (Jamestown Foundation), vol. 2, no. 178 (26 September 2005).

28 Also according to the RAND-MIPT Terrorism Incident Database, as reported in Jones (2006), p. 113.

29 As argued in Akram Gizabi, 'Landmark Afghan parliamentary election goes smoothly'.

30 Gregg Zoroya, 'Afghanistan insurgents extremely resolute and fought to the last man', *USA Today*, 16 November 2005; Naylor (2006); Akram Gizabi, 'Landmark Afghan parliamentary election goes smoothly'; Nivat (2006), pp. 81–2; 'A geographical expression in search of a state', *The Economist*, 6 July 2006; Tim McGirk, 'The Taliban on the run'; personal communication with diplomats and UN officials in Kabul, January 2006.

31 As noted in Kemp (forthcoming), p. 7.

32 Carlotta Gall, 'Despite years of U.S. pressure, Taliban fight on in jagged hills'; Sara Daniel, 'Afghanistan: "Résister aux talibans? À quoi bon!"', *Le Nouvel Observateur*, 10 August 2006; Françoise Chipaux, 'Dans le plus complet dénuement, la province afghane de Zabul mène la lutte contre les talibans'; 'Excuses des talibans pour une "petite erreur" ayant fait 16 morts', *Reuters*, 6 January 2004; Paul Watson, 'On the trail of the Taliban's support'.

33 Greg Grant, 'Emboldened Taliban emerging', *Army Times*, 3 July 2006; Wright (2006a); Ángeles Espinosa, 'La OTAN lucha en territorio talibán', *El País*, 14 September 2006; Kathy Gannon, 'Taliban comeback traced to corruption', *Associated Press*, 24 November 2006; Sami Yousafzai and Urs Gehriger, 'A new layeha for the Mujahideen'; Christopher Dickey,

'Afghanistan: the Taliban's book of rules', *Newsweek*, 12 December 2006; Graeme Smith, 'Inspiring tale of triumph over Taliban not all it seems', *Globe and Mail*, 23 September 2006; Carlotta Gall, 'Despite years of U.S. pressure, Taliban fight on in jagged hills'.

34 On this see Trives (2006).

35 Elizabeth Rubin, 'In the land of the Taliban'; Kate Clark, 'Cash rewards for Taliban fighters', *File On 4, BBC Radio 4*, 28 February 2006; interview with Massoud Kharokhel, Tribal Liaison Office, Kabul, October 2006.

36 Syed Saleem Shahzad, 'Taliban line up the heavy artillery'; Syed Saleem Shahzad, 'Afghanistan's highway to hell', *Asia Times Online*, 25 January 2007.

37 Bill Graveland, 'Canadians battling Taliban propaganda', *CNews*, 4 December 2006; Graeme Smith, 'The Taliban: knowing the enemy', *Globe and Mail*, 27 November 2006; Sami Yousafzai, 'Afghanistan: want to meet the Taliban? No prob', *Newsweek*, 25 December 2006; Syed Saleem Shahzad, 'How the Taliban prepare for battle', *Asia Times Online*, 5 December 2006; Syed Saleem Shahzad, 'The vultures are circling', *Asia Times Online*, 13 December 2006; 'Taliban military commander Mullah Dadallah: we are in contact with Iraqi mujahideen, Osama bin Laden and Al-Zawahiri', *MEMRI Special Dispatch Series*, no. 1180 (2 June 2006).

38 Tom Coghlan, 'Karzai questions NATO campaign as Taliban takes to hi-tech propaganda', *Independent*, 23 June 2006.

39 B. Raman, 'Al Qaeda and India', South Asia Analysis Group Paper no. 1498 (13 August 2005); Syed Saleem Shahzad, 'Taliban's call for jihad answered in Pakistan', *Asia Times Online*, 16 June 2006; Senlis Council (2006b), ch. 6; Bill Graveland, 'Canadians battling Taliban propaganda'; 'Propaganda masters: the Taliban is using emotionally-charged video discs in Afghanistan that play on ethnic and religious pride to recruit potential sympathizers', *AFP*, 17 July 2006; Elizabeth Rubin, 'In the land of the Taliban'.

40 'Propaganda masters ...', *AFP*, 17 July 2006. See <http://www.siteinstitute. org/>.

41 Rothstein (2006), p. 117.

42 This hypothesis is favoured by some high-ranking UN officials (personal communication, Kabul, October 2006).

43 Tim McGirk, 'The Taliban on the run'; 'Menace taliban dans le Sud', *AFP*, 20 February 2004.

44 'Canadian, American killed in Afghanistan firefight', *CBS News*, 29 March 2006.

45 Michael Smith, 'Key strike puts Taliban to flight', *Sunday Times*, 17 September 2006; Tim Albone, 'Amid the thud of artillery, soldiers stormed into a Taliban stronghold', *The Times*, 14 September 2006; personal communication with military attaché, Kabul, October 2006; personal communication with European Union official, 3 October 2006; personal communication with UN official, Kabul, October 2006; Carlotta Gall, 'After Taliban battle, allies seek advantage', *New York Times*, 2 October

2006; Murray Brewster, 'Taliban to be pushed into the mountains and marginalized: Canadian commander', *Canadian Press*, 7 February 2007.

46 This was implicitly admitted by NATO itself when its spokesman said that more attention should have been paid to sparing civilian lives: 'NATO laments Afghan civilian dead', *BBC News*, 3 January 2007.

47 Ahmed Rashid, 'Musharraf: stop aiding the Taliban', *Daily Telegraph*, 6 October 2006.

48 Bill Graveland, 'Taliban shows little resistance', *Canadian Press*, 24 December 2006; Syed Saleem Shahzad, 'Afghanistan's highway to hell'; 'Les taliban annoncent une offensive de printemps en Afghanistan', *Reuters*, 22 November 2006; 'A growing threat in Afghanistan', *Spiegel Online*, 4 December 2006; Jason Burke, 'Taliban plan to fight through winter to throttle Kabul', *Observer*, 29 October 2006; David Wood, 'Afghan war needs troops', *Baltimore Sun*, 7 January 2007; personal communication with ISAF source, Kabul, 7 December 2006; Ahto Lobjakas, 'Afghanistan: NATO seeks to preempt Taliban offensive in Helmand', *RFE/RL*, 31 January 2007; personal communication with Niamatullah Ibrahimi, Crisis States Research Centre, Kabul, January 2007; Alastair Leithead, 'Helmand seeing insurgent surge', *BBC News*, 11 February 2007; Sami Yousafzai and Ron Moreau, 'The mysterious Mullah Omar'; *Afghanistan*, 19 April 2007.

49 Syed Saleem Shahzad, 'Taliban raise the stakes in Afghanistan'; Marie-France Calle, 'Les talibans auraient infiltré les grandes villes', *Le Figaro*, 30 December 2003.

50 Shahin Eghraghi, 'Hekmatyar: the wild card in Afghanistan', *Asia Times Online*, 7 January 2004; Romesh Ratnesar, 'In the line of fire', *Time*, 8 September 2002; Syed Saleem Shahzad, 'Afghanistan strikes back at Pakistan', *Asia Times Online*, 9 November 2006; Syed Saleem Shahzad, 'Taliban line up the heavy artillery'; 'Interview with Afghan Islamist leader on jihad against U.S.', *MEMRI Special Dispatch Series*, no. 455 (6 January 2003); Abdul Qadir Munsif and Hakim Basharat, 'Conflicts keep away Taliban, Hizb-i-Islami', *Pajhwok Afghan News*, 12 December 2006; 'Hezb-E Islami claim to have taken control of Wormami district', *Arman*, 10 December 2006; ANA sources, January 2007; 'Afghan warlord wants "joint front" with Taleban', *AFP*, 10 March 2007; Zarar Khan, 'Afghan warlord sends mixed signals', *Associated Press*, 9 March 2007; Isambard Wilkinson, 'Warlord claims alliance with Taliban over', *Daily Telegraph*, 9 March 2007; Rahimullah Yusufzai, 'Hekmatyar denies offering unconditional talks to Karzai', *News International*, 9 March 2007.

51 Cordesman (2007); Noor Khan, 'NATO forces recapture Afghan territory', *Associated Press*, 12 September 2006; interview with police officers, Teluqan, May 2006; personal communication with UN source, Kunduz, March 2004; 'North is becoming unstable', *Anis*, 5 November 2006; Shoaib Tanha, 'Herat: distribution of statement by Hezb-e Eslami', *Pagah*, 10 October 2006; Kunduz governor rejects militants' comeback', *Pajhwok Afghan News*, 22 November 2006; *Pajhwok Afghan News*, 19 December 2006.

52 'New armed group announces "jihad"', *Pajhwok Afghan News*, 12 October 2006; van der Schriek (2005); Syed Saleem Shahzad, 'Osama back in the US crosshairs', *Asia Times Online*, 17 May 2006; Schiewek (2006), p. 163.

53 Syed Saleem Shahzad, 'Pakistan makes a deal with the Taliban', *Asia Times Online*, 1 March 2007; Claudio Franco, 'In remote Afghan camp, Taliban explain how and why they fight'; translation of biography of Arab jihadist, in *Global Terror Alert*, January 2006.

54 Michael Scheuer, 'Awakening Afghanistan's "old mujahideen"', *National Post*, 15 November 2006; Graeme Smith, 'The Taliban: knowing the enemy'; personal communication with UN official, Kabul, October 2005; personal communication with UN official, Kabul, March 2007.

55 Guy Dinmore and Rachel Morarjee, 'To a second front? How Afghanistan could again be engulfed by civil war'; 'Rocket attack on Maimana city', *Pajhwok Afghan News*, 10 December 2006.

56 Personal communication with UN official, Kabul, October 2003; Syed Saleem Shahzad, 'US turns to the Taliban', *Asia Times Online*, 14 June 2003; Victoria Burnett, 'US backs Afghan proposal to woo moderate Taliban', *Financial Times*, 31 December 2003; Rahim Faiez, 'Karzai says he has met with Taliban', *Associated Press*, 6 April 2007.

57 Saeed Ali Achakzai, 'Taliban says might join Afghan tribal peace talks', *Reuters*, 9 December 2006; 'Taliban says want no part of tribal peace talks', *Reuters*, 11 December 2006.

58 Fisnik Abrashi and Jason Straziuso, 'Deepening insurgency puts Afghanistan on brink', *Associated Press*, 8 October 2006; interview with Zaif, ex ambassador of Taliban in Pakistan, Kabul, October 2006.

59 Ismail Khan, 'Omar threatens to intensify war: talks with Karzai govt ruled out', *Dawn*, 4 January 2007; *Daily Times*, 28 October 2006; Muhammad Saleh Zaafir, 'Kabul against holding of one peace jirga', *The News*, 12 December 2006.

60 See 'Taliban military commander Mullah Dadallah: we are in contact with Iraqi mujahideen, Osama bin Laden and Al-Zawahiri', *MEMRI Special Dispatch Series*, no. 1180 (2 June 2006).

5
MILITARY TACTICS OF
THE INSURGENCY

Taliban tactics have been described as 'ingenious'[1] and there is certainly an element of truth in that. However, this applies to their use of available technology as well as to their tactics, as the Taliban were trying to make up for their shortage of both technology and skills.

5.1 MILITARY TECHNOLOGY OF THE INSURGENCY

Confronted with a far more technologically advanced enemy, the leadership of the Taliban seemed to have been well aware that motivation, commitment, determination, popular support and a sound strategy might not suffice to wear out the foreign contingents. In the early stages of the insurgency advanced weaponry was not necessary. However, as the Taliban escalated their activities in 2005–7, in order to inflict significant casualties an adequate military technology was required. Despite claims that the rebels were 'well armed' and had 'excellent weapons', throughout 2002–6 the weapons used by the Taliban were largely the usual Kalashnikov assault rifle (AK-47, -74, AKM) and RPG-7 rocket launcher, as well as primitive models of field rockets (BM-1) and machine guns, including a few heavy DShK. They also used hand-made IEDs of rather primitive design and antiquated types of land mines. 'Well armed', therefore, can only have meant that the Taliban have not just been using left-over Kalashnikovs and RPGs, but have also been purchasing brand new ones. By the standards of the early twenty-first century, these are quite obsolete weapons when the enemy being confronted is a state-of-the-art Western army, the more so since the ammunition available to the insurgents was mostly standard. Some improved penetration bullets, better able to pierce bullet-proof vests, were reportedly found in the Taliban's hands on a few occasions, while the Taliban seemed to be aware of the weakest spots in the body armour of US soldiers, but the ability to inflict mortal wounds on foreign troops seems to have been only marginally affected. The RPG-7 proved ill suited to inflict serious damage on the armoured troops transports commonly used by the foreign contingents in Afghanistan. Particularly in flat areas, the mobility awarded to the foreign troops by all-terrain transport and helicopters contrasted with the Taliban's reliance on foot soldiers, unable to move quickly and to counter enemy re-deployments effectively. In engagements taking place over large areas, the gap in communications technologies was also a major handicap for the Taliban.[2]

Although there are clear indications that the insurgents were trying to improve the quality of the equipment used, such desire clashed with the limited availability of advanced weaponry on the regional black market. Nonetheless, some progress was recorded in the arsenal of the Taliban. Two key weapons were non-conventional: IEDs and suicide bombers. There is no doubt about the rapidly increasing use of both, as shown in Graphs 1 and 3, but the ability of the Taliban to manage the technology also improved dramatically after 2002. Although the Taliban always lagged behind the sophistication of their Iraqi colleagues in the manufacturing of IEDs, the gap was estimated to have narrowed from an initial twelve months to six months during 2006, despite the alleged capture of 250 bombmakers by foreign and government forces. In the spring of 2006 the Taliban were already making experiments in stacking anti-tank mines together, while during 2006 linking together IEDs to improve the targeting of moving vehicles was also becoming common. Government forces and ISAF/CFC-A (until November 2006) were also improving their skills, though, and in January 2007 about half of all IEDs were identified and neutralised before exploding. Similarly, the technology used in suicide bombings improved, as did the skills of the suicide bombers. In 2004 suicide attacks were still estimated to have a failure rate of around 60–70 per cent. In 2005 the failure rate was down to 10–15 per cent, showing a dramatic improvement in the skills of the Taliban's 'bomb craftsmen' and of the suicide volunteers. Experts disagree on whether the improvement was the result of imported skills from the insurgents active in the Iraqi theatre or the result of local developments, but the Taliban themselves claim to have received help from the Arabs starting from no later than 2004. Certainly some technology seems to have come from abroad: in September 2006 fifteen 'highly sophisticated' bombs were seized by police in a mosque in Kabul, and they were thought to have been imported into Afghanistan.[3]

In terms of weaponry, most of the remaining progress achieved by the Taliban after 2002 was a matter of expanding the range available, rather than upgrading the technology used. The use of mortars was already reported in 2002 in attacks against US and Afghan bases. Since mortars require a relatively high degree of training to be used effectively, and are rather cumbersome on the battlefield for non-motorised infantry, it is perhaps not surprising that they started being employed in open engagements only in 2006 and even then played only a relatively limited role. The largest use of mortars took place during the most violent fighting of the conflict to date, in September 2006 in Pashmul (Kandahar), when it is estimated that the Taliban fired 1,000 shells, along with 2,000 RPG rounds and 400,000 rounds of automatic weapons. In general, NATO officers had disparaging views of the ability of the Taliban to use mortars effectively.[4]

The difficulty of the Taliban in dealing with armoured vehicles was by 2006 proving to be a major shortcoming, as they had started closing in on Kandahar and had made the decision to contest the mainly flat ground surrounding the city. The Taliban apparently referred to armoured vehicles as 'monsters' or 'beasts'. Although recoilless guns started being used in July 2006, because of being so cumbersome they were only used in engagements fought within the Taliban's strongholds of Helmand and Zabul and were not reported to have been used against armour. Anti-tank mines have been used by the Taliban since at least 2003,[5] but these were old models and often ineffective. More effective types were reportedly in use in 2005, but only occasionally. Moreover, the impact of mines on the battlefield can only be limited to defensive operations or to occasional ambushes. The Taliban tried to cope with the problem by organising ambushes in which salvos of several RPG grenades were fired at a single target (or kill zone), but again there are obvious limitations to the impact of these tactics. Foreign advisors to the police and officers of various foreign military contingents acknowledged that the Taliban were actively seeking heavier anti-tank weapons, with little success. During the autumn of 2006 there were unconfirmed reports of Chinese-made anti-tank weapons of more advanced types than the RPG-7 being found in Uruzgan, but it is not clear what models these would be.[6]

There were some other efforts by the Taliban to upgrade the technological content of their arsenal, but these too were limited. The capture of Russian-made silencers and night-vision equipment was reported as early as September 2003 in Paktika, and similar equipment was also employed in Uruzgan in 2004, but does not seem to have been commonly used. They might have been old devices captured during the anti-Soviet jihad, or small quantities of equipment belonging to individual volunteers, probably from Chechnya. For years rumours circulated that the Taliban were obtaining advanced equipment such as anti-aircraft guided missiles, including claims by the Taliban themselves. However, according to US and ISAF sources these had never been used in combat until late 2006. In 2006 rumours surfaced that Mullah Obeidullah, one of the leaders, had travelled abroad looking for anti-aircraft missiles to purchase. According to Taliban and UN sources, copies of Russian Strela 1 or 2 shoulder-fired missiles were first obtained in 2005, but the Taliban faced serious difficulties in training their fighters to use them and had to involve 'Arabs' in order to employ them on the battlefield or to receive appropriate training. At least two such missiles were fired against ISAF planes at the end of 2006 and another in early 2007, all of which missed their targets. In 2006 the Taliban also claimed to be trying to acquire more precise and powerful field rockets than the light Chinese and North Korean version they had been using since 2002, but it is not clear how they would have been able to move this heavy equipment around Afghanistan. The aiming and success rate of the field rockets undoubtedly improved in 2002–6, but this appears to have been due to the greater skills of those firing them than to the adoption of more advanced models.[7]

Given the features of the Afghan conflict and the low marksmanship levels of the Taliban rank-and-file, an obvious option to improve the ability to inflict casualties would have been the widespread deployment of snipers. Although laser pointers seem to have been utilised relatively often, they were rarely put to good use. In August 2005 the effective deployment of snipers by the Taliban was reported in the fighting at Mari Ghar, but the tendency among US officers was to attribute sniping skills to foreign volunteers, particularly Chechens. In any case, there was little report of appearances of skilled snipers after Mari Ghar. Taliban sources announced in July 2006 the ongoing training of teams of snipers and the acquisition of Russian Dragunov rifles as a major innovation. The case of sniper rifles is a confirmation of the Taliban's limited access to black market sources of advanced weaponry and of their dependence on Arab allies and sympathisers for the supply of more advanced military technology. All they could do was to hope that the Arabs' promises of bringing in more advanced equipment from the Middle East would be fulfilled.[8]

Some of the most important innovations in the Taliban's arsenal were not weapons. Reports that the Taliban were buying many hundreds of motorcycles during the summer of 2003, mainly 125cc Hondas, were later confirmed when these motorcycles started being used extensively inside Afghanistan as means of transport, reconnaissance, communications and battlefield coordination and also to carry out attacks against road-blocks. Substantial resources were also invested in improving telecommunications. Already during the summer of 2003 the insurgents were spotted using satellite phones in large numbers, presumably for long-distance communications. The motorcycles were usually all fitted with phone chargers, a fact which suggests that motorcycle-mounted reconnaissance scouts played an important role in the insurgents' operations at least for some time. Field radios made their first appearance during the summer of 2005, although it was not until 2006 that the Taliban started using them proficiently on the battlefield to coordinate groups of more than 100 combatants. However, the radios used by the Taliban up to the end of 2006 were always commercial types, not frequency-hopping military models. Precise US artillery and air bombardment, combined with advanced radio monitoring techniques, often resulted in the quick elimination of Taliban scouting teams. After some disastrous incidents involving radios and satellite phones, the Taliban became increasingly aware of the fact that their enemies were constantly monitoring their communications and started using them more carefully, resorting to coded messages or even dropping radios in favour of low-technology techniques like torch-signalling.[9]

5.2 MANOEUVRABILITY AND COORDINATION

As highlighted earlier, in order to upgrade their challenge to the enemy, the Taliban increasingly needed to concentrate larger numbers of fighters on the battlefield (see 4.8 *The third phase: 'final offensive'?*). This posed a number of problems. The first was how to command and control their men during the fighting. When the number reached over a hundred, shouting lost its effectiveness. The introduction of radios gave the Taliban the potential to manage the larger concentrations and the tactic appears to have been used effectively. NATO and US sources tend to agree that by 2005–6 the ability of the Taliban to quickly gather large numbers of men and to respond rapidly on the battlefield improved considerably. The insurgents also demonstrated an ability to split into small groups of four or five, as well as to scatter when ambushed and then reorganise. Some Taliban sources explain the improvement in operational capabilities in part with the cooperation between Jalaluddin Haqqani and other Taliban commanders less experienced in guerrilla warfare, as well as cooperation between Hekmatyar's Hizb-i Islami and the Taliban. While it is likely that Haqqani might have had a role, there is little evidence of any effective cooperation between Taliban and Hizb (see 4.9 *Alliances*), but former members of Hizb-i Islami absorbed by the Taliban could have played that role.[10]

The Taliban also placed great emphasis in establishing a thick network of informers, able to advise them of the movements of the enemy and enabling their forces to set up ambushes quickly. They also created their own motorcycle-mounted reconnaissance units, tasked with following NATO/US patrols and other potential targets, as well as with field reconnaissance. The use of Icom scanners to monitor radio and phone calls has also been reported.[11]

5.3 TACTICAL SKILLS

If tactical coordination was an area of evident improvement in 2005–6, other major shortcomings in the training of the insurgents remained. Initially at least, the training imparted to the new recruits was limited to forty days of 'physical and spiritual' instruction, including mainly lectures about the need for jihad and technical training on explosive devices and rockets. In practice, ideological training had pre-eminence over technical in many training camps. This did not always have negative repercussions on the tactical ability of the fighters, as at least it helped the Taliban to instil in them a strong determination. NATO and US officers were generally quite impressed by their resolution, particularly after 2004. Until 2004 the insurgents would normally break off contact as soon as air support was called in. Once ordered to stand and fight even while under air attack, however, the Taliban demonstrated the courage to do it. In a number of fights in 2005 and 2006 the Taliban did not even break contact after having been targeted by 2000lb bombs, often fighting to the last man, actually an odd tactic in guerrilla warfare. However, the stress on ideological indoctrination and on the formation of group comrade-ship came at the expense of tactical skills. Often in the early times of the insurgency little military training was imparted at all, resulting in disastrous outcomes on the battlefield. While this problem was at least in part resolved (see 5.2 *Manoeuvrability and coordination*), others were not. Particularly in the south, the aiming skills of the insurgents were very bad and they were often missing their targets even at very short distances, such as ten to fifty feet. US sources estimated that the Taliban only had a 5 per cent chance of killing an American soldier in the average engagement. Another shortcoming derived from poor training was weak radio discipline, despite the awareness that NATO/US forces were constantly monitoring the insurgents' communications. Poor training might have reflected the shortage of skilled cadres, which derived from the rapid expansion of the ranks, the extremely weak recruitment of educated individuals and the limited experience in guerrilla warfare. US forces on the ground also reported the preoccupation of Taliban units with protecting their leaders, even at the cost of high casualties, a fact which might be a reflection of this shortage of cadres. The loss of a commander could lead to permanent damage to the effectiveness of the insurgents. However, the lack of experience and training was evident when Taliban commanders would mistake mortar fire for air bombardment, or when they would underestimate the reconnaissance and communication abilities of the opponent, hiding in unsafe places.[12]

There were efforts to improve the situation. In 2005 some members of the Taliban reportedly started training in Iraq. Eight Afghans were allegedly part of a first group to travel there through Baluchistan and presumably Iran, to spend three months training. On their return to Pakistan, the trainees would impart to other Afghans the same training. However, the courses were mainly based on handling explosives and remote control detonators and while they might well have improved the insurgents' skills with IEDs, it is unlikely that they significantly affected their battlefield performance.[13]

The biggest tactical problem for the Taliban was how to avoid air strikes. They identified three basic options. The first was to split into small groups and flee. This was in fact the soundest option, but given the near omnipresence of air support, it would have amounted to forsaking any major offensive operation against international troops, ANA and from 2005 even Afghan police. Moreover, splitting into small groups and disappearing into the countryside was not always easy for non-local guerrillas who did not know the region where they were operating. A source close to the US military alleges that most losses among the Taliban ranks in the summer of 2006 were Pakistani volunteers, unable to melt in an unknown countryside.[14]

The second option was to seek cover whenever it was available once air power intervened on their enemy's side. Engagements were often refused when aircraft were present on the scene. Whenever possible the insurgents exploited the rugged terrain to avoid the superior firepower of US and NATO troops. In their own strongholds of northern Helmand, for example, the Taliban would dig ditches and channels or use existing ones and every other type of cover available.[15] The choice of Pashmul as a stronghold-to-be near Kandahar also appears to have been due to similar characteristics (see 4.8 *The third phase: 'final offensive'?*). The Taliban developed the ability to calculate the exact flight time of helicopters from their bases to the target area, preparing themselves to go into hiding with the arrival of the helicopter. However, the use of UAVs meant that US forces could survey an area of suspected Taliban concentration virtually indefinitely, often without the insurgents even realising it. Nonetheless, during the first few months of 2007 signs emerged that the Taliban were becoming increasingly proficient in avoiding offering easy targets to air attack. The US and allied air forces were being forced increasingly to rely on expensive guided missiles to eliminate small teams of insurgents, often as small as two or three individuals.[16]

The third option, adopted when it was deemed necessary to confront the adversary on the open ground or to attack its bases, was to carry out human wave attacks in order to close in as rapidly as possible. The tactic was first used as early as 2005 in the south-east, where the level of training and the skill of Taliban cadres were higher. They usually abstained from resorting to this tactic in flat areas or where the enemy had strong artillery support, or whenever the target was not worth it. The tactic later spread to the south, but was still used parsimoniously. In Kandahar province during 2006 there was a reduction in the number of ambushes and IED attacks by the insurgents compared to 2005, but a strong increase in 'outbreaks of open warfare', from twelve to twenty-eight, although many of these clashes were started by NATO troops. In terms of tactical effectiveness, human waves were clearly counterproductive. In Kandahar province estimates of casualties on both sides for the first five months of 2006 saw a much greater increase in civilian casualties and even more so in insurgent casualties than in the ranks of Afghan security forces and of the foreign troops. Moreover, the Taliban never succeeded in taking any objective defended by foreign troops, or inflicting large casualties on the foreigners. During 2005–6 the improved communication equipment of police and district headquarters meant that they were often able to appeal to ISAF for air support rather quickly, raising the cost of the Taliban's raids. In many cases, despite problems in USAF–US Army and US–British coordination, it might have taken as little as twenty minutes for air support to be deployed on the battlefield, making the task of closing in quickly enough a very demanding one for the Taliban field commanders. The political impact of the intense battles of 2006, however, was a different matter (see 2.7 *Changes in recruitment patterns*).[17]

The Neo-Taliban also demonstrated a fierce concern for the evacuation of casualties, including dead, and developed the ability to carry out this task efficiently.[18] Starting in no later than 2006, field hospitals were built in close proximity to enemy outposts and equipped with medical supplies.[19]

From late 2006 the Taliban began paying much greater attention to fighting off the infiltration attempts of the intelligence agencies of the government and of its external allies. As the insurgents moved closer to the cities and increased recruitment inside Afghanistan, they became increasingly vulnerable to the information gathering of their enemies. While Western officials recognised that penetrating the core of the Taliban remained almost impossible, their presence in many inhabited areas and the travels of the leaders across vast regions offered opportunities for villagers to supply key information to the Taliban's enemies. Searching individuals and in particular 'strangers' became routine for the Taliban and executions of 'informers' and 'spies' were constantly being reported in early 2007.[20]

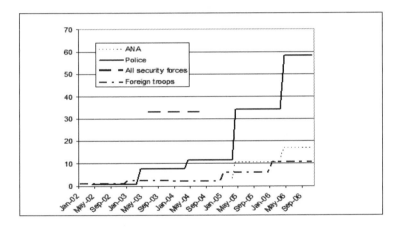

Graph 6. Combat losses suffered by Afghan armed forces and foreign contingents, 2002–7 (killed in action). 'All security forces' includes militias.

Sources: <www.icasualties.org/oef>, Ministry of Defence of Afghanistan press releases, Ministry of Interior of Afghanistan press releases, Law and Order Trust Fund—Afghanistan, press reports.

koran, kalashnikov and laptop

NOTES

1 Captain McKenzie, quoted in Christina Lamb, 'Have you ever used a pistol?', *Sunday Times*, 2 July 2006.

2 British officers quoted in Thomas Harding, 'Paras strike deep into the Taliban heartland', *Daily Telegraph*, 19 June 2006; McCaffrey (2006); *AFP*, 22 July 2006; Nick Allen, 'Sticks and carrots sway wayward Afghan town', *DPA*, 18 December 2006; David Rohde, 'G.I.s in Afghanistan on hunt, but now for hearts and minds', *New York Times*, 30 March 2004; 'Les talibans cherchent à se procurer des armes plus puissantes', *Afghan.org*, 8 May 2006, <http://www.afghana.org/html/article.php?sid=2092>.

3 'Increasing Afghan IED threat gives forces cause for concern', *Jane's Intelligence Review*, 1 August 2006; personal communication with UNAMA official, Kabul, May 2005; ANSO sources, quoted in Françoise Chipaux, 'En Afghanistan, des rebelles mieux organisés infligent de lourdes pertes aux forces américaines', *Le Monde*, 22 August 2005; Elizabeth Rubin, 'In the land of the Taliban', *New York Times Magazine*, 22 October 2006; 'Taliban military commander Mullah Dadallah: we are in contact with Iraqi mujahideen, Osama bin Laden and Al-Zawahiri', *MEMRI Special Dispatch Series*, no. 1180 (2 June 2006); Anna Badkhen, 'Foreign jihadists seen as key to spike in Afghan attacks', *San Francisco Chronicle*, 25 September 2006; 'Taliban seen adjusting tactics', *Reuters*, 13 February 2007; Kevin Dougherty, 'NATO and Afghanistan: a status report', *Stars and Stripes* (Mideast edition), 18 February 2007; UNDSS weekly presentation, 26 January–1 February 2007.

4 Tim McGirk and Michael Ware, 'Losing control? The U.S. concedes it has lost momentum in Afghanistan, while its enemies grow bolder', *Time*, 11 November 2002; Ron Synovitz, 'Taliban launches "spring offensive" with attack on Helmand base', *RFE/RL*, 30 March 2006; Peter Bergen, 'The Taliban, "regrouped and rearmed"', *Washington Post*, 10 September 2006; Christina Lamb, 'Have you ever used a pistol?'; Ahmed Rashid, 'Musharraf: stop aiding the Taliban', *Daily Telegraph*, 6 October 2006; Bill Roggio, 'Taliban losses in Afghanistan, gains in Pakistan', blog, *Fourth Rail*, 25 June 2006, <http://billroggio.com/archives/2006/06/taliban_losses_in_af.php>.

5 Owais Tohid, 'Arid Afghan province proves fertile for Taliban', *Christian Science Monitor*, 14 July 2003.

6 'Increasing Afghan IED threat gives forces cause for concern', *Jane's Intelligence Review*, 1 August 2006; Peter Bergen, 'The Taliban, "regrouped and rearmed"'; Tim Albone, 'Pathfinders on a four-day mission fight off eight-week Taliban siege', *The Times*, 27 September 2006; Nick Meo, 'In Afghanistan, the Taliban rises again for fighting season', *Independent*, 15 May 2005; 'Les talibans cherchent à se procurer des armes plus puissantes', *Afghan.org*, 8 May 2006, <http://www.afghana.org/html/article. php?sid=2092>; personal communication with researcher Armando Geller,

London, November 2006.

7 Carsten Stormer, 'Winning hearts, minds and firefights in Uruzgan', *Asia Times Online*, 6 August 2004; *AFP*, 21 September 2003; Scott Baldauf and Ashraf Khan, 'New guns, new drive for Taliban', *Christian Science Monitor*, 26 September 2005; Bill Roggio, 'Observations from southeastern Afghanistan', <http://counterterrorismblog.org/2006/06/observations_from_southeastern.php>; Graeme Smith, 'The Taliban: knowing the enemy', *Globe and Mail*, 27 November 2006; Tom Coghlan, 'Taliban train snipers on British forces', *Daily Telegraph*, 23 July 2006; 'Increasing Afghan IED threat gives forces cause for concern', *Jane's Intelligence Review*, 1 August 2006; 'Taliban claims it used surface-to-air missile to down helicopter', *Adnkronos International*, 22 February 2007; personal communication with UN official, Kabul, March 2007; Syed Saleem Shahzad, 'Pakistan makes a deal with the Taliban', *Asia Times Online*, 1 March 2007; 'Coalition strikes Taleban linked to anti-aircraft weapons', *AFP*, 10 March 2007.

8 David Rohde, 'G.I.s in Afghanistan on hunt, but now for hearts and minds'; Sean D. Naylor, 'Outnumbered and surrounded by Taliban, the Spartans came out on top in 54-hour fight', *Army Times*, 26 June 2006; Declan Walsh, 'In the heartland of a mysterious enemy, US troops battle to survive', *Guardian*, 5 December 2006; Tom Coghlan, 'Taliban train snipers on British forces'.

9 Ahmed Rashid, 'Safe haven for the Taliban', *Far Eastern Economic Review*, 16 October 2003; *AFP*, 21 September 2003; Andrew Maykuth, 'An Afghan rebuilding takes shape', *Philadelphia Inquirer*, 6 October 2003; Scott Baldauf and Ashraf Khan, 'New guns, new drive for Taliban'; Sean D. Naylor, 'The waiting game. A stronger Taliban lies low, hoping the U.S. will leave Afghanistan', *Army Times*, February 2006; Carsten Stormer, 'Winning hearts, minds and firefights in Uruzgan'; Wright (2006a); Elizabeth Rubin, 'Taking the fight to the Taliban', *New York Times Magazine*, 29 October 2006.

10 Sean D. Naylor, 'The waiting game. A stronger Taliban lies low, hoping the U.S. will leave Afghanistan'; Christina Lamb, 'Have you ever used a pistol?'; 'Taliban fighting with more sophistication: US-led coalition', *AFP*, 22 July 2006; Wright (2006a); Tom Coghlan, 'Taliban train snipers on British forces'; Claudio Franco, 'Islamic militant insurgency in Afghanistan experiencing "Iraqization"', *Eurasianet*, 8 November 2005.

11 Phil Zabriskie, 'Dangers up ahead: how druglords and insurgents are making the war in Afghanistan deadlier than ever', *Time*, 5 March 2006; Wright (2006a).

12 Owais Tohid, 'Taliban regroups – on the road', *Christian Science Monitor*, 27 June 2003; Sean D. Naylor, 'The waiting game. A stronger Taliban lies low, hoping the U.S. will leave Afghanistan'; Gregg Zoroya, 'Afghanistan insurgents "extremely resolute and fought to the last man"', *USA Today*, 16 November 2005; Scott Baldauf, 'Small US units lure Taliban into losing battles', *Christian Science Monitor*, 31 October 2005; Scott Baldauf, 'Taliban

play hide-and-seek with US troops', *Christian Science Monitor*, 12 October 2005; Christina Lamb, 'Have you ever used a pistol?'; Declan Walsh, 'In the heartland of a mysterious enemy, US troops battle to survive'; Tom Coghlan, 'Taliban train snipers on British forces'; Sean D. Naylor, 'Outnumbered and surrounded by Taliban, the Spartans came out on top in 54-hour fight'. For an example of the impact of poor training as described by a militant see Philippe Grangereau, 'Comment le Pakistan redonne des forces aux talibans afghans', *Libération*, 4 September 2003; Cordesman (2007).

13 Sara Daniel and Sami Yousufzai, 'Ils Apprenent en Irak les secrets du Djihad Technologique', *Le Nouvel Observateur*, 3 November, 2005.

14 James Dunnigan, 'The secret war in Afghanistan', *Strategy Page*, 1 January 2007.

15 Wright (2006a).

16 Anthony Loyd, 'It's dawn, and the shelling starts. Time to go into the Taleban maze', *The Times*, 14 February 2007; personal communication with Declan Walsh, who was embedded as a journalist with British forces in Helmand, April 2007.

17 Nick Meo, 'In Afghanistan, the Taliban rises again for fighting season'; Lee Greenberg, 'Renewed Afghan fighting comes amid signs of Taliban buildup', *Ottawa Citizen*, 30 October 2006; Senlis Council (2006c), pp. 32, 37; 'Afghan firefight kills 55 militants', *Associated Press*, 30 October 2006; on some problems of USAF–US Army coordination in the use of close air support, see Greg Jaffe, 'Getting U.S. forces together poses challenge for war plan', *Wall Street Journal*, 11 February 2003. For a more detailed analysis see Pirnie (2005).

18 'A double spring offensive', *The Economist*, 22 February 2007.

19 Laura King, 'Taliban offensive expected in spring', *Los Angeles Times*, 18 February 2007.

20 'Informer killings show growing Taleban control', *Afghan Recovery Report*, no. 243 (26 February 2007).

6

THE COUNTER-INSURGENCY EFFORT

In the beginning neither the Americans nor the Afghan government took the Neo-Taliban insurgency very seriously, although for different reasons. The United States had other places in the world in their sight and the Afghan campaign was left without much political or strategic direction. The Afghans were relying on what they perceived as the United States' overwhelming power to rid them of their enemies in the remote countryside and across the Pakistani border and did not invest much energy or resources in the counter-insurgency effort or in seeking to prevent the conditions which made the spread of the insurgency possible. In fact, Karzai and his circle continued to busy themselves with building a power system without paying any consideration to the effects these efforts would have either on the ongoing insurgency or on the popularity of the government. When criticism of the Karzai administration's conduct started to surface among Afghans and expatriates alike, opinion polls were produced showing very high popularity ratings for Karzai (on the reliability of polls see 2.1 *How strong are the Taliban?*). Those travelling around the country during the early years of the insurgency had different feelings about the popularity of the government, but were not listened to by the over-confident Americans and pro-Karzai Afghans. By 2006, when reality struck back with a vengeance, the insurgency was already well past the incubation stage.

The military counter-insurgency effort in Afghanistan was the work of several different components. At the top, in terms of combat potential and decisional power, ranked the US Task Force assigned to the Afghan theatre. Until 2006 the only other foreign contingents

to see significant fighting were a 200-man detachment of French special troops based in Spin Boldak and a Romanian battalion based in
Kandahar as well some Australian special troops. From 2006 British,
Canadian, Australian and Dutch troops were also actively involved.
On the Afghan side, until 2004 the only forces active against the
insurgents were various Afghan militias, the police and Afghan units
directly recruited by the Americans. This section focuses mainly on
the Afghan component of the counter-insurgency, in part because of
its neglected importance and in part because the qualities and limitations of the Western armies involved are better known.

A very important component of the counter-insurgency effort
which is not discussed at length is the National Security Directorate
(NSD), Afghanistan's intelligence service. Due to its inevitably se-
cretive character, not much is known about its activities and capabilities. Its strength is variously estimated at 15–20,000, to which a large
number of informers should be added. Starting from 2004 the NSD
tried to expand its network of informers, aiming to have at least one
in each village, but it is doubtful that it succeeded, at least in the in-
surgency-ridden regions of the south. The Directorate certainly con-
tains a comparatively large number of professionally-trained officers,
largely coming from the Soviet school. What is of particular concern
to the scope of this book is that the NSD's methods of information gathering remain to date largely 'traditional' and technologically
primitive. One of the consequences of having a relatively limited
network of informers is that cross-checking information is often difficult, a fact which makes the NSD vulnerable to 'bad tips'. Many
former jihadi fighters and former Taliban seem to believe that the
NSD's Soviet-trained officers are deliberately targeting them for revenge purposes, but it is likely that misreporting and false accusations
might derive from the limitations of the informers' network, which
can be easily exploited by information suppliers to pursue personal
feuds. There are also indications that in order to recruit informers
in sensitive areas and in specific sectors of the population the NSD
might resort to harassment and intimidation. The other main source

of information apart from informers is the interrogation of suspects. Beatings and torture appear to be used routinely for this purpose. Since many of those arrested are then released, if for no other reason than a lack of capacity in NSD's prisons, these practices are likely to have driven many into the hands of the insurgency.[1]

6.1 INTERNATIONAL ACTORS

As far as the foreign contingents involved in the counter-insurgency are concerned, suffice it to say that they were all composed of professional troops, with a strong presence of Special Operations Forces (about 2,000 in late 2006) and élite troops such as paratroopers and others. The equipment did not include tanks until the arrival of fifteen Canadian ones at the end of 2006, but it did include armoured troops transports. Artillery was available at the main bases. Air support was available through A-10s, F-16s and AH-64s based in Bagram, Kandahar and Kabul, as well as plenty of UAVs and B-52s and B-1s flying from distant US bases and circling over Afghanistan waiting for a call. The actual number of troops increased from some 15,000 in 2002 to around 47,000 in March 2007. While the numbers were far too small to secure all or even a substantial part of Afghanistan, in terms of tactical potential these troops far outclassed anything the Taliban could field (see also 5.1 *Military technology of the insurgency*). Based on released figures, in direct engagements the average casualty rate (including dead and wounded) would appear to be as high as ten or twenty to one, although the overall rate (including military victims of road bombs, suicide attacks and Afghan government forces) was significantly lower at maybe three to one. Criticism vented at the foreign contingents involved in the counter-insurgency has focused on a reliance on massive firepower, mostly delivered from the air, a lack of attention for developing local knowledge and familiarity and a failure to maintain whatever knowledge was accumulated through the successive rotations of personnel.[2]

Another weakness of the foreign contingents was found in their relations with the local population. The AIHRC registered forty-four complaints against the behaviour of US forces in June 2003–June 2004[3] and 113 in June 2004–May 2005,[4] of which at least eighty were from southern Afghanistan. These ranged from lack of respect for local customs to arbitrary arrest and killings. Unauthorised access to homes was a major source of discontent, to the extent that it soon forced US forces to rely on Afghan militias and security forces rather than their own troops. Using Afghan troops was not always possible or even seen as desirable by some US commanders, so that house searches continued even if at a diminished pace. Efforts by the local authorities to restrain such activities by US troops were sometimes at least partially successful, such as in Khost province, but the 'disrespectful' attitude towards house searches would then resurface elsewhere, for example in Nangarhar. Smaller incidents, such as the 'recreational' looting of agricultural fields, also contributed to generate a climate of resentment towards the foreign troops. In general, there was little understanding among the population for US security requirements, such as the ban on drivers overtaking US convoys. This background helps to explain how simple road accidents could spark whole riots, as happened in Kabul in May 2006. Even officials of the reconciliation commission established by the government (see 6.8 *Reconciliation efforts*) tried to stay clear of US representatives, fearing that meeting them would reflect negatively on their popularity. Other foreign contingents were not necessarily welcome either, in part because the rural population failed to distinguish between them and in part because of historical memories. The heritage of two nineteenth-century wars against the British was still felt in southern Afghanistan, where the British are often described in 'derogatory' terms.[5]

As the counter-insurgent force took an increasingly multinational character during 2006, issues related to the unity of intents and to the formulation of a common strategy became paramount. The rift within ISAF during 2006, pitting in particular Germans against Americans and British, concerned exactly the unity of intents and contributed to create a climate of uncertainty, which was perceived by the Afghan population too.[6] Tension had been simmering throughout 2004–6 as

NATO struggled to organise its takeover of the international security effort in Afghanistan and to ensure a greater presence of its member countries. It started boiling over during 2006 as British and Canadian troops were stretched thin in the south and other countries showed little solidarity. According to British MPs, German commanding officers refused to commit their reserves to help Canadian troops in southern Afghanistan despite a request for assistance. However, high-ranking British officers in Afghanistan expressed reservations about the value of having half-committed and casualty-shy troops in the south.[7] The idea that an under-equipped Polish battalion would be able to replace a US battalion in eastern Afghanistan in 2007 also aroused criticism. The tension within NATO, however, was wider than a simple divide between 'gung-ho' and 'battle-shy' nations and concerned the diverging strategies adopted by the foreign contingents deployed to the south. Only the Australians seemed inclined to accept whatever approach the lead country in their area of operations (Uruzgan) would take. The Dutch found themselves quite apart from the other countries (see 6.5 *Strategy*), and a rift emerged between the Americans and the British concerning the role of truces in Helmand, the administrative line-up there (see 6.7 *Improving 'governance'*), the attitude towards Pakistan and the approach towards poppy eradication. The attitude of General Richards, the British commander of ISAF in Afghanistan, was judged to be 'too political' by some partners, in particular the Americans. Different attitudes towards key problems also contributed to prevent the shaping of a coherent strategy. While for example in Helmand British troops carefully avoided interfering with the eradication effort, even abstaining from seizing opium when coming across it, in Kabul US officials were lobbying the government to start spraying the poppy fields in 2007. A decision in this sense was taken in December 2006, irritating British, Canadian and Dutch diplomats who reacted by trying to prevent the adoption of aerial eradication, eventually forcing the Afghan government at least to postpone the plan to spray the crops and rely instead on 'traditional' techniques.[8]

In terms of the impact of foreign intervention against the insurgency, the picture is a blurred one. It certainly did not lead to increased security in the south, nor to a strengthening of government presence. Quite the contrary, the situation rapidly deteriorated in Helmand and Kandahar at least. Numerous districts were lost by the government, while violence escalated. Was it a nationalistic or xenophobic reaction to the presence of large numbers of foreign troops? Definitive evidence in this regard was lacking at the time of completing this book. However, it is more likely that the main factor in the deterioration of the situation was the perception of a threat to the *status quo* from communities and powerful individuals, for example those active in the narcotics business.

6.2 AFGHAN MILITIAS

At the outset of the insurgency in 2002 the main component of the Afghan counter-insurgent effort consisted of a range of militias, including the so-called Afghan Military Forces (AMF), under the orders of the MoD, some private militias mainly referring to provincial governors, village militias and US-recruited local militias called ASF. The ASF started developing in late 2001, as US Special Forces formed and trained their first militias. Their role in the war was completely subordinated to the requirements of US units; they had no autonomy. Deployed in units of 100–150 men at US firebases, they would provide external security to those bases and accompany US troops on missions. Their most valuable contribution was as screens protecting US troops and in tasks such as house searching and information gathering, which were problematic for the Americans. At their peak they must have numbered no more than 3,000 men distributed among twenty-six US firebases. The ASF were gradually disbanded from 2005 as the existence of militias was drawing a lot of flak from NGOs and the UN, but were provided incentives to join the ANA or the ANP.[9]

Of greater impact were the AMF, due to their larger numbers and to their more widespread presence across the territory. In early 2002 the various anti-Taliban militias and guerrilla armies coalesced in part into a 'transitional' army, later dubbed 'Afghan Militia Forces' or 'Afghan Military Forces' (AMF), formally under the command of the MoD. The new central government legitimised the commanders of these non-state armed groups by appointing them officers and assigning to their formations names of military units. It could be described as a form of privatisation of security reminiscent of the feudal model. Some 200,000 militiamen were included in the personnel charts of the AMF. Some of their units had been receiving cash payments from the CIA to fight against the Taliban, but starting from the early months of 2002 such transfers of cash were limited to *ad hoc* payments whenever a militia was mobilised to accompany US troops in some operation against the remnants of the Taliban and Al Qaida. As the militiamen were not being paid significant sums and the commanders did not need to keep large numbers mobilised any more, the AMF began to shrink. UNAMA estimated during 2002 that there were some 75,000 active militiamen in the AMF, but over the following year the size of the mobilised AMF constantly declined, mainly due to the failure of the MoD to pay salaries; often even food allowances were paid late. By the end of 2003 they did not exceed 45,000 active militiamen, although many more were still included in the personnel charts, despite having been demobilised.[10]

The AMF suffered from a number of problems. The Minister of Defence in 2002–4, Mohammed Fahim, was mainly interested in turning it into a patronage machine for his own political ambitions. Hence an inflation in military ranks which resulted in the existence of 2,500 officially recognised generals on the payroll of the Ministry of Defence by the end of 2002. In order to expand the number of high-ranking officers and incorporate more militias into the system, even as the AMF personnel strength was shrinking, the number of units continued to rise. By the spring of 2002 the AMF boasted over forty divisions, with a few more being established later in the year. In other words, the AMF were anything but a meritocracy. Initially that did not bother too many within the government or within the diplomatic corps, as the war was assumed to be essentially over. Once the insurgency began to spread, however, the AMF's indiscipline, lack of a clearly defined chain of command and primitive organisation were soon recognised as serious problems. The Ministry of Defence never succeeded in bringing under its control the militias that nominally answered to it. In practice the chain of command remained very weak and the commanders of the largest units maintained a nearly complete autonomy in running what were still their private armies. When new commanders were appointed by the MoD to lead AMF units, they proved unable to control them.[11] In turn, unit commanders had difficulties in maintaining the discipline of their own troops. Most units had to be ordered out of cities and towns, in order to contain episodes of looting and violence targeting the urban population. While the order was obeyed in many towns and cities, in Kabul many troops continued to hang around and were reported to be behind a crime wave hitting the capital. Outside Kabul, patrolled by ISAF troops and Afghan police, several AMF units were maintained in active service—and sometimes issued with uniforms—with the task of trying to collect weapons from the population. The remaining units of the AMF were gathered in improvised garrisons and asked to hand over their weapons, in order to have them registered and stored.[12]

With some isolated exceptions, little effort was made to re-train these soldiers or their officers, mainly because of a lack of funding, since most international help in the security sector was directed at forming a new army from scratch. Under international pressure, plan after plan was proposed to reorganise the AMF:

- summer 2002: an MoD plan to assess the current level of education and preparation and then train the officers and soldiers of the AMF's forty-plus divisions, which did not succeed in attracting any funding;
- summer 2002: a plan to modify the organisational chart of the AMF according to the effective personnel strength of the units rather than the political connections of their commanders, which was never implemented;

- beginning of March 2003: a plan to bring in line the ranks of the commanding officers of the transitional army with the type of units they were actually commanding; many of the thousands of Afghan generals would have faced demotion, but it was never implemented;
- spring 2002: a proposal by the Ministry of Defence to appoint professional deputies to the untrained commanders of the old private militias was partially implemented;
- first half of 2003: a plan to reform the AMF was circulated, envisaging the incorporation of a greater number of former regular army officers and their appointment to more senior positions, but it was never adopted;
- a plan to transfer commanders away from their strongholds for training and other purposes, with the effect of weakening their hold over their 'private armies', was partially implemented in 2003–4.[13]

By the end of 2003 the US command had given up any prospect of reforming the AMF as a whole. However, being increasingly worried about the deterioration of security in the country and the slow start of the ANA, by the end of the year it was toying with the idea of 're-forming' and retraining at least some AMF units and using them as a mobile reserve to provide security during the forthcoming elections, scheduled for June 2004. This 'interim security force' or 'National Guard' was to number 5,000 men, but again it never saw the light of day.[14]

Most of these plans were intended by the MoD to meet criticism of the AMF from international sources and were not implemented because in the end the Coalition and external donors were more interested in pushing for the dismantling of the existing military structures, mainly through the plan to demobilise former mujahidin fighters incorporated in the MoD (DDR). Their disarmament was completed nationwide in 2005 and even sooner than that in the south, where AMF units were already in a state of particularly advanced decline. Lack of government support and in some cases of local resources affected the AMF nationwide, besides which in the south the resurgent Taliban had been targeting them since 2002. By 2003 the ragtag southern AMF militias were wholeheartedly demoralised and unable to oppose a significant resistance to the Taliban except in their own strongholds in Popolzai, Barakzai, Achakzai, Alkozai and Alizai villages (see 4.3 *Demoralisation of the enemy*). Their role was limited to occasionally accompanying US troops in 'clear and sweep' operations, but their services were in decreasing demand because of their ineffectiveness and unreliability. In the south-east and east the AMF was in better shape and somewhat more effective. The 25th Division in Khost, for example, succeeded in keeping the insurgents at bay until it was disbanded in 2005. It had been established with former professional army officers in Khost with local funding thanks to the efforts of the governor of Khost. Insurgent activity in the area started increasing and penetrating deeper after its disbandment, although whether there was a causal connection between the two developments is not clear (see 2.6 *Recruiting local communities*).[15]

The third type of militia fighting the Taliban was the private armies of various strongmen and governors. The Karzai administration endorsed and encouraged the practice of allowing governors to maintain small private armies to consolidate their hold over their provinces, but several of them did not have the means to recruit significant numbers. In comparatively poor Zabul, for example, the local strongmen appointed by President Karzai to run the province did not have a sufficient revenue base to maintain a large force in the face of Taliban opposition. Where the resources existed, the private armies survived their role of 'governor's militias'. In Helmand, for example, Sher Mohammed maintained a militia even after his removal from the governorship. In any case, given the extreme weakness of the government security forces, having a private army was often a matter of survival for governors. Even the new governor of Helmand, Eng. Daoud, who did not have a past in the militias and had not fought in the war, before accepting the post at the beginning of 2006 insisted that he be allowed to form his personal militia. The government imposed, however, a formal limit of 500 men to such militias, which also existed at least in Ghazni, Kunar, Daikundi and Farah.[16]

Those hired by private contractors, such as private security companies, for the protection of specific activities were a fourth type of militia/security force in evidence. The largest contractors were two American companies, USPI and Dyncorp, but tens of others existed, including several Afghan ones. These forces were involved in the fighting mainly as the object of attacks from insurgents. For example, one Afghan security company (NCL) had lost seven of its 250 guards by early 2007. However, such militias would generally refuse to play an active role in the conflict.[17]

As violence seemed to spin out of control in the south during the spring of 2006, President Karzai once again tried to promote private armies as one at least partial solution to the security problem. At the beginning of the summer of 2006 he announced the formation of highly-paid mobile militias in four southern provinces, to be led by local strongmen and former governors. In Helmand such a militia was established immediately by Sher Mohammed, without even waiting for a formal decision. By October reports of corruption and of commanders pocketing the pay of ghost militiamen had already surfaced.[18] The plan was soon vetoed by the British and replaced with an alternative proposal to recruit an 'auxiliary police' (see below). Nonetheless, even without official status the Sher Mohammed militia continue to exist and to operate alongside government and British forces, often drawing accusations of abuses against the population. In Uruzgan both Jan Mohammed and Matiullah maintained militias after their sacking, but the Dutch refused to cooperate with them. Jan Mohammed's militia withdrew from the battlefield in protest, but Matiullah's continued to fight on its own and alongside the US Special Operations Forces.[19]

This leads us to the fifth and last type of militia involved in the counter-insurgency effort, that is village militias. They first re-emerged as tribal militias in 2002 in south-eastern and eastern Afghanistan, where local tribes have a tradition of organising so-called *arbakai*, tribal militias, at the orders of the elders. This was a reaction of tribal elders to both the insurgency and the ineffectiveness of the government's law enforcement. Despite the opposition of Minister of Interior Jalali, several such formations were created and by the end of 2003 several thousand tribal militiamen existed. In terms of protecting local installations and individuals, they did their job. Although there were fears in some quarters that creating militias of this kind might re-ignite tribal rivalries and in the end push some other tribes into the arms of the Taliban and other opposition groups, this had not yet happened by 2006. Because the role of the *arbakai* in the conflict was mostly judged positively, it might have contributed to the formulation of a proposal to create the 'auxiliary police', initially described as a village-based militia to be deployed in the provinces most affected by the insurgency. In October 2006 President Karzai approved a plan for the deployment of more than 11,000 such 'auxiliary police' to strengthen the weakened ANP. They were to be quickly trained in ten-day courses, to be topped up by four additional weeks of training once operational, and operate under the orders of district CoPs. The pay would be the same as regular police, but they were to be on yearly contracts. The candidates were to be screened by a committee of district officials and local elders and then vetted by the CoP. The rationale of having village militias was presented as providing an income for young men in the villages and motivating them to actively defend their communities against the encroachment of the insurgents, but in the end the auxiliary police was not deployed in the villages. However, as the programme was just starting, it immediately drew criticism because of the low recruitment standards and the little training provided. Drop out rates were high. Even with such low standards the recruiters were forced to reject many volunteers because they did not meet the requirements, mostly because of drug use. Quite a few of those left in the ranks looked suspicious too and infiltration by the Taliban was seen as a possibility by those involved in training and monitoring.[20]

If it is accepted that a major problem of counter-insurgency in Afghanistan is the inability to control the villages, a logical conclusion would be that the formation of village militias is a necessity. Neither police nor ANA would ever have been available in numbers large enough to be deployed everywhere. The formation of militias aroused passions in Afghanistan, as people tended to associate the term with the formations which fought the civil war, which were undisciplined and had an inclination towards abusing the civilian population. Certainly, the record of mobile militias, able to operate away from their villages, had been a negative one even after 2001. Village-bound militias could do better as the incentive to misbehave diminishes if an armed formation operates in its own village, but much would depend on the ability of the National Police to supervise them.

6.3 AFGHAN POLICE

The police force was involved in the counter-insurgency effort from the very beginning and bore the brunt of it from the implementation of DDR in 2004–05 until 2006, when the ANA was deployed in greater numbers to the south. The Afghan police force was not very different in its origins from the AMF. It too had been created out of the factional militias in 2002, with militia commanders becoming chiefs of police at the district or provincial level and their sub-commanders being appointed as officers. As such, the police force was almost completely untrained and unskilled, with the exception of a sprinkling of professionals appointed here and there, mainly in investigative, administrative and logistical tasks.[21] While the AMF was being disbanded, in most provinces the police continued to exist with little improvement, except that the replacement of commanders by the MoI in many cases weakened its *esprit de corps* and broke the relationship between the strongmen and their old militiamen. There was also some mixing of former militiamen from different districts and provinces, particularly in Kandahar. In Zabul, the police force had been to some extent professionalised after the top authorities in the province had been replaced in 2005. In Kandahar the first signs of an attempt to discipline the police surfaced in early 2007. However, Uruzgan and Helmand police, as well as Kandahar's border police, were still *de facto* mostly homogeneous militias, often coming from a single tribe. As such, they were somewhat more effective fighting forces, but at the same time were liable to keep creating conflictual situations with other communities. The presence of the Achakzai-dominated border police behind the Taliban contributed not only to create a conflict with the Noorzais in Panjwai, but also to maintain it even after the battle of Pashmul and the occupation of the area by Canadian and Afghan troops (see 2.6 *Recruiting local communities*).[22]

The heritage of the factional militias was reflected in the performance of the police. Where the police force was relatively well trained and well led, it did better in terms of containing the Taliban. In Zabul, for example, after the appointment of a professional CoP of good reputation in 2006 and his personally led reform of the unit, the ANP was at least able to control the main highway and contain losses. Elsewhere it might have been more a liability than an asset. A long-term training programme organised by the German authorities only started to produce, slowly, professional policemen in 2003 and its impact on the provinces by 2007 had been minimal. The short-term training programme run by US private security company Dyncorp in 2004–5 had little impact too as it was based on very short courses (two to eight weeks), so that the capabilities of the police in terms of enforcing law and order would at best have been limited in any case.[23] Because of the high staff turnover, the number of trained police was actually declining in 2006 and a substantial percentage of policemen serving in the south in 2006 had not received any training at all. During 2006 Afghan police units received policing and military training from British and Canadian advisors and appear to have improved some of their skills, for example with regard to their ability to identify and neutralise IEDs.

In terms of the direct impact of the police on the counter-insurgency effort, there is plenty of evidence to suggest that the indiscipline and corruption of Afghan security services, including police, was a contributing factor to the insurgency (see 2.6 *Recruiting local communities*). The MoI compounded the situation by usually paying police units their meagre salaries (US$16–70) months late. Sometimes policemen would not be paid for as long as a year, while police chiefs often had to buy fuel and supplies on credit. Inevitably this encouraged the police to impose their own 'taxes' on the population. Although President Karzai tried to diminish the importance of corruption in fuelling the insurgency, allegations of police corruption were already flourishing in 2003.[24] Some examples of the police's illegal activities include:

- in November 2003 a district governor accused his own chief of police of being involved in the narcotics trade;
- in 2006 sources within the AIHRC pointed out that the practice of arresting people in order to extract bribes from them was common in Helmand province;
- the practice of releasing prisoners on payment of a bribe was reported as widespread in Ghazni in 2006;
- Nangarhar's border police reportedly allowed smugglers and insurgents to cross the border during 2006;
- widespread bribing of police to save the poppy fields was also reported in 2006;
- in a rare case of police being brought to account, the authorities confirmed arrests of corrupt police in Helmand in 2006;
- ANA sources alleged that the police of Gereshk (Helmand) were taking money from drivers in early 2007;
- the involvement of the police in the drugs trade was recognised by expatriate anti-narcotics officers in 2007;
- looting of private property in Musa Qala in 2006;
- use of hashish, marijuana and opium was also reported in 2006–7, resulting in the need to squeeze even greater amounts of cash from the population;
- police would sometimes vent their frustration against civilians, as in one case in Kandahar at the beginning of 2007, where they

started shooting traders in the bazaar accusing them of complicity with the Taliban;

- a seizure of 500kg of opium in Helmand in 2007 was divided between police and ANA and only 15kg handed over to foreign troops.[25]

Even US Ambassador Neumann accepted that the Afghan police force was widely viewed as corrupt by the population. Its reported abuses include not only taking bribes, but also more malign ones, including the arrest of relatives and of unarmed civilians in villages where the presence of Taliban had been reported, torture and extrajudicial executions.[26] While the AIHRC does not distinguish between different security agencies when releasing statistics about

2004–5	South-east	West	East	Kabul region	South	All Afghanistan
Illegal detention	464	49	132	47	336	942
Destruction of property	6	9	9	17	17	76
Torture	54	59	19	73	141	439
Extra-judicial killings	31	30	44	33	63	261
Extortion	35	38	40	139	19	410
Other violations	318	281	146	179	304	1,683

Table 7. Abuses by Afghan security agencies as reported by AIHRC's offices in regions affected by the insurgency.

Source: AIHRC, 2004–5 report.

2005–6	South-east	West	East	Kabul region	South	All Afghanistan
Illegal detention/imprisonment	320	19	34	37	127	602
Property destruction	5	12	8	11	3	71
Extortion	15	17	24	54	12	210
Torture and rape	8	24	44	71	36	290
Extra-judicial Killings	11	11	23	11	7	147
Violations of women's rights	289	76	134	39	50	1,041
Other violations	268	105	129	187	126	1,193
Total	916	264	396	410	361	3,554

Source: AIHRC, 2005-6 report.

human rights abuses, it is likely that most abuses were the work of the police (see Table 7).

The potential impact of police's abusive behaviour in turning the population towards the Taliban seems obvious to this author. In any case, this opinion was shared by both UN and Afghan officials, as well as common Afghans. In Panjwai, UN sources explicitly reported that the abusive behaviour of national and border police seemed to have been a key contribution to turning part of the local population towards the Taliban.[27] Demoralised and corrupt police units were often reported refusing to enforce law and order, forcing locals to rely on the Taliban. In Zabul the new, reformist CoP confirmed the presence of widespread corruption within his force, to the extent that the population was forced to turn to the Taliban to resolve disputes and obtain law enforcement. He also alleged that salaries for the police were being embezzled before reaching their destination. The inhabitants of Musa Qala were so unhappy about the exactions of the ANP and ANA that they felt better off once the town had been transferred to the control of the local elders.[28]

Apart from impacting negatively on the feelings of the population towards the government, corruption and low pay ended up corroding the will and ability of the police to oppose the Taliban. The average district in the south would have a force of forty policemen (in fact ranging between fifteen and fifty). Even when the insurgency was not yet a major problem, only about fifteen out of forty would be available to patrol and act as an intervention force. Typically another ten would serve as escort to the district governor, five as escort to the Chief of Police, five as prison guards and five as garrison. As a result, real patrolling was very rare and police would not venture into villages unless tipped off about the presence of anti-government elements. Even in provinces where the threat of the Taliban was not so strong, like Farah before 2006, the police hardly ever visited the villages. Unsurprisingly, the situation worsened once the Taliban became a more fearsome presence. As Taliban strength grew, escort requirements for the local authorities absorbed an ever greater percentage of available resources. In the once safe district centres surrounding Kandahar city, most government officials were relying on the protection of just a couple of policemen until 2005. By 2006 they were being escorted by as many as twenty. Consequently, and because of the increased risk, police would stop patrolling altogether. Hence, the Taliban were able to visit houses and villages next to the district centre without risking the intervention of the police. In general, whenever possible the police would try to avoid confronting the Taliban and would avoid actively pursuing them. Even when manning roadblocks, policemen were often reported to be failing to act on spotting Taliban around the area. In some cases, police units fled their barracks even before the Taliban managed to mount their attacks. The ability of the police to operate with effectiveness was weakened even more by the constant replacement of chiefs of police. Some police stations saw their commander change every fifty days.[29]

The weakness or non-existence of reserve forces able to intervene in support of district centres under attack contributed to demoralise the police, which would often flee when faced with a threat.[30] For a time in Kandahar under CoP Hashem Khan two well trained ANP units were deployed, but were later withdrawn. Afghan police units would also often complain about not receiving help from either the ANA or the foreign contingents and of being left alone to fight off the insurgents despite heavy casualties and bad equipment. Weekly visits by the foreign troops and repeated, unfulfilled promises of new and better equipment only added to the frustration. During 2005 police detachments started receiving communications equipment that enabled them to communicate with US forces and request help, including in the form of air strikes. Previously, Afghan police detachments had been unable to communicate even with each other. This to some extent helped the police to become more resilient against the Taliban, but it did not always work and often police requests of support would not be answered positively. Losses were heavy. In Maiwand district (Kandahar), where the Taliban arrived in 2005, by mid-2006 a quarter of the sixty local policemen had already been killed. During six months of intense fighting in Sangin district (Helmand) fifty-two policemen were killed. In Kandahar province, during less than two months in winter–spring 2006 forty-one policemen were killed. During the Pashmul battle in September 2006 the ANA lost a single soldier, but twenty police were killed. Official figures on total losses (see Graph 6) might even be underestimated if it is true, as stated by unofficial sources within the ministry, that during just March–September 2005 325 policemen were killed throughout Afghanistan. Almost all these losses had occurred in fighting the insurgents. In January 2007 about eighty-five police casualties were reported nationwide by UNDSS.[31]

Demoralisation and rising risk also resulted in large-scale desertions, or in the failure to re-enlist. In Kandahar, out of 6,000 policemen who were trained in 2003–6, half had left the force by June 2006. Seventy of 350 policemen in a Helmand unit deserted in 2006. Kandahar and Helmand were not the worst spots in this regard: in Zabul's Dai Chopan district the local police had already evaporated entirely by the end of the summer of 2003. Sometimes whole units were defecting, as in the case of forty highway policemen in Ghazni province in March 2006, who according to their commander quit because of a delay in the payment of their salaries. Some of these defectors were to join the Taliban, although the numbers were small. However, cooperation between the police and the Taliban seems to have been more widespread. Such instances were already reported in Khost in 2004. In Kandahar, sources within the police force reported that even within Kandahar city the officers of several police stations were in contact with the Taliban. In some cases, police units were accused of collaborating with the Taliban and even of fighting against foreign troops, not only in northern Helmand, but also in Gereshk, a district close to the centre of the province.[32] To a smaller extent such cases were reported also in other parts of Afghanistan. These attitudes towards the Taliban are likely to have been at least in part the result of deep-rooted hostility towards the presence of foreign troops among some members of the Afghan police, as well as of their involvement in the narcotics trade and in their desire to avoid being attacked by the insurgents. The foreign contingents were aware of that, but their reaction often contributed to stoke hostility further, or to undermine the ability of police to work among the population. In at least one instance, US forces confiscated team weapons (machine guns and RPGs) from a government police station in Helmand in 2004, presumably in order to prevent them from falling into the hands of the Taliban. In other cases the Americans, desperate to staff police stations in Taliban strongholds, would make odd choices. Two Hazara militia commanders were appointed as CoPs in the districts of Khakeran and Arghandab Zabul. Although they could certainly be expected not to collaborate with the Taliban, they were also hardly able to communicate with the population or win the sympathy of the very conservative Pashtun villagers, both because of being Shi'as and because of their ethnicity.[33]

For all its weaknesses, the Afghan police force did on some occasions put up a decent fight against the Taliban, particularly when the policemen came from communities or militias that had rivalries with those supporting the insurgents. This is particularly true when the weak equipment of the police is taken into consideration. Its standard included mainly Kalashnikovs, light machine guns and RPG-7 rocket launchers, usually with a limited supply of ammunition. Some of these 'militias in police clothes' fought to the end against the Taliban, particularly in northern Helmand. When this is considered, it is not surprising that the Americans resisted attempts by people like Eng. Daoud, with British support, to terminate their activities (see 6.5 *Strategy* and 6.6 *Tactics*). Ongoing plans to reform the MoI had limited impact in the provinces, although a proposed salary increase to $100 a month seemed to be close to approval as of May 2007. A number of professional provincial chiefs of police had been appointed in the south in early 2006, but faced much resistance in reforming local police forces. During 2007 the MoI seemed intent on replacing them with former militia commanders, who it expected to be more effective in battling the insurgents. The MoI seemed once again to be giving precedence to counter-insurgency over actual policing, oblivious to the great demand for law enforcement in the villages.[34]

6.4 AFGHAN NATIONAL ARMY[35]

The new national army created from May 2002 was a substantially different force from both the various militias and the police. It was in fact the only Afghan security force to be created from scratch on a professional basis. It was widely touted as one of the few success stories of post-2001 Afghanistan, and compared to abject failures such as the formation of a police force worth the name it was indeed a success. However, from the beginning the ANA showed intrinsic limitations, which would later affect its ability to engage the insurgency successfully. Some analysts criticise the ANA model as based on the US light infantry unit model, suitable for presence patrols and 'clear and sweep' operations, rather than non-conventional ones. However, given the human resources available, it is doubtful whether an ANA modelled after the Special Forces would ever have been a realistic option. There is some evidence that initially the ANA was essentially intended by its financial supporters (the US government) to become in the short and medium terms little more than an auxiliary force accompanying US forces in the field, rather than an army capable of autonomous action.[36] This created some friction with both the government and the MoD. The latter objected, for example, to the involvement of ANA battalions in raids deep into Taliban territory and would have preferred to secure more control over ANA units by concentrating them around the main population centres. President Karzai tried to claim greater control over the activities of the ANA, but without success. As disengagement from Afghanistan became an issue for the Bush Administration in 2006, the need for an ANA capable of autonomous operations became obvious, but up to then little had been done to create it. From January 2003 the ANA was heavily dependent on embedded US (and later also Canadian, British and others) 'mentors', who were present down to the company level. The initial neglect of logistics and communications made it impossible for ANA units to operate independently and as a rule each ANA battalion would be attached to a US or NATO unit. Until then the ANA did not even have vehicles to move autonomously and trainees had to be taken to the training centre every day with trucks hired from the bazaar. Even as the ANA started developing some logistical capabilities in mid-2006, its deployment was still subject to the 'dual key' system, which implied negotiations between the government and the Coalition before any deployment or mission. As of September 2005 ANA units were still unable to operate in units larger than a company.[37]

Initially formed by US, British and French trainers, and then by specifically trained Afghan officers under foreign supervision, the basic training course was ten weeks, which later oscillated between eight and fourteen weeks. The creation of fully trained and disciplined units was expected to take six months. The development of the ANA, however, proceeded much slower than first expected and by April 2003 the army had far fewer than the 12,000 men initially planned. The reorganisation and rationalisation of the training process, together with improvement in the living conditions of the troops and the injection of additional funding into the training, led to an acceleration of the process from early 2004 (see Graph 7). However, this rapid and on-target expansion of the personnel charts was not matched by a similar rise in effectively deployable troops, which constantly lagged well below. The initial inflow of recruits was insufficient to staff the battalions fully, which moreover suffered high attrition rates during training due to the low quality of the recruits, itself a consequence of the lack of commitment to the ANA within the MoD. Under the pressure of US political and military authorities, a new system of recruitment, virtually autonomous from the MoD and like the rest of the ANA *de facto* under American control, was introduced in the summer of 2003. This led not only to a rapid increase in the inflow of recruits from the end of 2003, but also to a significant improvement in their quality, which in turn resulted in the reduction of the training attrition rate.[38]

This was not the end of the early problems experienced by the ANA, as the newly trained battalions suffered throughout 2002–3 from a very high desertion rate, although it was positive that desertions were mostly concentrated among private soldiers and were proportionally much lower among NCOs and almost non-existent among officers. A study carried out under the aegis of the Coalition's Office of Military Cooperation-Afghanistan (OMC-A) discovered that low wages and problems accepting military regulations figured among the prominent reasons for deserting, a fact confirmed by anecdotal evidence. Hazing and other abuses also reportedly contributed to high desertion rates, at least until abusive NCOs and officers were relieved by late 2003. Moreover, many among the fist batches of ANA trainees were not genuine volunteers, as they had been sent to the Army by the village elders. That desertions were not politically motivated is confirmed by the fact that until at least 2006 hardly any ANA soldier ever deserted to the Taliban. A number of measures were taken to address the problem, including pay rises from US$50 a month to US$70 for private soldiers plus field deployment indemnities, and the situation improved from the end of 2003 (see Graph 8). However, the ANA never really resolved the problem. The post-2003 improvement was in part a statistical reflection of the fact that most desertions occurred just after the completion of the training and of the lenient attitude adopted towards AWOL troops, who were allowed to return to their units without punishment. This in turn led to the routinisation of the practice of going on unauthorised leave on pay day or whenever needed, which contributed to ANA battalions being permanently below strength (300–400 men instead of 600). There are clear indications that the attractiveness of a long-term ANA job was still limited in 2005–6. The desertion rate started increasing again once ANA units were deployed in battle. This was the result of casualties and of threats by the insurgents against the families of the soldiers hailing from areas affected by the conflict.

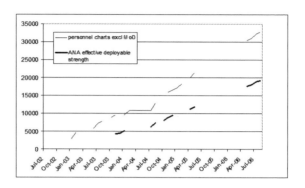

Graph 7. Personnel charts of ANA and deployable ANA strength.
Sources: MoD, Coalition, press reports.

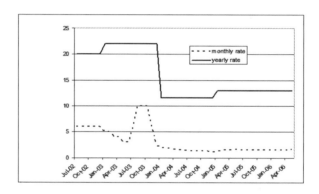

Graph 8. Desertions in the ANA (per cent), 2002–6.

Sources: elaboration from MoD, Coalition and press reports.

Note: the yearly rate takes into account soldiers who returned to their units after having gone AWOL and therefore it is not consistent with monthly rates.

Moreover, when the first battalions reached the end of their three-year contract in spring 2005, re-enlistment rates were a mere 35 per cent. Intimidation and threats by the Taliban might also have contributed to lower recruitment and retention. Captured ANA soldiers were routinely tortured and executed.[39]

Until the beginning of 2005 the ANA had seen only marginal deployment to the battlefield. Its casualties were consequently low, with only about thirty servicemen killed up to March 2005. These deployments were, however, sufficient to push the desertion rate back up, as most soldiers now resented being based away from home and unable to visit their families often (see Graph 8). Over the following year the ANA's involvement in the counter-insurgency grew significantly, even if only a minority of battalions were deployed in conflict-affected areas at any given time. Casualties rose to 130 killed over the March 2005–March 2006 period, corresponding to a rate of about 15 per cent (killed and wounded) for the two corps deployed on the frontline, but the impact was reduced by the rotation of the battalions, with the six permanently deployed in the south and south-east being relieved periodically. For the period March 2006-7, ANA losses rose to 200 killed. However, it has to be considered that the number of battalions deployed to the southern region increased dramatically from the spring of 2006. The desertion rate climbed much higher as far as the units deployed in the areas of operations were concerned. Several detachments in Paktika lost more than half of their men, while Corps 205 in Kandahar in September 2004–June 2005 lost between 1,200 and 1,500 men out of a personnel chart of 2,400, and desertions continued later in the year. Because of the long distances and difficulty in travelling home, AWOL rates increased further for units deployed in the conflict area, shooting up to as high as 50 per cent. As a result, one of the ANA units in the south operated with only 27 per cent of its personnel chart in November 2006. Retention rates also dropped further and by the second half of 2006 were down to just 20 per cent.[40]

The deployment of embedded mentors allowed ANA battalions to take up an operational role from February 2003, although battalion-size operations started only in 2004, almost two years after the training had started. Although the initial plan was to maintain embedded trainers in each unit for a period of two years, until at least the end of 2006 no ANA unit had ever been deployed without embedded advisors, even in the case of the two-dozen battalions which in early 2007 were claimed to be able to operate 'on their own with minimal support'.[41] In practice mentors often served as commanding officers in the place of Afghans, to the extent that occasional displays of initiative by ANA officers were seen as major events. The best units, able to operate in relative autonomy, were soon overworked. Most reports suggested that ANA soldiers fought bravely in small units, although there are also examples of officers avoiding contact with the enemy. However, that ANA officers were not allowed to grow professionally by a mentoring programme which worked more like nursing is shown by the fact that even the more combative ANA officers maintained the tendency not to plan operations and to seek immediate contact with the enemy, forcing their mentors to restrain them. After an initial show of enthusiasm, ANA units would often scatter under enemy fire, forcing the 'mentors' to intervene and re-group them. These difficulties in forming the officer corps are not surprising when it is considered that due to the recruitment policies adopted at the outset, and to the limited attractiveness of ANA service, the illiteracy rate remained very high among officers. For example, as late as February 2006 50 per cent of the officers of Army Corps Kandahar were illiterate. Bearing witness to the dissatisfaction with the capabilities of the ANA, in 2006 the training process was revised once again to shift the focus of training away from 'quantity' and towards 'quality'.[42]

Another problematic aspect of the ANA was its ethnic composition, which became a serious issue once battalions started being deployed against the insurgency. Patronage politics at the centre resulted in an over representation of Tajiks, particularly among officers. When the MoD came under pressure to resolve this issue, a vetting system was introduced to re-balance the higher ranks of the Ministry, while the new recruitment system introduced in 2003 addressed the problem among the rank-and-file with provincial quotas.

However, among field officers the imbalance largely remained (see Table 8). Allegations continued to surface that the training staff, by then completely Afghan and mostly Tajik, was trying to weed out non-Tajiks from the army by pressurising them and forcing them to quit the training courses, or by discouraging selected recruits from joining the army altogether in ethnically mixed provinces. Ethnic differences were reported to affect sometimes the functionality of units, as in the case of one unit where the pay clerk was not filling out the pay forms. Other instances of ethnic tension in the ANA were reported in the press. Apart from the existence of ethnic tensions within the ANA, which are also demonstrated by the fact that punishment existed for soldiers using ethnic slurs, the presence of so many Tajik officers led to difficult relations with the local authorities and population in the conflict-ridden south. For example, the Tajik commanders of the ANA battalions deployed in Kandahar in early 2005 refused to speak Pashto to the local authorities and entertained bad relations with the local police. Problems between the Tajik component of ANA units and the Pashtun population were reported by

	Troops	NCOs	Officers
Pashtuns	52.7	35.8	32.0
Tajiks	36.8	52.9	55.9
Hazaras	5.1	7.2	6.5
Uzbeks	2.7	3.2	3.4
Others	2.7	0.9	2.2
Total	100.0	100.0	100.0

Table 8. Ethnic breakdown (per cent) of ANA by rank, summer 2004. Source: elaboration based on Coalition sources.

US sources as well, again in part due to the refusal of some ANA officers to speak Pashto.[43]

One of the main selling points of the ANA was originally its human rights and no-corruption record. While there is no doubt that these are much better for the ANA than they are for the AMF or ANP, as

ANA units came under pressure in the south and south-east, much of what had been taught by their trainers in terms of respect for human rights appears to have been readily forgotten. Canadian soldiers intervened at least twice to stop summary executions of suspected Taliban fighters. Accusations of abuses against the civilian population, accused of supporting the Taliban, also surfaced. At least one case of beating of UN national staff was confirmed. In Ghazni villagers were complaining in 2006 of ANA soldiers robbing their homes and of brutal behaviour.[44]

Although the reputation of the higher ranks of the ANA and MoD was never very good, allegations of corruption among field officers too started surfacing in 2006, when even some trainers were convinced that officers were pocketing part of the soldiers' wages. There were reports of military equipment being sold, which resulted in shortages on the frontline, and rumours abounded about the involvement of some ANA units in the narcotics trade. Consumption of hashish in the ranks was also reportedly common. At least one report exists concerning a police seizure of narcotics in an ANA vehicle and there are allegations of a much wider involvement. Reports started to emerge that ANA soldiers too, like the police, indulged in 'taxing' road travellers when manning checkpoints, even in the presence of foreign troops, although whether the latter were aware of such activities is not clear. As a result of this as well as a lack of contact with the population and a lack of any public relations efforts, among the southern and south-eastern population the reputation of the ANA was being eroded during 2006.[45]

At least the ANA does not seem to have suffered significant desertions to the Taliban. In the summer of 2006 it was reported that the Taliban had started offering ANA soldiers three times their pay to switch sides, but it is not clear whether this had any impact. To most soldiers it would of course have meant abandoning their family, an unlikely option. The offer, if true, was probably meant to demoralise ANA troops rather than attract any serious number. Some sources allege that many who quit the police or ANA in 2002–3 later joined the Taliban, particularly in Zabul province, but even if true this is more likely to refer to rejected volunteers. More recently, the Taliban claimed that a number of ANA soldiers defected to them in late 2006, but there is no independent confirmation of this.[46]

6.5 STRATEGY

Following the successful campaign to remove the Taliban regime from power, the US armed forces restructured their military commitment to Afghanistan. During 2002 the roughly 500 US Special Forces that had been the main presence on the ground during Operation Enduring Freedom were integrated into conventional US troops. Their main task was to hunt down the remnants of the Taliban and particularly Al Qaida, leaving to the multi-national contingent known as ISAF the task of securing the government and stabilising the country. Throughout the first four years of its existence, ISAF was mainly based in Kabul, successfully preventing a coup against President Karzai, but had little presence in the provinces, including those where the insurgency was beginning to emerge. Only in 2006 did ISAF contingents start being dispatched to the south in any strength, under NATO command.

With the US regular army taking the lead in 2002, an attitude prevailed that was radically different from that initially adopted by the Special Operations Forces in the search for the remnants of the Taliban and their Arab allies. Rather than operating in small units and spending weeks in the same location trying to forge links with the local population, the new arrivals carried out large sweeps covering many districts with large concentrations of force ('clear and sweep'). The conventionalisation of the US campaign in Afghanistan was the result of the creation of Combined Joint Task Force 180 under the command of a regular army general, a development which marginalised the Special Operations Forces. Several analysts argued the ineffectiveness of 'clear and sweep' operations in rooting out the insurgents and some regular army officers seem to have agreed. In practice, there are some doubts concerning the viability of an alternative model in Afghanistan, since covering the territory affected by the insurgency would have required not only more Special Operations Forces than were in Afghanistan at that time, but even more than were available anywhere. One estimate is that 200,000 troops would be required to control Afghanistan's territory.[47] This figure might have been lower for Special Operations Forces, but with only around 17,000 troops available to the Special Operations Command worldwide, sufficient numbers could never have been mustered for Afghanistan. Moreover, as some of the analysts mentioned above admit, Special Operations Forces too changed their tactics in 2002–4, abandoning operations focused on occupying and pacifying the villages (and establishing local security forces) and shifting instead to raiding suspected enemy hideouts. As the conventional troops lacked specific training on how to handle counter-insurgency, reports rapidly surfaced of their heavy-handed behaviour, in particular with regard to violating the privacy of Afghan homes and of Afghan women. Moreover, the difficulty of the Americans to identify the Taliban among the population often deprived them of the ability to make arrests. Quite the contrary, it often led to the arrest and harassment of the wrong people. Journalists and analysts who spoke to Special Forces members found that they were very critical of the approach adopted by the regular troops. Already during 2002 there were signs that this behaviour was one of three main factors beginning to turn local opinion against the United States (see 6.1 *International actors*), and complaints were still being reported in early 2007. The other two factors were civilian casualties of air strikes (see 6.6 *Tactics*) and the reliance on anti-Taliban local strongmen for their insurgency effort, even when these had a reputation for abusing the population (see 1.2 *'Rebuilding' the Afghan state* and 6.2 *Afghan militias*).[48]

An interesting and involuntary 'counter-factual' experiment took place in Orgun district (Paktika) during 2002, when a single Special Forces detachment continued to use population control tactics while the rest of the Special Forces were focusing on hunting 'terrorists'. The Special Forces in Orgun sidelined a corrupt militia commander who was alienating the local population and proceeded to establish a relationship with the local elders, start a local development programme and recruit an ASF militia. As a result the detachment was able to gather much local intelligence from the population. This limited effort was, however, abandoned in September 2002, after just three months, under pressure from the Task Force command. The main problem, however, was that conducting the experiment in a single district, which had not even been a major focus of opposition activities, made it all too easy for the insurgents to move to another area of operations. How successful the same approach would have been if the insurgents had opposed a stronger resistance is not clear. It is also important to consider that not all was necessarily well with the SOF either, as reports of severe abuses against the civilian population have been emerging since at least 2005.[49]

US Army regular troops were not totally oblivious of hearts and minds tactics when carrying out their operations, but these were implemented in a mechanical and ultimately ineffective way. A typical conventional counter-insurgency operation would involve rapidly occupying a village, rounding up the men, interrogating them, arresting a few and then proceeding with hearts and minds deliveries, such as providing medical services for humans and animals, hygiene kits and medicines, and bringing in some local authorities so that the villagers could vent their grievances. In such operations, the hearts and minds component was compromised by the aggressive entry into the village and by the fact that the troops would soon withdraw, leaving the village to its fate. Similarly, reconstruction and development work in the Pashmul area was compromised by what the farmers perceived as the threat of being expelled again from their villages if the foreign troops were attacked, even if the evacuation of the civilians was meant to be for their own safety.[50]

By 2003 the Task Force command had concluded that this approach was counter-productive, probably helped by the change at the top with the end of Gen. McNeill's tour of duty in August and his replacement by Lieutenant General Vines. The Task Force had by then been renamed Combined Joint Task Force 76. While the lack of permanent presence in the villages had turned out to be a major limitation of counter-insurgency operations, better results were achieved around the US Forward Operating Bases (FOBs), because the Americans were permanently based there and could afford some protection to the villagers. As a result, and for other reasons, US forces were spread wider over Afghanistan, with the number of bases increasing from eleven in 2003 to twenty-six in 2004 and to twenty-nine in 2005. A softer attitude was adopted, involving communicating with the local population, building schools, digging wells and clinics. Platoon-size US units were dispatched to spend time in the villages in order to forge ties with village elders and to gather information about the insurgents' activities. During 2004 US forces reported a marked improvement in the cooperation of locals, who turned to the US military more than a hundred arms caches, compared to just thirteen in 2003. Discoveries of arms caches continued to increase in later years regardless of the strategy adopted by the United States or ISAF and by early 2007 about 600 of them had been found. However, this might well have been the result of more caches being there in the first place. Furthermore, it is likely that much of the cooperation enlisted by the troops was the result of handsome cash payments, as opposed to a vaguely friendly inclination of the villagers.[51] By the spring of 2005 US forces were reporting further increases in cooperation among local villagers at least in areas such as Kandahar and provinces, compared to six months earlier. According to US troops, the idea was that engaging people, by distributing aid and providing jobs in the reconstruction effort, would turn them against the Taliban/Al Qaida and into pro-government informers. An alternative explanation is that anti-Taliban elements already present in the villages might have felt that coming out was no longer so dangerous. In any case, a number of US garrisons had discretionary funds for US$6 million to spend yearly, with larger amounts for critical areas such as Zabul. The total 2004 budget for these operations was US$40 million. On top of that, US FOBs would allow locals access to army clinics six days a week and 7,300 people were treated by November 2005. Later, a similar benefits-for-information approach was also adopted by the British when they deployed in Helmand (2006), and by other contingents as well, often with a greater dose of cash injected into their counter-insurgency strategies; for example the Turkish PRT in Wardak was planning to spend US$24 million when it was set up in early 2007. At the roots of the new approach was the claim that what the military called 'development' (and in fact rather resembled patronage) was the best counter-insurgency strategy and that the Americans 'like the Romans' wanted to leave behind something which would last. The traditional lull in the fighting during winter was seen as a window of opportunity for advancing the reconstruction process, so that in spring the returning Taliban would find a hostile population. One such scheme was the Temporary Work for Afghans, which in September 2005 was employing 11,000 Afghans in reconstruction projects. Initially there seemed to be signs that this could work. There were, however, problems in the implementation of the strategy: Special Troops operating in Afghanistan told an analyst that there was a 'disconnect between aid programs and military operation'. Despite the lack of cooperation of villagers in providing information, 'military commanders remain[ed] unable to stop the flow of aid to them'. Where local security was established, it often seemed to the villagers to be coming from the pro-government strongmen's militias rather than from US troops. More important, once again it was to be proved that counter-insurgency is much easier when insurgents are not around. Possibly because they sensed that the Americans were making some inroads, the Taliban quickly developed counter-measures to the benefits-for-information approach. By 2006 it was widespread knowledge in the Afghan countryside that the Taliban would retaliate against anybody supplying information to their enemies (see also 4.2 *Rooting out government presence*). The attempt to rehabilitate the Kajaki dam, which used to supply electricity to much of southern Afghanistan, was similarly hampered by the dogged determination of the Taliban to keep harassing the British troops deployed to protect the area.[52]

Although other factors might also have contributed to turn the population against the foreign presence, the Taliban's countermeasures seemed to be working. Rapidly, a dark shadow started being cast over the viability of the patronage-based counter-insurgency. Often foreign troops would face the steadfast refusal of the villagers to even accept help such as building bridges or schools, although it is not clear to what extent this was due to fear of Taliban reprisals or to genuine distrust of the foreigners. Anecdotal evidence suggests that there was genuine hostility towards the foreign presence in Kandahar, where it was often interpreted as part of a wider attempt to dominate the Muslim world. In some cases, and certainly in Ghazni, local villagers, following the instructions of their mullahs and fearful of retaliation, handed over to the Taliban cash help provided by US forces for reconstruction projects. Reportedly the Taliban often entered the villages just after a visit by US forces, confiscating and destroying any goods or propaganda material left behind.[53]

The shift away from big 'clear and sweep' operations and towards more village-focused ones reached its apex in the first half of 2005. Soon, however, a backlash followed, with yet another new command of Combined Joint Task Force 76 assessing that the local focus of military operations was leaving the enemy unaffected in most areas, allowing it to reorganise. During the second half of 2005, therefore, US forces changed tack again and started pursuing the Taliban more aggressively into their sanctuaries, leading to more intense fighting and heavier casualties on both sides. With the appointment of British General Richards to lead an expanded ISAF in 2006, there was once again a return to a more patronage-based strategy. The Bush Administration seemed to have come around to supporting similar concepts and in early 2007 it announced an increase in its support for Afghanistan, to the tune of US$10.6 billion for the following two years. If approved by Congress, it would bring the rate of US transfers to Afghanistan to over US$5 billion a year, up from less than US$3 billion a year in 2002–6. Although most of this money was meant for the security sector, a substantial part of it (US$2 billion) was targeted at reconstruction.[54]

The actual impact of different strategies is difficult to assess, not least because changes occurred so frequently that there was no time for the outcome of a particular approach to become obvious. Task Force and ISAF commanders were rotated as often as every nine months, although some stayed longer. However, it is clear that US/ISAF forces struggled to achieve one of the stated main aims (particularly by the British), that is to 'separate the insurgent either physically or psychologically from the populace'. US officers were well aware that this task would have required the presence of troops in every village within the area of activity of the Taliban, but such troops were not available.[55] The strategy of occupying territory permanently, therefore, might well have been the right one, but it was impossible to apply consistently in practice. Occupying only small portions of the country left the insurgents with the options of moving to different areas or of lying low until the Americans eventually moved on to pacify a different area. The task of occupying territory was therefore left to the ragtag Afghan armed forces, which proved not to be up to the task.

Petty political concerns also often interfered with the formulation of military strategies, particularly once the insurgency started becoming seriously threatening. As non-US contingents started deploying to the area of conflict in the spring of 2006, they came under pressure not only from the United States to actively hunt down the insurgents in large scale operations, but also from the Kabul government to protect government administrative centres in areas where the threat was stronger. The British, in particular, were compelled to split their forces into small units and deploy them in the mountainous districts of northern Helmand. Before that US forces had already been establishing garrisons in several district centres of Zabul, incorporating the administrative centres into the fortified garrisons, but did not try to use them to expand control over the surrounding territory, nor was much of Zabul of the same strategic importance to the Taliban. In combination with deploying forces to protect the districts, British troops would continue staging raids deep into Taliban strongholds, to show that the insurgents did not have firm control over any part of Afghanistan's territory, to prevent them from consolidating their organisation inside Afghanistan, and to provoke them to react and fight against superior firepower. However, British hopes to drive the Taliban out of Helmand by the end of the summer of 2006 turned out to have been mere wishful thinking. Faulty intelligence led British commanding officers to claim that the Taliban were unable to amass forces for a counter-attack and that they had 'fewer and fewer places to go and hide'. When the Taliban reacted and it became apparent that there were at least 1,500–2,000 of them in northern Helmand, as opposed to the few hundreds estimated by US intelligence in early 2006, the small British raiding units were often forced to seek shelter and in some cases ended up being besieged for many days in small villages and towns. Similarly, the small district garrisons came under siege too. By the autumn of 2006 the British decided it was wiser to reduce their commitment to controlling the northern district headquarters.[56]

As the Taliban were beginning to concentrate large forces close to a key city like Kandahar in August 2006, what was by now NATO's strategy had to be adapted once again. It now appeared imperative to clear and hold on to at least key parts of the territory. The new strategy incorporated elements of the patronage-based model of counter-insurgency with the 'clear and sweep' one: some key parts of the territory would be consolidated and occupied and more remote and strategically less significant areas would be kept in check through periodical raids. The first component of the new strategy was evident in the battle of Pashmul, when the plan was to conquer territory, hold it, and turn it into an anti-Taliban stronghold without withdrawing (see 4.8 *The third phase: 'final offensive'?*). A large amount of cash was allocated for distribution to the soon-to-be-displaced population and to rebuild the areas destroyed by air raids. After the Pashmul fighting, USAID alone rushed US$14 million to southern Afghanistan in assistance to displaced people, of which US$8 million was destined for the Pashmul area, with relatives of dead civilians being promised US$8,000 in compensation for each victim. The Ministry for Rural Rehabilitation and Development was given another US$18 million to spend in Kandahar province. Canadian troops re-opened schools and established medical clinics. Early indications from the UN about the Pashmul post-battle impact were that hiring young villagers in the reconstruction effort had positive effects on security. However, by mid-January 2007 the promised aid, to be delivered during the 'winter lull', had not yet materialised, with the exception of a new road which was built on the property of angry locals. By early March work had started on only sixteen of fifty projects in the whole province. Lack of coordination between the military and the civilians in charge of reconstruction projects and the lack of security for aid workers were blamed for the failure to deliver. Assessing compensation claims also proved more complicated than originally thought. The same problem of missing coordination between civilians and military and of missing reconstruction aid was experienced in Musa Qala in late 2006 and early 2007. Although British forces claimed to have completed eighty-three projects in Helmand worth US$9 million in all by December 2006, the population seemed to have hardly noticed. Significantly, reports emerged after the battle of Pashmul that despite the presence of foreign troops, insurgents remained active in the area with local support and their number was estimated at 300–400, a relatively large number for just a couple of districts. In December it was necessary to launch another 'clear and sweep' operation to purge Panjwai and Zhare districts of Taliban. After that NATO and Afghan authorities could finally claim that the locals were cooperating with them and reporting the location of roadside bombs, but also admitted that re-infiltration was very likely. Indeed, by March the frequency of IED attacks was rising fast in Panjwai and Zhare, while the Canadians had to scale down their ambition to hold positions tens of miles west of Kandahar city due to high risk to the supply convoys.[57]

If in the context of southern Afghanistan (2006) delivering development was problematic, an even greater difficulty was presented by the fact that even a successful delivery might not have impacted on the counter-insurgency effort. One reason is that development and assistance matter little as long as security is not reliably provided. In the Pashmul area, as the reconstruction process was starting, following devastating air strikes in September 2006, the locals often seemed less than impressed and remained wary of finding themselves between two fires. Often villagers and town dwellers alike were unaware of whatever reconstruction aid had effectively been delivered to their localities and in any case were more concerned about the lack of security and the death of relatives at the hands of foreign troops. Another reason was that even when the 'foreigners' could reasonably argue to have delivered something in terms of reconstruction, they stood accused of having catered only for their own self-serving interests. The Kabul–Kandahar highway, for example, was the first highway to be rebuilt with aid money after 2001. However, it was often seen as being intended to facilitate the movement of foreign and government troops to the south rather than to benefit the local economy. A third reason was that the expectations of the villagers, inflated by excessive promises, were hard to meet. The inhabitants of a village endowed with no less than sixteen wells dug by aid agencies were still reported to be complaining about the lack of development aid and about what they considered the unjustified arrest of villagers on allegations of aiding the insurgents.[58]

Some controversy surrounds the role of Dutch troops in Uruzgan and their adoption of a different approach in dealing with the Taliban (the 'Dutch approach'), which they had already 'tested' in Kabul and in Baghlan in 2002–5. Until the autumn of 2006 the Dutch described their own role as establishing contact with the population and privileging support for local government as opposed to focusing on killing insurgents. Secure bases would be established from where stability, security and reconstruction projects would win the trust of the local population and gradually spread elsewhere. In fact, the Dutch were even reported to have insisted on restraining the activities of two detachments of US Special Forces deployed in Uruzgan with them. The appointment of a new governor with a background in the Taliban regime helped to develop informal contact with some groups of insurgents. The Dutch started from negotiating with the local insurgents, before despatching patrols away from their bases. According to their own radio intercepts, they succeeded in delivering the message that a new 'type of foreigner' was now in Uruzgan, more interested in negotiating than fighting. The Dutch troops made a point of paying as many visits as possible to the households of the area to reinforce the message and of offering to mediate between villagers and US military authorities for the release of Afghan prisoners or at least find out about their fate. According to the Dutch, they were also trying to protect villagers from predatory members of the Afghan security forces, taking the controversial militias off the battle front and confining them to guard duties. During the first four months of their presence in Uruzgan, the Dutch suffered only two injured and none killed in action; the level of enemy military activity against them was comparatively modest, standing at seven ambushes and eighteen roadside bombs. British and US officers did not always appear to be fully convinced of the validity of the Dutch approach and objected that they remained confined in the region of Tarin Kwot, sheltered from some of the Taliban's largest concentration of forces by a mix of US and Australian troops. Some Dutch troops, in particular commandos, also complained about not being allowed by the 'politicians' in Amsterdam to hit the Taliban as hard as required to improve local security. It certainly should be considered that the Taliban do not normally prioritise fighting foreign troops, unless ordered to do so by their leadership. Hence, in the absence of aggressive activities from the Dutch side, the Taliban might have had little incentive to mount a major effort against them. The Dutch approach was adopted by the smaller Australian contingent too, which had earlier fought aggressively alongside the American Special Forces in the same province.[59]

From the beginning much tension was reported between the Dutch and the Americans in Uruzgan, with the former pointing out how the latter were very arrogant and focused on destroying the 'Taliban' without even knowing exactly who these were. The US Special Forces were reported by the Dutch as being very gung-ho and all too keen to call in air strikes, which the Dutch opposed as likely to cause much collateral damage. As the end of 2006 approached, in any case, nobody was talking of the 'Dutch approach' any more. Dutch sources attributed the development to the worsening violence in Uruzgan, which prevented the carrying out of any development activities, as well as to the insufficient numbers of ANA and ANP troops. The Dutch were critical of the US approach to delivering aid, for example mentioning schools were built without involving the locals and without follow-up; soon the schools were burnt down. However, reports published in the Afghan press suggested that the Dutch were not doing very well in terms of delivering reconstruction to Uruzgan, even compared to the US. All that was left of the Dutch peculiarity in late 2006 seemed to be the refusal to carry out poppy eradication activities and the insistence on advising the authorities of Uruzgan to do likewise. It is, however, worth noting that the change of 'approach' took place just after the Dutch parliamentary elections of November 2006 and might have been due to the pressure of NATO allies.[60]

General Richards made a strong point to the press that NATO needed to show the Afghans that it was ready to stand and fight when it deployed to southern Afghanistan in 2006. However, his hope that a first round of tough fighting in the summer of 2006 might have been sufficient to deliver the message would later appear quite optimistic. ISAF/US strategy remained largely reactive throughout 2002–6, until in 2007 ISAF started increasingly taking more of a proactive role, committing itself to exercise continuous pressure on the Taliban and to force them to withdraw to the mountains and slowly wither away. It is not clear how successful such a strategy can be in a country like Afghanistan, where mountains represent the largest part of the country. Moreover, divergences continued to exist, as Americans were pushing for increased air strikes and for the targeting of commanders, the British were claiming to be refocusing their efforts in terms of identifying 'tired Taliban' and convincing them to stop fighting.[61]

6.6 TACTICS

At the tactical level, the main problem for the United States and their allies was to draw the insurgents out of their hideouts to fight against their far better armed enemy. Until at least 2003 avoiding casualties remained a major concern of US commanders and US patrols would usually try to break off contacts as soon as possible. However, a radically opposed approach emerged between 2004 and 2005. Small units were deployed in areas of activity of the insurgents in order to lure them into battle and then inflict heavy casualties with the help of air power. Other tricks used included the issuing of provocative statements about the 'cowardice' of the Taliban and provoking them by burning Taliban corpses, even though the latter practice was condemned by the Afghan government who feared its unpopularity. When the Taliban of their own initiative started launching attacks against small NATO and Coalition outposts in 2006, the development was welcomed as an opportunity to inflict heavy casualties on the enemy, despite some apprehension that the small outposts might be somewhat vulnerable. However, as has been pointed out by A. Cordesman, the Taliban displayed a remarkable ability to replace casualties, while these US tactics were not able to inflict losses where the Taliban might have been more vulnerable, that is the cadre structure. The NATO command seems to have realised this weakness and by December it was claiming to have shifted its focus towards targeting Taliban commanders; the killing of Osmani in December 2006, of Dadullah in May 2007 and the alleged capture of Obeidullah in February were attributed to this new approach. It is worth adding that NATO and US commanders appear not to have realised the political impact of the rising violence of the conflict in the south (see 2.7 *Changes in recruitment patterns*). Claims of huge losses inflicted on the Taliban during the spring and summer of 2006, whether accurate or not, backfired as they implicitly demonstrated to the Afghan public that either the Taliban were many more than officially estimated, or many civilians were being killed and branded as Taliban.[62]

The perception that US troops lacked conviction and were afraid of fighting except when strongly supported by air power might have contributed to embolden the resistance, strengthening the feeling that Americans could not stomach a long conflict in Afghanistan. The reliance on air power was particularly accentuated in 2006. Between June and November 2006 alone, the US Air Force conducted more than 2,000 air strikes in Afghanistan, a figure which represented a massive acceleration on previous years. The 2006 monthly rate of aircraft ammunition expenditure was ninety-eight bombs and 14,000 bullets, compared with twenty-two bombs and 3,000 bullets in 2001–4. During early 2007 a further increase in air activity was reported. Reliance on air power led inevitably to significant casualties among the population and to the accusation of excessive force, particularly when 2,000lb bombs were extensively used to deal with small groups of insurgents. In the few cases investigated, civilian casualties were regularly reported to be higher than initial NATO/US estimates. Locals often argued that civilian casualties were underreported by NATO and the United States and that civilians were often mistaken for Taliban and targeted in air raids.[63] Health authorities also tended to disagree with NATO reports of low civilian casualties. UNDSS reported that about one third of the civilian casualties of January 2007 (about sixty) were to be attributed to ISAF and ANA and the rest to the Taliban. Whatever the actual number of civilian casualties, because of the lack of territorial control, Taliban propaganda claims that tended to inflate the number of civilian victims of the bombardments were difficult to dispute convincingly. Such propaganda appeared successful insofar as it led in some cases to local residents fearful of 'collateral damage' asking for a withdrawal of foreign troops from the Panjwai and Zhare areas of Kandahar, in part inspired by the example of Musa Qala and Sangin districts in Helmand. Afghan authorities in Kabul and in the provinces came under pressure to pay at least lip service to these widespread feelings. Even the most pro-US members of the local authorities, like Governor Asadullah Khalid of Kandahar, were forced to complain about excessive use of force by the Americans. It should also be considered that the intense fighting around Kandahar in 2006 led to a negative economic turnaround in the city, compounding the economic problems.[64]

6.7 IMPROVING 'GOVERNANCE'

Once the contradictions of the state-building process in Afghanistan (see 1.2 *'Rebuilding' the Afghan state*) became increasingly evident, pressure started mounting for a change in the government's approach. Improving 'governance' in Afghanistan became the new motto of the international community. The underlying idea was that by delivering a good and efficient administration, the root cause of grievances would be removed and the political situation would improve. This author takes it that what is meant by governance is that an institutionalised administration replaces a patrimonial one based on the personal power base and attitudes of appointees, although there is rarely any clarity about governance in official documents.[65] According to a UN analysis, in 2005 about one third of 1,500 political killings in Afghanistan and three quarters of all violent incidents were not linked to the insurgency but to land or resource conflicts and to the 'lopsided distribution of power in local administrations'.[66] Hence, improved governance could likely have reduced these types of conflict, thereby possibly contributing to prevent a spread of the insurgency too. As a result, starting from 2004 the Karzai administration was forced to start removing the most controversial governors in the south. The first to fall was Gul Agha Shirzai, governor of Kandahar, whose alliance with the Karzai circle was shakier (see Introduction). In early 2006, faced with British and Dutch ultimatums, Karzai had to sack Sher Mohammed in Helmand and Jan Mohammed in Uruzgan and to replace them with Eng. Daoud in Helmand, who had a reputation as a good administrator, and Abdul Hakim Monib in Uruzgan, who had potential as a mediator with the insurgents. Monib had been Junior Minister for Tribal Affairs under the Taliban and as a Ghilzai he was thought to be well positioned to talk to the insurgents in Uruzgan. At the same time, as an outsider (he hailed from Paktia) he could be seen as an impartial broker by different factions. However, he was not liked by either the Americans or many in the government and, starved of funds, was incapable of exercising a significant role. In early 2007 he offered his resignation in protest of the lack of funding and of the activities of the US Special Forces, which hampered his attempts at negotiations. In Zabul, which had seen a succession of ineffective governors after 2001, Karzai appointed Haji Arman, who also had a reputation as a good administrator. Despite widespread optimism about the impact of these developments, it might already have been too late. The government failed to quickly follow up the appointment of new governors with improvements in policing (except in Zabul) and the judiciary. Moreover, local communities had already been mobilised against the government and 'good governance' was no longer sufficient to appease them. The Taliban were by now well established in most of the countryside and were in a position to sabotage any attempt to deliver better 'governance'. In Zabul the administrative skills of Haji Arman had little impact outside Qalat, as whatever was left of district level administration was barely surviving under the direct protection of the ANA and US forces. Administrative offices were often housed in the same fortified compounds where US troops were based, making interaction with the population very hard. Being associated with the US presence might even have played against the ability of the local administration to interact with the population, not least given the decreasing popularity of foreign troops in the south. Similarly, the hosting of government radio stations within US military compounds in the south-east was seen by many Afghans as a sign of the inability of the government to maintain a degree of autonomy *vis-à-vis* the foreigners. The presence of the administration in the districts was merely symbolic, as district administrators would spend most of their time in the safer environment of the provincial capital.[67]

While the 'better governance' project harvested few positive results due to an already compromised situation and the resistance of elements of the central government, the replacement of the old governors created a vacuum of power, as communities that had sided with the pro-Karzai strongmen were now unhappy and afraid of their forthcoming marginalisation or in any case of losing the privileges and positions they had acquired (see 2.6 *Recruiting local communities*). The fact that the new governors and particularly Eng. Daoud were under pressure to support poppy eradication measures contributed to weaken their hold and prevent them from establishing a working relationship with much of the population. The choice to focus the eradication programme on the south rather than on the north-east, the other main poppy growing area, was seen as controversial and was attributed to the personal interest of Deputy Minister of Interior for Counter-narcotics Daoud Khan. Eng. Daoud's attempt to strike a balance between opposite sources of pressure consisted of avoiding compulsory eradication and trying to convince farmers to give up planting the poppies. The situation, however, had deteriorated to the extent that a reputedly honest administrator like Daoud, trying to resist the arbitrary behaviour of the security forces and to endorse to some extent the eradication agenda, found himself almost completely isolated. Less than a year after his appointment, Daoud became the object of a strong backlash from local allies of former governor Sher Mohammed Akhundzada, who had maintained good relations with Karzai (who appointed him senator) and continued to meet him often in Kabul. Sher Mohammed and his family had assiduously been building their own 'power bloc' in Helmand between 2001 and 2006. Not only had he staffed the police and administration with cronies, but during previous attempts to eradicate the poppies in Helmand, landlords connected with Sher Mohammed had usually been spared, while others were seeing their crops eradicated. Strengthened as it was by powerful connections in Kabul, Sher Mohammed's 'power bloc' proved quite resilient. Some of the Kabul press reported the 'criticism', by former and current government officials from Helmand, of Daoud, whose attempts to restrain and isolate the rogue militias and police forces of Helmand were described in terms of collaborationism with the Taliban. Daoud reacted by accusing the local 'drug mafia' of plotting against him and tried to convince President Karzai to leave him in his post, but not even British Prime Minister Tony Blair's efforts sufficed to save him. Karzai sacked Daoud in the autumn of 2006. His replacement, Asadullah Wafa, was widely seen as a weak figure who for several months even refused to deploy to Lashkargah. Daoud's chief of police, a professional named Muhammad Nabi Molakhel, was also transferred. After the sacking, British sources would blame the United States for having supported the removal of Daoud, while Defence Secretary Des Browne was reportedly very upset. Karzai had adopted a similar strategy in the past, grudgingly accepting to appoint individuals sponsored by the international community only in order to discredit and then remove them at the first sign of difficulty. From the perspective of this book, however, the most salient point is that Daoud's replacement was in line with the continuous change in the military and political strategies adopted to deal with the insurgency. It can be argued that changing strategy every six to twelve months is tantamount to having no strategy whatsoever, particularly if that is not justified by changes in the insurgents' own strategy.[68]

6.8 RECONCILIATION EFFORTS

In early 2002 the Afghan government offered an amnesty to all members of the Taliban regime, except for those 142 listed by the UN as 'leaders'. The original intention of the Karzai administration seems to have been an even wider amnesty which would have included even Mullah Omar, but US objections led to a more careful formulation, first excluding Mullah Omar and then all the 'leaders'. This amnesty had a degree of success in that most 'old Taliban' went back to their villages and stayed quiet there, at least initially. However, harassment by local security forces often pushed them back into the Taliban fold. In April 2003 Karzai, with a public speech, re-opened the door to 'moderate' Taliban, inviting them to join the political process. He reiterated the offer during an interview with the BBC in October of that year and a few days later Chief Justice Mawlawi Fazl Hadi Shinwari stated that talks were already underway with some Taliban. In the end the main prize of the negotiations was former Minister of Foreign Affairs Mutawakkil, who signed a reconciliation deal with the government and later put forward his candidature in the parliamentary elections of 2005. Mutawakkil, however, was in detention at the time of the deal and had never been a military commander. Former field commander Salam Rocketi also made peace with Kabul, but he had never joined the Neo-Taliban and did not bring with him substantial numbers of combatants.[69]

By 2005, after at least two years of efforts to attract 'moderate Taliban' to the government side through secret negotiations, the government had little to show. In an effort to approach the rank-and-file directly, bypassing the leadership, the Peace Strengthening Commission was established in March 2005 in Kabul and at the regional level. As of the summer of 2006 the Peace Strengthening Commission was still trying to expand throughout the country, establishing offices at the provincial level. Working with limited manpower, the Commission led by Segbatullah Mojaddedi relied on tribal and religious notables to establish contact with opposition elements at the local level. After the initial contact, individuals and groups willing to reconcile with the government would meet the provincial governor and the regional representatives of the Commission. In the case of a successful agreement, the reconciled oppositionists would be given a letter in three copies, one to keep and the remaining two to be handed over to NATO or the Coalition and to the government. By October 2006 2,400 individuals had been granted such letters, of whom 700 in the south-eastern region (including Logar).

Government sources showed a strong tendency to overstate the success of the reconciliation programme. When 169 mostly former members of the 'old Taliban' surrendered in western Afghanistan in March 2006, local officials described them as '169 high-ranking Taliban commanders'. This supposedly happened in a region which until then had seen little or no Taliban activity (Herat, Farah, Ghor and Badghis).[70] When asked to identify the most important Taliban commanders who joined the reconciliation process, one of the representatives of the Commission mentioned a number of officials who had not even been active after 2001:

- Abdul Hakim Mojahed, who had been the unofficial representative of the Taliban regime at the UN and later one of the founders of Jamiat-i Khudam-ul Koran (see 3.1 *Cohesiveness of the Taliban*);
- Pir Mohammed Rohani, who had been rector of Kabul University under the Taliban regime;
- Arsala Rehmani, another founder of Jami'at-i Khudam-ul Koran and Deputy Education Minister under the Taliban;
- Abdul Wahid, former Taliban commander in Baghran, who never fought actively against the government or the Coalition after 2001 and moreover was alleged to be maintaining contacts with the Taliban.[71]

UN sources in eastern Afghanistan alleged that many of the applicants to the Commission had never been with the insurgency or with the Taliban and were just refugees trying to return to Afghanistan under privileged conditions. A US officer admitted in 2005 that none of the thirty or so relatively high-ranking Taliban officials to accept amnesty was a former military commander. Moreover, several of them continued to support the Taliban politically even as they enjoyed government protection in Kabul's safehouses. Of the 2,400 who joined the process, about 1,000 were former fighters, with very few recently active commanders of any rank among them. On the whole the reconciliation programme scored some successes in provinces like Paktia, Laghman and Kunar, where even some mid-rank field commanders of the insurgency joined the process, but not much anywhere else. In Kandahar the environment was so far from conducive to reconciliation that local officials of the Commission were just contacting non-active former Taliban in the hope that these could at some point drag in some active fighters.[72]

Although only a handful of those accepting reconciliation then went back to fighting, lack of trust in the genuine character of the government's offer continued to affect the chances of success of the Commission. A number of other problems also existed. The performance of the Commission was allegedly hampered by the sometimes dubious choice of staffing, often responding more to patronage logic than to a concern with the effectiveness of the programme. The appointment of a new and more respected chief of the Commission in Kandahar in September 2006 (Agha Lalai), for example, produced an immediate increase in the number of individuals accepting to support the government, particularly in Agha Lalai's own district of Panjwai, where over 10 per cent of the local insurgents were reported to have quit fighting in just seven months. There were also allegations that some elements in the National Security Council in Kabul, an institution modelled on the US original, opposed reconciliation and tried to sabotage it by mistreating applicants. According to officials of the Commission, another limitation was the lack of resources to provide the reconciled elements with shelter, jobs and protection, except for a few top defectors housed in Kabul under NSD protection. In fact, some former Taliban who expressed their support for the government were assassinated, such as former Deputy Interior Minister Mullah Abdul Samad (January 2006). Allegations also flourished that the Pakistani security services actively tried to prevent Taliban militants from accepting the government's reconciliation offer. The demand that defectors from the Taliban be provided with jobs and housing, however, sounds quite demagogic in a country where unemployment was estimated at 30–40 per cent of the workforce; it would have been seen as rewarding the wrongdoers at a time when the needs of most of the population were being ignored. In the end, it is obvious that as long as the Taliban were thinking that the insurgency was making progress, 'reconciliation' or surrender were not going to be attractive options. Reconciliation was not going to take off until the Taliban would appear militarily defeated. Until the end of 2006 the main role of the reconciliation process was to offer an alternative to former Taliban who were not inclined to fight for their own reasons.[73]

6.9 LOCAL TRUCES

When the focus of the counter-insurgency campaign was not on the south and more on the east and south-east, where Al Qaida elements were present in strength, truces with individual Taliban commanders in the south were well accepted by the Americans. However, these had little lasting positive impact. The case of Rais-e Baghran, alias Mullah Abdul Wahid, the strongman in control of Baghran district (Helmand), who had been aligned with the Taliban since 1995, is illustrative. Negotiations with him had been going on since the fall of the regime in 2001, but integrating him and his supporters within the power system of Sher Mohammed, governor of Helmand, proved impossible. The original deal between the two men was ready in 2002, but had immediately collapsed because of a lack of trust between the two parties. Although after more than three years of truce Sher Mohammed successfully renegotiated Abdul Wahid's 'surrender' in March 2005, allowing him to keep his weapons and his militia, by the end of the year the two were once again at odds.[74] In the end Abdul Wahid continued to linger in a limbo between the government and the Taliban, maintaining contacts with both of them, while Baghran district returned to its old status of a Taliban stronghold.

Other negotiations between provincial authorities and local Taliban commanders took place in Zabul province in 2003, but they seem to have brought no results. Allegedly an informal deal existed in Nangarhar province between Taliban, Hizb-i Islami and governor Din Mohammed, according to which the city and the surrounding districts would be spared violence from both sides, but whether the deal was ever endorsed by Kabul is not clear; it might have been purely informal. Despite some bellicose statements by NATO officers during the summer of 2006, by September the exhaustion of British troops in Helmand following intense fighting forced the British to accept truces in Musa Qala and Sangin districts, negotiated by the local elders. The two truces held until the beginning of December, despite some tension over the terms of the agreement. The deals were supported by UNAMA and were also strongly sponsored by then governor of Helmand, Eng. Daoud, but Afghan officials in Kabul and in Helmand were often unhappy, describing the truces as 'surrender to the Taliban'. Even President Karzai expressed some doubts, while some cabinet members such as Foreign Affairs Minister Spanta openly expressed their opposition. By early 2007 relations between Great Britain and Afghanistan were seriously strained, impacting negatively even within Kabul's government itself. A strong argument against the deals was that it allowed the local elders, whoever they were, effectively to choose the district governor, CoP and even individual policemen, against an established practice of appointments from above. It was feared that similar demands might surface in other districts if fully endorsed from Kabul, endangering the ultra-centralised character of the Afghan state. By contrast, the reaction among the population of Musa Qala town appeared positive, as shown by a burst of reconstruction efforts aimed at repairing and rebuilding houses and shops. In the opinion of cynics, the forthcoming poppy planting season might have contributed to the peace-making mood of the locals. Nobody, however, argued that the Taliban disbanded or disarmed and the elders had only committed themselves to 'try to limit' the number of the insurgents, who continued to be allowed into the town, although without carrying arms. Some locals argued that the elders were not really independent of the Taliban, who were in a position to pressure them.[75]

In early February the truce in Musa Qala collapsed amid recriminations over who was responsible. Sources in the British Army alleged that the truce-breaking airstrike which killed the brother of the local insurgent commander was deliberately intended by the Americans to sabotage the truce. It also appears that pressure from Kabul and from the United States might have pushed the British towards adopting a more aggressive approach. Confirmation that government pressure played a role came from the fact that shortly afterwards the governor of Helmand, Eng. Daoud, who had been instrumental in negotiating the truces, was removed from his post (see 6.7 *Improving 'governance'*). The new governor, Asadullah Wafa, expressed his opposition to such truces. Pressure for more truces had started building up after these initial deals, particularly around Panjwai, a development which must not have been welcome in NATO headquarters. In any case the truces were then re-established under a new plan to hand over to local elders control over the recruitment of police and reconstruction aid in exchange for assurances of loyalty to Kabul. By offering a better financial deal to the elders, while at the same time tying them to specific undertakings to respect the sovereignty of Kabul, it was hoped the aim of separating the insurgents from the population might be made more attainable. As of January 2007 similar deals were being negotiated in Sangin and Garmser, although there were sceptics within the British ranks too, arguing that it was likely too late to drive a wedge between the population and the insurgents. Reports from Musa Qala in February 2007 suggested however that at least in this regard the truces might have succeeded, as a delegation of elders reached Kabul to appeal for help against the repression unleashed by the Taliban. The new deals might not have been welcomed by the Taliban, who argued that they would never negotiate deals in the future. Taken aback, as of February 2007 the British had little option left apart from dropping leaflets in the hope of scaring the non-core Taliban to give up the fight. The situation appeared to be at a standstill, but the new commander of ISAF in Afghanistan, US General McNeill, was widely expected to cancel such deals after taking over that month.[76]

Another unwanted effect of the local truces, together with the deal between militants and the Pakistani government in Waziristan, was the spread of rumours concerning negotiations with the Taliban leadership, stimulated also by the fact that individuals around the increasingly beleaguered Bush Administration had started talking about the possibility or indeed even the need for a political solution. This was most notoriously the case of Bill Frist, Senate Republican majority leader.[77]

6.10 WHAT COUNTER-INSURGENCY?

US counter-insurgency in Afghanistan wavered between the old Cold War approach, targeted at fighting strategies mainly inspired by left-wing ideologies, and an alternative identifying prevention through development and aid as the only possible solution to the 'war of the flea'. The classical approach postulated that would-be Taliban strongholds had to be periodically raided in order to prevent the insurgents from consolidating their presence and developing the means to move on to the next phase of the insurgency. The development-based approach argued that since there was no point in trying to kill off all the 'fleas', the solution was to prevent the 'fleas' from infesting the 'dog' by undermining conditions that would allow the 'fleas' to breed. 'Development' was to clean the country of insurgents in much the same way as good hygiene would rescue the dog from the fleas. 'Fourth generation' counter-insurgency warfare, being a new proposition, had not yet filtered down to policy makers by early 2007 and since it implies a major restructuring of the US armed forces, it might never do so. Nonetheless, the wavering between the first two options resulted in the Taliban still being able to develop their strongholds, if with some delay, during the lulls in the raiding by enemy forces. It also resulted in attempts to combine the dispensation of patronage ('development') with counter-insurgency being patchy, *ad hoc* and implemented on and off. Similarly, the approach towards eradication, combining verbal commitment, strong rhetoric and little and unbalanced action, was sufficient to irritate and scare large sections and the population, without removing what was alleged to be an important source of funding for the insurgency.

This pattern continued well into 2007. While the Americans were actively lobbying in favour of eradication, the British were favouring the targeting of traffickers and of the refining business and the Dutch were communicating their desire to stay out of it altogether.[78]

By 2006 few people in southern Afghanistan were impressed with the benefits of this wavering approach. This author's view, however, is that even if either of the two strategies had been implemented consistently, it is unlikely that they would have resulted in the defeat of the insurgents, although they might have made their life more difficult. Classical counter-insurgency might have been able to further slow the development of Taliban strongholds and therefore the formation of small insurgent 'armies' and the passage to the third phase of the insurgency. This, however, would have been a mixed blessing, because the Taliban would have been forced to drop their risky plans to take Kandahar and focus on the 'war of the flea', spreading it wider and wider into Afghanistan. Classical counter-insurgency would only have succeeded in blocking the development of the insurgency (but not yet defeating it) if it had been possible to wipe out the strongholds entirely, depriving the Taliban of the ability to support infiltration deeper into Afghan territory. This, however, would have demanded a greater concentration of forces and their permanent deployment in the mountainous areas where the strongholds were being established. In the context of 2003–6, this was not possible because of the commitment of almost all US ground forces to Iraq. It is also unlikely that any US government would have wanted to commit a large portion of its armed forces to Afghanistan for long periods of time.

Patronage-based counter-insurgency, combined with extensive use of special troops for population control, could have been useful in the early days of the insurgency, when it was not yet widespread. It might then have been possible to suffocate it before it spread. Once the Taliban became active in tens of districts, there were never going to be sufficient special troops or 'development' funds and workers to cover such large areas. However, during the incubation stage of the insurgency nobody in either Kabul or Washington was taking it seriously, hence the chance of a major investment in resources to suffocate it in its early days never really existed. By the time it actually started being implemented, success in one district would only have meant that the insurgents would move to another one, where the ground had in the meanwhile been prepared by the elusive infiltration teams, and intensify military operations there. This strategy was also confronted with the hard facts of the corruption of the central government. In early 2007 US and British defence officials were reported to have estimated that up to half of all aid to Afghanistan failed to reach 'the right people'. Not only the authorities seemed to be siphoning off much of the aid, but even much of what was delivered by them was hoarded by village elders and notables and not distributed to the villagers. The existence of such attitudes is confirmed by the experience of development workers inside Afghanistan, whose best efforts at providing services for the population, such as deep wells, were often hijacked by local notables for their exclusive benefit.[79]

It has been argued that a better integrated effort would have benefited the counter-insurgency war. While there is truth in this, this is not the main point. Analysts are fond of citing successful British experiences in defeating insurgencies in Malaya, Kenya, Oman and Borneo as models of an 'integrated, coordinated, interagency approach' to be emulated.[80] However in a fashion typical of those who focus on tactics more than on strategy, and on military aspects more than political ones, they miss the main factor in securing victories in those cases: the British wisely chose to fight only wars they could win. If the British had known of some magic formula to defeat any insurgency, they would not have given up their Empire once nationalist mobilisation started building up in India and elsewhere. They dropped struggles which were leading nowhere and looked unsustainable in the long term, even in cases where the military challenge itself looked manageable in the short term. Even the celebrated 'victories' in Malaya, Kenya, Oman and Borneo were in fact a result of the political willingness to compromise and abandon control of

215

those territories, in exchange for guarantees regarding the protection of some vital British interests there. This is exactly the contrary of what the Bush Administration did in Afghanistan and elsewhere. By ideologising the struggle against radical and extremist groups in the Middle East as the 'War on Terror', the American leadership unwittingly trapped itself in a situation where strategic and tactical flexibility could no longer exist. While ideologisation might work in a context of confrontation between states of similar strength, in the post-9/11 context it legitimised the claim of a relatively small nucleus of terrorists to be the leadership of a much larger movement incorporating mainly national and local grievances. When the Bush Administration accepted to be dragged into an ideological war, as the planners of the 9/11 attacks likely wished it would be, it accepted to fight on the ground chosen by the enemy, pitting its weaknesses against the enemy's strengths.

To the extent that the Afghan insurgency was becoming part of a wider jihadist movement, there was little that political and military authorities based in Afghanistan could do, except make a deal which also satisfied the regional powers, including Pakistan, or make a grand attempt to claim political ground from the insurgency in order to marginalise it. Reducing counter-insurgency to a mere technical/technological problem could only lead towards proposing unviable solutions, such as imposing population control through the establishment of a national identification card system.[81] To the extent that local communities were not yet merged into the Taliban and maintained a separate identity and specific grievances, serious progress towards the solution to the conflict in Afghanistan might have been achieved by addressing the outstanding political issues. Given the advanced state of the insurgency, possibly nearing its 'metastasis', mild measures such as slowly improving governance skills seem insufficient, not to mention the fact that the 'power blocs' that had developed in many provinces often opposed reforms and new appointments aimed at improving 'governance'. In this author's opinion, better results might have come from developing new and more institutionalised ways of managing subnational administrations in Afghanistan, more inclusive of local communities, strongmen and interest groups, ensuring at the same time that checks and balances were established to prevent 'bad' authorities from tyrannising large sectors of the population. The provincial councils established in 2005 were powerless entities which could only advise local authorities and were usually paid little or no attention. Any reform moving in this direction should have been packaged as a major political campaign aimed at changing the way the Afghan state behaves in relation to the population and should have recognised past wrongdoings in order to have a significant impact on the areas affected by the insurgency.[82]

koran, kalashnikov and laptop

NOTES

1 Personal communications with NSD officers, Kunduz, 2003–4 and Pul-i Khumri, 2006; personal communications with individuals harassed by the security services and their relatives, 2006–7; 'Afghans tortured prisoners captured by Canadians', *Pajhwok Afghan News*, 23 April 2007; Lee Carter, 'Canadian row over Afghan "abuse"', *BBC News*, 24 April 2007.

2 Cordesman (2007).

3 Afghan Independent Human Rights Commission (2004), p. 20. 'Eleven of the complaints were related to the bombing of civilians. The other 33 complaints included cases of beatings, detention of innocent people, and damage to houses, injuries to people and a lack of respect for Afghan culture during coalition raids', <http://www.aihrc.org.af/mon_inv.htm>.

4 Afghan Independent Human Rights Commission (2005), p. 37.

5 Interview with Afghan security officer, Kandahar, January 2006; Elizabeth Rubin, 'In the land of the Taliban', *New York Times Magazine*, 22 October 2006; Eric Schmitt and David Rohde, 'Afghan rebels widen attacks', *New York Times*, 1 August 2004; Chris Sands, 'Afghanistan: battle for hearts and minds lost', *PalestineChronicle.com*, 11 December 2005; Amin Tarzi, 'Afghanistan: Kabul riots appeared spontaneous', *RFE/RL*, 6 June 2006; interview with Maulana Obeidullah, Peace Strengthening Commission, Kandahar, January 2006; Declan Walsh, 'We'll beat you again, Afghans warn British', *Guardian*, 28 June 2006; interview with Haji Mir Khan, MP from Khost, Kabul, February 2007; interview with Afghan notable from Khugyani, Jalalabad, February 2007.

6 For a summary of the early differences within NATO, see Gallis (2006).

7 Personal communication, Kabul, October 2006.

8 Konstantin von Hammerstein *et al.*, 'NATO chaos deepens in Afghanistan', *Der Spiegel Online*, 20 November 2006; Cordesman (2007); Robert Fox, 'CIA is undermining British war effort, say military chiefs', *Independent*, 10 December 2006; Jason Burke, 'Fear battles hope on the road to Kandahar', *Observer*, 25 June 2006; Declan Walsh, 'Afghanistan's opium poppies will be sprayed, says US drugs tsar', *Guardian*, 11 December 2006; Murray Brewster, 'Canada trying to deter spraying of poppy fields', *Canadian Press*, 22 January 2007; Raymond Whitaker, 'Opium war revealed ...', *Independent*, 21 January 2007; Syed Saleem Shahzad, 'Afghanistan's highway to hell', *Asia Times Online*, 25 January 2007.

9 See 'Afghan Security Forces demobilize, join ANA, ANP', *Freedom Watch* (CENTCOM), January 2006, <http://www.cfc-a.centcom. mil/Freedom%20Watch/2006/01-January/Jan%2023.pdf>. For more information see Giustozzi (2007a).

10 On the AMF see International Crisis Group (2003b). On the warlords' system behind the AMF, see Giustozzi (2003). UNAMA source, Kabul, 2003; UN sources, Kabul, January 2004.

11 For an example in Herat see *Erada Daily*, 28 October 2003; *RFE/RL Newsline*, vol. 7, no. 140, part III, 25 July 2003; *RFE/RL Newsline*, vol. 7, no. 156, part III, 18 August 2003.

12 Personal interviews with local authorities in various provinces of Afghanistan, October 2003–February 2004.

13 Ministry of Defence of Afghanistan (2002); General Pezhanwai, quoted in *RFE/RL Newsline*, 5 March 2003; General Atiqullah Baryalai, quoted in *New York Times*, 25 January 2003; General Gulad, quoted in *Christian Science Monitor*, 27 March 2002; personal interview with General Nurul Haq Ulumi, May 2003.

14 Personal interview with UNAMA military liaison officer, February 2004.

15 See Giustozzi (2007a); International Crisis Group (2003b).

16 Owais Tohid, 'Arid Afghan province proves fertile for Taliban', *Christian Science Monitor*, 14 July 2003; UN and ISAF sources, Kabul, October 2006; David Rohde, 'Afghan symbol for change becomes a symbol of failure', *New York Times*, 5 September 2006; International Crisis Group (2006a), p. 17.

17 Personal communication with NCL employee, Kabul, February 2007. For the case of Kajaki see 'A double spring offensive', *The Economist*, 22 February 2007. See also Giustozzi (2007a).

18 Interview with Afghan journalist returning from the south, Kabul, October 2006.

19 Tom Coghlan, 'Taliban flee Afghan-led NATO offensive', *Daily Telegraph*, 30 March 2007; *Arman-e Milli*, 11 April 2007; 'Men in uniforms rob civilians in Helmand', *IRIN*, 24 Apr 2007; interview with tribal notable from Chora, April 2007; personal communication with UN officials and foreign diplomats.

20 Trives (2006); Scott Baldauf, 'Key to governing Afghans: the clans', *Christian Science Monitor*, 24 June 2004; Scott Baldauf, 'Outside Kabul, militias bring security to Afghanistan', *Christian Science Monitor*, 24 April 2003; 'Jalali rejects formation of tribal units in Afghanistan', *Pakistan Tribune*, 1 August 2003; International Crisis Group (2006a), p. 17; Pamela Constable, 'A NATO bid to regain Afghans' trust', *Washington Post*, 27 November 2006; Declan Walsh, 'Special deals and raw recruits employed to halt the Taliban in embattled Helmand', *Guardian*, 4 January 2007; Fisnik Abrashi, 'Taliban, criminals may be among militiamen recruited as auxiliary police in Afghanistan', *Associated Press*, 25 November 2006.

21 On the problem of corruption and abuses in the police see Amnesty International (2003). Kandahar police has 120 professionally trained policemen out of a total force of 3,000 in 2003 (p. 9).

22 Graeme Smith, 'Chief cracks down on Kandahar police', *Globe and Mail*, 24 January 2007; personal communications with UN officials, Kandahar and Kabul, January, February and October 2006; Graeme Smith, 'Inspiring tale of triumph over Taliban not all it seems', *Globe and Mail*, 23 September 2006; Graeme Smith, 'The Taliban: knowing the enemy', *Globe and Mail*, 27 November 2006; Pamela Constable, 'A NATO bid to regain Afghans'

trust'.

23 See *Interagency Assessment of Afghanistan Police Training and Readiness* (2006).

24 Interview with Afghan journalist returning from the south, Kabul, October 2006; Phil Zabriskie, 'Dangers up ahead: how druglords and insurgents are making the war in Afghanistan deadlier than ever', *Time*, 5 March 2006; James Rupert, 'Corruption and coalition failures spur Taliban resurgence in Afghanistan', *Newsday*, 17 June 2006; Elizabeth Rubin, 'In the land of the Taliban'; Terry Friel, 'Resurgent Taliban strangles southern heartland', *Reuters*, 16 November 2006; Andrew Maykuth, 'An Afghan rebuilding takes shape', *Philadelphia Inquirer*, 6 October 2003; Kathy Gannon, 'Taliban comeback traced to corruption', *Associated Press*, 24 November 2006; Murray Brewster, 'Kandahar cops making progress says RCMP', *Canadian Press*, 3 February 2007.

25 Jason Burke, 'Stronger and more deadly, the terror of the Taliban is back', *Observer*, 16 November 2003; Kate Clark, 'Cash rewards for Taliban fighters', *File On 4, BBC Radio 4*, 28 February 2006; Sara Daniel, 'Afghanistan: "Résister aux talibans? A quoi bon!"', *Le Nouvel Observateur*, 10 August 2006; Senlis Council (2006d), p. 27; Elizabeth Rubin, 'In the land of the Taliban'; Jason Burke, 'Fear battles hope on the road to Kandahar'; David Leask, 'In some areas of Helmand, the police are your worst enemy', *Herald*, 10 January 2007; Syed Saleem Shahzad, 'Afghanistan's highway to hell'; Harm Ede Botje, 'We zitten darr goed', *Vrij Nederland*, 6 January 2007 (courtesy of J. van den Zwan, Crisis States Research Centre, London); Graeme Smith, 'Chief cracks down on Kandahar police'; Tom Coghlan, 'Profits are vast but only the big fish survive', *Daily Telegraph*, 8 February 2007; 'Living under the Taleban', *Afghan Recovery Report* (IWPR), no. 249 (4 April 2007).

26 David Rohde and James Risen, 'C.I.A. review highlights Afghan leader's woes', *New York Times*, 5 November 2006; Elizabeth Rubin, 'Taking the fight to the Taliban', *New York Times Magazine*, 29 October 2006; Elizabeth Rubin, 'In the land of the Taliban'.

27 Quoted in Graeme Smith, 'Inspiring tale of triumph over Taliban not all it seems'.

28 Senlis Council (2006a), p. 11; Kathy Gannon, 'Taliban comeback traced to corruption'; Syed Saleem Shahzad, 'Rough justice and blooming poppies', *Asia Times Online*, 7 December 2006.

29 James Rupert, 'Corruption and coalition failures spur Taliban resurgence in Afghanistan'; 'ANP don't control the villages', *Arman-e Milli*, 10 December 2006; Kim Barker, 'Taliban flexes renewed muscle', *Chicago Tribune*, 3 July 2006; Phil Zabriskie, 'Dangers up ahead: how druglords and insurgents are making the war in Afghanistan deadlier than ever'; Borhan Younus, 'Taliban call the shots in Ghazni', *Afghanistan Recovery Report*, no. 213 (25 April 2006); Eric de Lavarène, 'La province de tous les dangers', *RFI*, 19 March 2006; interview with Afghan security officer, Kandahar, January 2006; David Rohde, 'G.I.s in Afghanistan on hunt, but now for hearts and minds', *New*

York Times, 30 March 2004; Amir Shah, 'Police flee after Afghan bomb attack', *Associated Press*, 19 February 2007.

30 For the case of Chora district of Helmand, 2006 see Kim Barker, 'Taliban flexes renewed muscle'.

31 Interview with Afghan security officer, Kandahar, January 2006; David Rohde, 'G.I.s in Afghanistan on hunt, but now for hearts and minds'; Paul Watson, 'On the trail of the Taliban's support', *Los Angeles Times*, 24 December 2006; Declan Walsh, 'We'll beat you again, Afghans warn British'; 'Why are Helmand's districts falling to the Taliban?', *Abadi*, 13 December 2006; Hamid Mir, 'The Taliban's new face', *Rediff* (India), 27 September 2005; Murray Brewster, 'Kandahar cops making progress says RCMP'; Jason Straziuso, 'Race is on to prevent Taliban's return', *Associated Press*, 6 February 2007; UNDSS weekly presentation, 2–8 February 2007.

32 For two cases in Helmand see Tim Albone, 'Pathfinders on a four-day mission fight off eight-week Taliban siege', *The Times*, 27 September 2006, and Thomas Coghlan and Justin Huggler, 'A ruthless enemy, a hostile population and 50C heat', *Independent*, 9 July 2006.

33 Françoise Chipaux, 'Les talibans consolident leur emprise dans le sud de l'Afghanistan', *Le Monde*, 9 June 2006; Kathy Gannon, 'Taliban comeback traced to corruption'; Andrew Maykuth, 'An Afghan rebuilding takes shape'; 'Forty Afghan police flee checkpoints with weapons after not paid in full', *Pajhwok News Agency*, 30 March 2006; Scott Baldauf, 'Small US units lure Taliban into losing battles', *Christian Science Monitor*, 31 October 2005; 'Sept policiers afghans tués par des collègues alliés aux taliban', *Reuters*, 5 June 2006; David Rohde, 'G.I.s in Afghanistan on hunt, but now for hearts and minds'; interview with Afghan police officer, Kandahar, January 2006; Elizabeth Rubin, 'Taking the fight to the Taliban'; Kathy Gannon, 'Taliban comeback traced to corruption'; Eric Schmitt and David Rohde, 'Afghan rebels widen attacks'; personal communication with Niamtullah Ibrahimi, Crisis States Research Centre, Kabul, October 2006.

34 Kim Barker, 'Taliban flexes renewed muscle'; Terry Friel, 'Resurgent Taliban strangles southern heartland'; David Rohde, 'G.I.s in Afghanistan on hunt, but now for hearts and minds'; 'Why are Helmand's districts falling to the Taliban?', *Abadi*, 13 December 2006; personal communication with UN officials, Kabul, April and May 2007; personal communication with police advisor, Kabul, May 2007.

35 This paragraph is based mainly on Giustozzi (2007b), where the reader can find more details and data.

36 For an elaboration of this point see Giustozzi (2007b).

37 Dyke and Crisafulli (2006), pp. 9, 10; Naylor (2006); Michael A. Fletcher, 'Bush rebuffs Karzai's request on troops', *Washington Post*, 24 May 2005; *C4I News*, 17 February 2005; Carlotta Gall, 'U.S.–Afghan foray reveals friction on antirebel raids', *New York Times*, 2 July 2006.

38 Giustozzi (2007b).

39 Interview with former ANA soldier, January 2007; Giustozzi (2007b);

'Taliban tortures two kidnapped Afghan soldiers to death', *Xinhua*, 1 September 2006; personal communication with US military advisor in Afghanistan, May 2007.

40 Giustozzi (2007b); interview with Afghan journalist returning from the south, Kabul, October 2006; Dyke and Crisafulli (2006), p. 10; Cordesman (2006), p. 4.

41 Tim Kilbride, 'As Afghan troops build capacity, decisive battles loom', *American Forces Press Service*, 2 March 2007.

42 Giustozzi (2007b); 'A double spring offensive', *The Economist*, 22 February 2007.

43 Cordesman (2006), p. 5; Kemp (forthcoming), p. 10; drug trader interviewed in Elizabeth Rubin, 'In the land of the Taliban'; interview with Afghan journalist returning from the south, Kabul, October 2006; Giustozzi (2007b).

44 Mirwais Atal, 'US hearts and minds cash goes to Taliban', *Afghan Recovery Report*, no. 236 (28 November 2006); Giustozzi (2007b).

45 Aryn Baker, 'Can the Afghans defend themselves?', *Time*, 3 January 2007; 'Narcotics found in Afghan army vehicle', *UPI*, 29 March 2006; Syed Saleem Shahzad, 'Afghanistan's highway to hell'; David Loyn, 'On the road with the Taliban', *BBC News (BBC Radio 4)*, 21 October 2006; interview with former ELJ commissioner, Kandahar, 26 January 2006; interview with Afghan security officer, Kandahar, January 2006; interview with Alkozai notable and Sufi leader from Dand district, Kandahar, January 2006; Giustozzi (2007b); Tom Coghlan, 'Profits are vast but only the big fish survive'.

46 Kathy Gannon, 'Taliban comeback traced to corruption'; Senlis Council (2006b), ch. 6, pp. 13–14; Giustozzi (2007b).

47 Jones (2006), who bases his estimate on James T. Quinlivan, 'Force requirements in security operations', *Parameters*, vol. 25, no. 4 (winter 1995–6), pp. 59–69 and Dobbins (2003); Dobbins *et al.* (2005).

48 Kemp (forthcoming), pp. 12–14; Rothstein (2006), pp. 113, 129; Dyke and Crisafulli (2006), pp. 8–9; Charles Heyman, 'Special forces and the reality of military operations in Afghanistan', *Jane's World Airlines*, 5 November 2001; John Simpson, 'US special forces are worried because they are leaving', *Sunday Telegraph*, 15 September 2002; Françoise Chipaux, 'Les talibans font régner leur loi dans les provinces pachtounes du Sud', *Le Monde*, 7 October 2004; Sher Ahmad Haidar, 'Residents flay home-search in Ghazni', *Pajhwok Afghan News*, 21 January 2007; Elizabeth Rubin, 'In the land of the Taliban'.

49 Dyke and Crisafulli (2006), pp. 55–7; Kevin Sack and Craig Pyes, 'Cloak of secrecy hides abuse in Afghanistan', *Los Angeles Times*, 26 September 2006; R. Jeffrey Smith, 'Army files cite abuse of Afghans', *Washington Post*, 18 February 2005.

50 Elizabeth Rubin, 'Taking the fight to the Taliban'; Rothstein (2006), p. 141; Murray Brewster, 'Afghan villagers told they'll be expelled again if

Canadian troops attacked', *Canadian Press*, 13 February 2007.

51 For an example of offers of rewards to the villagers see a flier reproduced at <http://www.huffingtonpost.com/h-candace-gorman-/why-i-am-representing-a-_b_29734.html>.

52 Eric Schmitt and David Rohde, 'Afghan rebels widen attacks'; David Rohde, 'G.I.s in Afghanistan on hunt, but now for hearts and minds'; Tim McGirk, 'The Taliban on the run', *Time*, 28 March 2005; Eric de Lavarène, 'La fin des Taliban?', *RFI*, 1 March 2005; 'A geographical expression in search of a state', *The Economist*, 6 July 2006; Naylor (2006); Patrick Bishop, 'Taliban or tractor? British try to win over peasants', *Daily Telegraph*, 16 September 2006; Ahmad Khalid Mowahid, 'PRT to spend $24m in Maidan Wardak', *Pajhwok Afghan News*, 18 January 2007; 'Afghanistan: le manque d'Etat nourrit la rébellion des talibans (armée US)', *AFP*, 22 September 2005; Carlotta Gall, 'Despite years of U.S. pressure, Taliban fight on in jagged hills', *New York Times*, 4 June 2005; Rothstein (2006), p. 115; Bill Graveland, 'Canadians battling Taliban propaganda', *CNews*, 4 December 2006; Anthony Loyd, 'It's dawn, and the shelling starts. Time to go into the Taleban maze', *The Times*, 14 February 2007; Anthony Loyd, 'Missiles drive US staff from dam that Royal Marines fought to save', *The Times*, 15 February 2007; Tom Coghlan, 'British "quick fix" aid for Afghans brought to halt by insurgents', *Daily Telegraph*, 19 February 2007; Kevin Dougherty, 'NATO and Afghanistan: a status report', *Stars and Stripes* (Mideast edition), 18 February 2007.

53 Elizabeth Rubin, 'Taking the fight to the Taliban'; Senlis Council (2006c), p. 34; Mirwais Atal, 'US hearts and minds cash goes to Taliban'.

54 Naylor (2006); Michael Evans and Anthony Loyd, 'I will build more and kill less, says NATO's Afghanistan general', *The Times*, 1 November 2006; Michael Abramowitz, 'Bush plans new focus on Afghan recovery', *Washington Post*, 25 January 2007.

55 Naylor (2006).

56 Christina Lamb, 'Have you ever used a pistol?'; Alastair Leithead, 'Unravelling the Helmand impasse', *BBC News*, 14 July 2006; Thomas Harding, 'Paras strike deep into the Taliban heartland', *Daily Telegraph*, 19 June 2006; Tim Albone, 'Pathfinders on a four-day mission fight off eight-week Taliban siege'.

57 Les Perreaux, 'NATO urges Afghans to vacate volatile Panjwaii district', *Canadian Press*, 31 August 2006; David Rohde and James Risen, 'C.I.A. review highlights Afghan leader's woes'; Pamela Constable, 'A NATO bid to regain Afghans' trust'; Carlotta Gall, 'NATO's Afghan struggle: build, and fight Taliban', *New York Times*, 13 January 2007; Declan Walsh, 'Special deals and raw recruits employed to halt the Taliban in embattled Helmand'; Akram Naurzi, Najib Khilwatgar, 'Expectations go unfulfilled in Helmand', *Pajhwok Afghan News*, 24 December 2006; Murray Brewster, 'A ride through Taliban country', *Canadian Press*, 17 January 2007; Graeme Smith, 'Inspiring tale of triumph over Taliban not all it seems'; Graeme

Smith, 'The Taliban: knowing the enemy'; Bill Graveland, 'Taliban shows little resistance', *Canadian Press*, 24 December 2006; Gethin Chamberlain, 'Afghan army takes fight to Taliban's heartland', *Sunday Telegraph*, 17 December 2006; 'At site of NATO's largest Afghan ground battle, race is on to prevent Taliban return', *Associated Press*, 30 January 2007; Jason Straziuso, 'Race is on to prevent Taliban's return'; John Cotter, 'Increased roadside bombs, rocket attacks in Afghanistan', *Canadian Press*, 25 March 2007; Damien McElroy, 'Afghan hearts and minds refuse to be won', *Daily Telegraph*, 26 March 2007.

58 Pamela Constable, 'A NATO bid to regain Afghans' trust'; Michael Evans *et al.*, 'Aid effort fails to impress war-weary Afghans', *The Times*, 27 January 2007; Elizabeth Rubin, 'In the land of the Taliban'; Senlis Council (2006c), p. 34; Fisnik Abrashi and Jason Straziuso, 'Deepening insurgency puts Afghanistan on brink', *Associated Press*, 8 October 2006; Tom Coghlan, 'British "quick fix" aid for Afghans brought to halt by insurgents'.

59 Karimi (2006), pp. 148–9, 154, 168ff (courtesy of J. van den Zwan, Crisis States Research Centre, London); Harm Ede Botje, 'We zitten darr goed'; Graeme Smith, 'Doing it the Dutch way in Afghanistan', *Globe and Mail*, 2 December 2006; personal communication with high-ranking NATO officer, Kabul, October 2006; Joeri Boom, 'Martelende gesprekken', *De Groene Amsterdammer*, 24 November 2006; Vik Franke, author of documentary on the Dutch in Uruzgan ('De Wereld draait door'), interviewed on *Vaara TV*, 20 November 2006 (courtesy of J. van den Zwan, Crisis States Research Centre, London); Cordesman (2007); Paul McGeough, 'Winning hearts and minds is keeping the Taliban at bay', *Sydney Morning Herald*, 22 February 2007.

60 Harm Ede Botje, 'We zitten darr goed'; Marina Brouwer, 'Geen zachte aanpak meer in Afghanistan', *Radio Nederland*, 22 December 2006; 'Vredemissie verliest het van wapengeld', *NRC Handelsblad*, 16 November 2006 (courtesy of J. van den Zwan, Crisis States Research Centre, London); 'Reconstruction of Uruzgan is proceeding slowly', *Paktia Ghag*, 18 December 2006; 'Dutch troops won't participate in destruction of poppy crops in Afghanistan', *Associated Press*, 30 January 2007; 'Dutch scale back strategy in southern Afghanistan', *DPA*, 16 February 2007.

61 Michael Evans and Anthony Loyd, 'I will build more and kill less, says NATO's Afghanistan general'; David Wood, 'Afghan war needs troops', *Baltimore Sun*, 7 January 2007; Murray Brewster, 'Taliban to be pushed into the mountains and marginalized: Canadian commander', *Canadian Press*, 7 February 2007; Richard Norton-Taylor, 'Britain switches tactics to undermine the Taliban', *Guardian*, 27 February 2007.

62 'Sud-est de l'Afghanistan: "Ici, c'est la guerre!"', *AFP*, 20 September 2003; Scott Baldauf, 'Small US units lure Taliban into losing battles'; 'SBS shows troops burning Taliban bodies', *Australian Associated Press*, 20 October 2005; Ghufran (2006), pp. 85–94; Cordesman (2006), pp. 15–16; Sardar Ahmad, 'Forces in Afghanistan shift focus to Taliban leaders', *AFP*, 2 January 2007;

Matthew Pennington, 'Afghanistan body count raises skepticism', *Associated Press*, 15 September 2006.

63 For some of these allegations see Senlis Council (2006a), pp. 10 and 43.

64 Syed Saleem Shahzad, 'The vultures are circling', *Asia Times Online*, 13 December 2006; David S. Cloud, 'U.S. airstrikes climb sharply in Afghanistan', *New York Times*, 17 November 2006; David Rohde and Taimoor Shah, 'Strike killed 31 Afghans, NATO finds', *New York Times*, 14 November 2006; Ángeles Espinosa, 'La OTAN lucha en territorio talibán', *El País*, 14 September 2006; 'Civilian casualties trigger anti-govt sentiments', *Pajhwok Afghan News*, 21 August 2006; Cordesman (2006), pp. 15–16; 'Some in southern Afghan province call for ISAF's withdrawal', *RFE/RL Newsline*, 8 November 2006; Kathy Gannon, 'Taliban comeback traced to corruption'; Graeme Smith, 'Inspiring tale of triumph over Taliban not all it seems'; Tom Vanden Brook, 'Bombing campaign intensifies in Afghanistan', *USA Today*, 8 February 2007; UNDSS weekly presentation, 2–8 February 2007.

65 Katzman (2006); Sedra and Middlebrook (2005); for a critical discussion of the governance concept as used by international organisations and diplomats, see Allan (2003).

66 Schiewek (2006), pp. 156–7.

67 Harm Ede Botje, 'We zitten darr goed'; Kate Clark, 'Cash rewards for Taliban fighters'; interview with Afghan journalist returning from the south, Kabul, October 2006; personal communication with foreign diplomat, Kabul, February 2007; Philip G. Smucker, 'Afghanistan's eastern front', *U.S. News & World Report*, 9 April 2007.

68 Senlis Council (2006d), pp. 18, 21; Smith (2005), pp. 7–8; Raymond Whitaker, 'Opium war revealed …'; 'Why are Helmand's districts falling to the Taliban?', *Abadi*, 13 December 2006; 'Key Afghan governor supports spraying of opium poppies, reaching out to Taliban', *Associated Press*, 5 January 2007; Christina Lamb and Michael Smith, 'Sacked Afghan leader blames opium mafia', *Sunday Times*, 10 December 2006; Jeremy Page and Tim Albone, 'Blow for Britain as Helmand's "cleanest" governor is sacked', *The Times*, 9 December 2006; Robert Fox, 'CIA is undermining British war effort, say military chiefs'; Kim Sengupta, 'Helmand governor escapes blast as he battles for job', *Independent*, 13 December 2006.

69 Clark (2002); Bradley Graham and Alan Sipress, 'Reports that Taliban leaders were freed shock, alarm U.S.', *Washington Post*, 10 January 2002; Vernon Loeb and Bradley Graham, 'Rumsfeld says no amnesty for Taliban leader', *Washington Post*, 7 December 2001; Elizabeth Rubin, 'In the land of the Taliban'; Tim McGirk, 'The Taliban on the run'; 'Afghan administration reportedly opens negotiations with Taliban', *RFE/RL Afghanistan Report*, vol. 2, no. 35 (9 October 2003).

70 Interview with Habibullah Mangal, head of Peace Strengthening Commission for Paktia, Gardez, October 2006; interview with Afghan security officer, Kandahar, January 2006; Peter Bergen, 'The Taliban,

"regrouped and rearmed"', *Washington Post*, 10 September 2006; '169 Taliban commanders surrender to gov't in Afghanistan: official', *Xinhuanet*, 28 February 2006.

71 Interview with Habibullah Mangal, head of Peace Strengthening Commission for Paktia, Gardez, October 2006; interview with Afghan security officer, Kandahar, January 2006.

72 Personal communication with UN official, Jalalabad, February 2007; Tim McGirk, 'The Taliban on the run'; interview with Habibullah Mangal, head of Peace Strengthening Commission for Paktia, Gardez, October 2006; interview with Afghan security officer, Kandahar, January 2006; Peter Bergen, 'The Taliban, "regrouped and rearmed"'; Kemp (forthcoming), pp. 12–14; interview with Maulana Obeidullah, Peace Strengthening Commission, Kandahar, January 2006.

73 Peter Bergen, 'The Taliban, "regrouped and rearmed"'; Elizabeth Rubin, 'In the land of the Taliban'; Tim McGirk, 'The Taliban on the run'; interview with Maulana Obeidullah, Peace Strengthening Commission, Kandahar, January 2006; Pamela Constable, 'Afghan city's rebound cut short. Battles between NATO forces, resurgent Taliban make ghost town of Kandahar', *Washington Post*, 19 August 2006; 'Former Deputy Interior Minister killed in S. Afghanistan', *Xinhua*, 15 January 2006; Doug Schmidt, 'Buy Taliban weapons, tribal leader proposes', *Windsor Star*, 8 February 2007.

74 See Giustozzi (2006).

75 'Afghan government opens talks with Taliban in troubled south', *AFP*, 1 September 2003; Syed Saleem Shahzad, 'Taliban deal lights a slow-burning fuse', *Asia Times Online*, 11 February 2006; Les Perreaux, 'NATO urges Afghans to vacate volatile Panjwaii district'; 'ISAF clarifies position on Sangin', *Pajhwok Afghan News*, 27 October 2006; Rahimullah Yusufzai, 'Taliban warn UK troops to vacate Musa Qala district', *The News*, 4 October 2006; Alastair Leithead, 'Can change in Afghan tactics bring peace?', *BBC News*, 17 October 2006; speech of Minister Dadfar Spanta at Chatham House, London, 1 February 2007; Carlotta Gall and Abdul Waheed Wafa, 'Peace accord in provincial Afghanistan dividing opinion', *New York Times*, 2 December 2006; Amin Tarzi, 'Governor of southern Afghan province proposes talks with Taliban', *RFE/RL Newsline*, vol. 11 no. 28 (13 February 2007); personal communication with UN official, Kabul, March 2007.

76 Samad Rohani, 'Whodunit? Violation of truce in Musa Qala', *Pajhwok Afghan News*, 5 December 2006; Ahmed Rashid, 'Britain out of step with NATO allies', *Daily Telegraph*, 6 January 2007; Michael Evans *et al.*, 'Aid effort fails to impress war-weary Afghans'; Declan Walsh, 'Special deals and raw recruits employed to halt the Taliban in embattled Helmand'; James Bays, 'Afghan tribes negotiate with NATO', *Al Jazeera*, 16 November 2006; Tom Coghlan, 'Afghanistan: local leaders offered the chance to recruit their own police force', *Daily Telegraph*, 23 January 2007; Syed Saleem Shahzad, 'Afghanistan's highway to hell'; Carlotta Gall and Taimoor Shah, 'Afghan town is overrun by Taliban', *New York Times*, 3 February 2007; 'Taliban

appears to reverse position on deal over southern Afghan', *Afghan Islamic Press*, 6 February 2007; Murray Brewster, 'Taliban to be pushed into the mountains and marginalized: Canadian commander'; Christina Lamb, 'Karzai bids for peace in furore with London', *Sunday Times*, 11 February 2007; Abdul Waheed Wafa and Carlotta Gall, 'Town's elders plead for help with Taliban', *New York Times*, 26 February 2007; personal communications with UN and British officials.

77 Shaheen Sehbai, 'Bush adopts Musharraf's policy in Afghanistan', *The News*, 4 October 2006.

78 Tim Albone and Claire Billet, 'Ruined poppy farmers join ranks with the Taleban', *The Times*, 27 February 2007; Richard Norton-Taylor, 'Britain switches tactics to undermine the Taliban'.

79 Gethin Chamberlain, 'US military: Afghan leaders steal half of all aid', *Sunday Telegraph*, 28 January 2007; personal communications with NGO and UN staff, Afghanistan 2003–6.

80 See for example Hammes (2006), p. 230, who is, however, one of the most articulate and sophisticated of these analysts.

81 Long (2006), pp. 72–3.

82 On the current debate concerning this topic, see Lister and Nixon (2006).

CONCLUSION

It has been argued that excluding the Taliban from the negotiations in Bonn was a mistake which is at the roots of the subsequent insurgency.[1] Whether there was ever a real chance of including the Taliban in the Bonn process is not clear. The Movement was in a state of disarray at the end of 2001 and it would not have been in a position to win significant representation in the new Transitional Administration, the more so given the strenuous opposition of other Afghan parties and groups. The emergence of a hard-core Taliban opposition, therefore, was probably inevitable. It has also been argued, particularly within the UN,[2] that if the Karzai administration had been keener to cultivate the support of the clergy, large sections of it would not have supported the Taliban. Indeed, President Karzai at times took initiatives aimed in that direction, such as when he appointed ultra-conservative Mawlawi Fazel Haq Shinwari as head of the Supreme Court in 2002, when he sponsored plans by the Council of Ulema to launch its own television station, when he announced the creation of a 'moral police' in 2006, or when he created 500 positions within the Ministry of Hajj and Endowments for Ulema to be on the government's paybook. However, in the context of international intervention in Afghanistan and given the very conservative leanings of the majority of the clergy, it is unlikely that Karzai could ever have gone far enough to appease the latter without deeply upsetting some of his foreign allies. In the absence of a political strategy to bring the clergy closer to the government, the only alternative would have been a massive investment in patronage. Given the sheer size of the clergy (200,000–300,000), including all or most of them on the government payroll might only have been feasible with large-scale support from abroad. Then, elders and tribal leaders too would also have demanded government support, with obvious consequences in terms of financial burden. The resulting inflationary process would have forced the government periodically to increase hand-outs and state salaries, in a vicious cycle which inevitably would have tested the patience of even the most committed donor. Finally, reaching out to the village clerics and incorporating them in a state-sponsored patronage system would probably have resulted in government-sponsored clerics moving to the towns and once again leaving a vacuum in the villages, which could have been filled by the opposition.[3]

Although the insurgency cannot be described in terms of a rural jacquerie against changes imposed from an urban-based government, there are elements of rural revolt which contributed to make the insurgency possible. The foreign-educated élites that made up part of the Afghan cabinet and much of the top ministerial staff were not well equipped to communicate with the remote countryside, or to understand the processes going on there. The reverse is also true, as the rural population had little understanding of the processes going on in Kabul and of the rationale and technicalities of foreign intervention. Nonetheless, it was more than simply a cultural and communication gap. Different and often opposed interests were at stake. The Kabul-based élites wanted to bring the countryside back under some form of central control and used a number of approaches to obtain that, including allying with local strongmen and empowering them as administrators. This attitude was in line with the policies of the Afghan state since at least the nineteenth century, but in the context of the post-2001 period it proved to be hardly sustainable. The emergence of an increasingly politically conscious and ambitious clergy and its attempts to mobilise dissatisfied villagers had been going on amid many ups and downs for over 150 years, dating back to the First Anglo-Afghan War. The crisis of Afghan rural society has not been the subject of many studies, but it can be assumed that the doubling of the population between 1978 and 2002 and the loss of much agricultural land and livestock during the wars of that period intensified it. Hence the rural population and recent immigrants in the cities were likely to become receptive to criticism of the government, of its foreign backers and of their local allies once the original expectations of generous hand-outs and rapid development were not met. Finally, the consensus on the value of Afghanistan as a buffer state among regional powers had been in crisis since 1947 and was well defunct by 2001, creating the conditions for external support to internal opposition. The old model of the Afghan state could hardly survive in the new conditions.

If a clergy-supported and Pakistan-based insurgency was probably inevitable in practice, what could possibly have been avoided was the mobilisation of large constituencies by the remnants of the 'old Taliban' in many parts of southern and south-eastern Afghanistan. In 2002–3 a de-patrimolialised subnational administration could probably have removed one of the main causes of the alliance between the clergy, the militants and the villagers, that is abusive and factionalised local authorities. This could have been a key contribution to preventing the insurgency from escalating from a nuisance to a major problem. The situation, of course, was different at the end of 2006, as the Taliban had by then firmly established themselves in many areas. The alliance between the insurgents and sections of the village population was also favoured by the foolish promises initially made by officials of international organisations, NGOs and government development agencies, who went much beyond what could realistically be offered and even more so beyond what could be delivered, given the conditions of the infrastructure and of the administration. As a result international intervention in Afghanistan was caught between a 'revolution of rising expectations', which they unwittingly encouraged, and the inability to even remotely match them (see 6.5 *Strategy*).

The option of ending the war through negotiations still existed in 2007, although the negotiating leverage of the Taliban had dramatically increased by then, while that of their adversaries had greatly declined. Despite the claims by diplomats and military commanders that no negotiations were possible with the Taliban,[4] contacts seem to have occurred and might occur again in the future, although an eventual success appears a tall order, given the huge disparity of views and ideologies between would-be partners in the negotiations. However, if it was true, as this author has speculated (see 1.3 *The role of Pakistan*), that Pakistan has control over the delivery of support to the Taliban, then Islamabad might play a key role in successful negotiations by simply threatening to cut off the Taliban's lifeline. The Pakistani authorities, of course, would demand to be rewarded with substantial concessions. For the Pakistani leadership the loss of influence over Afghanistan was a major blow both psychologically and in terms of image, given how much had been invested in establishing control over Afghanistan as Pakistan's best (first?) success story in foreign policy. After a half-hearted and ill-fated attempt to create a 'Taliban party' as a vehicle for obtaining some power-sharing in Kabul (see 3.1 *Cohesiveness of the Taliban*), the temptation to exploit Kabul's obvious weaknesses and force the northern neighbour to the negotiating table in a position of inferiority must have been strong in Islamabad. The Durand Line has been mentioned often during 2006 as a key bone of contention between Afghanistan and Pakistan,[5] but recognising the Durand Line would be very costly for any Afghan government and would not necessarily suffice to appease the Pakistanis, as a future Afghan government might still raise the issue again. In the end, any agreement will have to revolve around Pakistan's implicit demand of a significant stake in Afghan government, which likely implies control over at least a key ministry by trusted partners. Such a demand might be difficult to swallow for a government, like Karzai's in 2006, partly built around Pashtun nationalist circles. It would certainly have been unacceptable in 2002, when the Transitional Administration exuded self-confidence and was certain of US support. During 2006 the emergence of many former members of Hizb-i Islami as one of the key components of the cabinet and more in general in the state structure appeared to hint at the direction of a possible solution to the dilemma. Hizb-i Islami maintained good relations with both Pakistan and Iran, but some of its former members incorporated in Karzai's entourage had also accumulated a substantial dose of credibility among Karzai's foreign patrons. However, if the Pakistanis were granted such a stake in Kabul, other regional powers such as India, Iran and Russia would likely also demand similar concessions. If a balance could be stricken, Afghanistan would return to its old status of buffer state.

As long as time is not ripe for a negotiated solution, and short of some major change in the counter-insurgency approach, or in the structure of the Afghan state, the war might go on indefinitely. As of March 2007 the strategic situation was one of stalemate, with a slight advantage for the Taliban. The insurgents were still unable to challenge the ISAF and the US forces on the battlefield, but the latter were unable to check the Taliban's spread across Afghanistan's territory and were failing to maintain control of the population, the most important aim in counter-insurgent warfare. If the Taliban and their allies succeed in spreading to the northern half of Afghanistan, then the ISAF would face a strategic conundrum. Unable to muster larger numbers of troops and given the doubtful inclination to fight of many of its member contingents, the ISAF might turn out to be unable to cope. The main risk for the Taliban seemed one of failing to stand up to the claims made during 2006, that a countrywide jihad was starting and that the war had progressed to a new stage of strategic challenge or even of 'final offensive'.

In terms of mounting a credible insurgency in Afghanistan, the Taliban faced major challenges in 2002. Their original rank-and-file was largely demoralised by the unexpectedly quick collapse of the regime under the attack of the United States and the internal opposition. Moreover, they had little experience in organising a large scale insurgency. Finally, and perhaps most important, the population was tired of war and wanted peace and was also buying into promises of rapid reconstruction and development once Afghanistan rejoined the international community. Despite these constraints, whether by their own efforts or more likely with the help of international jihadists and of at least some elements of the Pakistani state, after a slow start in

2002 they succeeded in mounting a credible threat to the government in Kabul. By skilfully exploiting local grievances against the government and against local authorities, they successfully mobilised much of the southern population against the government and foreign contingents and forced a collapse of the structure of government in whole provinces. Their human losses were heavy but although precise figures will never be available they do not seem to have been out of line with the casualty rates experienced by other insurgent movements in the 1950s–1990s when fighting against superior armies supported by locally recruited troops. For what this type of statistic is worth, according to available figures in Vietnam (1963–75) the casualty ratio was around one to one, when losses from all actors and killed and wounded are included. During the Malayan emergency, it was two to one in favour of the British and their local allies. In Algeria it might have been closer to four to one, while for the Taliban this author estimates it at three to one in favour of their adversaries (see 6.1 *International actors*). Insurgencies can do much worse than that, as shown by the Mau-Mau in Kenya, where the ratio was around fifteen to one against them. The Taliban performed particularly badly in direct engagements, where their casualty ratio might have been similar to that of the Mau-Mau, but managed to reduce greatly the casualty ratio through the use of relatively new insurgency techniques such as IEDs and suicide bombing.

The Taliban subordinated tactics to a strategy. The latter also happened to be mostly sound and consistent in identifying the weaknesses of the enemy and focusing on those. The Taliban did commit a number of blunders, but these were the result of the need to test new tactics and potential weaknesses of the enemy. In other words, the Taliban showed that they could learn from their mistakes, or at least that they had good advisors and were listening to them. However, the Taliban's struggle was also marked by clear differences from the 'classic' insurgencies of the 1940–1980s, Maoist or otherwise. If it is true, as argued in section 4.11, that the Neo-Taliban's strategy was turning into a global jihadist one, then what the leadership wanted was not to expel the 'foreigners' as quickly as possible, but keep them in and wear them out, as was being done in Iraq. That is the opposite of what a classic 'war of national liberation' would have tried to do. Victory was to be achieved at the global level or not be achieved at all.

If they had been fighting a war of national liberation, the greatest strategic limitation of the insurgents would have been their confinement to a single portion of the country, at least until 2006. However, as a global jihadist insurgency, the Neo-Taliban were not affected as much by this limitation. Outside the southern region, the Taliban and their advisors relied only partially on direct infiltration to establish their presence, often opting to use various incentives to mobilise local insurgents, particularly in areas remote from the border. Hence the importance of creating a 'Tet effect' with highly visible initiatives such as the intensified fighting around Kandahar in the summer of 2006, hoping that this would help them mobilise new allies. Undoubtedly, they did succeed in attracting the attention of the Afghan public and in shaking the faith in the ability of the foreign contingents to maintain control of the situation. A substantial number of pragmatically minded but small 'conflict entrepreneurs' seem to have responded to the call of the Taliban, generating low-level violence in many areas. As of March 2007, however, it was still difficult to say whether this would suffice to convince major new players to enter the conflict on the Taliban's side. Indirect mobilisation is cheap and implies little risk-taking for the centre of the insurgency, but it comes at a price. Whether joined by a multitude of small conflict entrepreneurs or by a few large military-political leaders, the insurgency would face a challenge in terms of coordination and control. If the insurgency continues to spread both geographically and politically, it will likely start to resemble more and more the Afghan jihad of the 1980s, which was a chaotic movement with no effective overall leadership. The main tool of control will increasingly become the monopoly over sources of funding, which in turn could be successfully maintained only if endorsed and actively supported by the Pakistani authorities and other regional players. Difficult command and control would, however, not prevent the spread of chaos and insecurity throughout the country.

Although their tactical skills remained weak throughout 2002–6, they made 'creative' use of the modest human resources available. Indeed, compared to the 'old Taliban' of 1994–2001, the insurgents of 2002– deserve to be described as *Neo*-Taliban. If the Kuran and the Kalashnikov continued to describe well the ethos of the Movement, as they did for the old Taliban, the Neo-Taliban developed a passion for the new technologies completely at odds with the ostracism showed in the old days. It is not clear whether the top ranks of the Movement, who played a key role in 1994–2001 too, also personally adopted the new technologies or whether they only allowed their subordinates to use them. The first, shy attempts to court educated constituencies also seemed to hint at the fact that the Taliban might be willing to amend their earlier stance. The internationalisation of the Taliban is a third feature marking the Movement as *'neo'*. The influence of the Arab jihadists was evident in this case. But does the adoption of new technologies and of international jihadist rhetoric imply a more substantial change? What we have been seeing in 2002–6 is probably a process of transition, from an ultra-orthodox and narrowly focused interpretation of Islam towards an ultra-conservative but more 'political' and 'internationalist' interpretation. However, the 'ideological' dimension of the Neo-Taliban does not seem well defined yet. After all, the jihadist component started emerging strongly only in 2005 and it is unlikely that it found deeper roots within the old leadership, who might have adopted it somewhat pragmatically. This pattern of adaptation could still take different paths. The Neo-Taliban could become fully radicalised and incorporated into a global jihadist perspective, or in the event of a negotiated deal their evolution could boil down towards something resembling the Islamic parties of Pakistan, which combine 'reactionary' attitudes with, for example, the acceptance of electoral competition.

The counter-insurgency effort by contrast has been characterised by the extremely inefficient use of the considerable financial and technological resources available. Continuous changes in the military strategy prevented the achievement of durable results, while the high expenditure on strengthening Afghan forces had yielded comparatively modest results by 2006. By all standards the formation of the ANA was a slow process: almost five years after the start of the training programme, the army still had a deployable force of less than 20,000 men (see 6.4 *Afghan National Army*). Just to mention a single example, in a similar situation of having (or choosing) to rebuild an army from scratch and immediately facing an insurgency, the Sandinista government in Nicaragua organised an army of 18,000 men in less than a year (1979–80), without receiving much help from outside. Although the effectiveness of this army was limited, once it started receiving substantial help from abroad (Cuba and Soviet Union) in 1982, it became able to control the insurgency of the Contras in just one year, over which period its strength rose to 24,000.[6] Moreover, the Sandinista army was fighting without embedded mentors or trainers and without the help of foreign military contingents or air forces.

Intelligence gathering and analysis was also far from being up to the task. There was little consistent effort at identifying the weak spots of the enemy and focusing on those. The approach to counter-insurgency was mainly reactive and defensive. The government showed little interest in what was going on in remote parts of the country, being mainly concerned with securing the cities, their surrounding areas and the highways. Understandably US and Afghan officials often issued propaganda statements, as happens in any war, announcing continuous defeats of the Neo-Taliban and imminent victory. These statements were likely often motivated by career and image concerns, exacerbated by the short rotation time and by President Karzai's habit of frequently reshuffling government positions. What is worrying, however, is that often they seemed inclined to believe their own propaganda. Only once the Taliban had started approaching Kandahar and the highway linking it with Kabul and Herat did the government start taking the insurgency seriously. The efforts of both the Karzai administration and its international sponsors could be characterised as 'too little, too late':

- when in 2006 Karzai proposed Peace Jirgas to mobilise tribal leadership against the Taliban, the tribal elders which the jirgas were supposed to mobilise had already lost much power and control to the insurgents, as well as faith in the government;
- concern for governance issues emerged only at a stage where the situation on the ground had already been compromised;
- the half-hearted formation of village militias (auxiliary police), which could have prevented the infiltration of the Taliban at an earlier stage, was only proposed in the south in mid-2006, when the Taliban already had sufficient military strength to threaten to overwhelm them; it was never implemented;
- the decision to bring more development and aid to the southern regions was only taken once the insurgency had taken control of the countryside, greatly complicating the task.

It is also worth noting that patronage-based counter-insurgency and improved governance were at odds, as were reconstruction and fighting tactics heavily reliant on firepower. In the end, whereas the Taliban leadership was doggedly pursuing a strategy of destabilisation, neither the United States nor the Afghan government ever had a consistent strategy lasting more than a year. There was evidently a problem of weak political leadership: the Bush Administration was not interested in Afghanistan and left the direction of its local political affairs to its Ambassador, Zalmay Khalilzad, and of military affairs to the fast-rotating commanders of Task Force 180 or 76. While the US military controlled the ANA, they did not control most militias or the police, a fact which led to weak coordination. The government, apart from not having a military policy, did not have much of a political strategy either. The various initiatives were the result of much talking and lobbying by various actors, chiefly UN agencies, a few foreign embassies, NATO and the US armed forces.

The complex and flawed decisional process resulted in delays and in inconsistent policy making. In some cases, the lack of political will in Kabul to go along with external requests led to the implementation of agreed decisions being further delayed, often by many months. Worse still, under pressure the government would often approve policies and reform initiatives and then pay only lip service to them.

At the beginning of 2007 there were still scant signs that a radical change of direction was about to happen either in Kabul or in Bagram (the US HQ), except for an increased military aggressiveness. The talk was still of separating the mass of 'mercenary' fighters from an isolated leadership and of the virtues of 'development' in healing insurgencies. It was not clear, however, how the 'misled' fighters of southern Afghanistan would be made to see the light, or how patronage was going to be delivered to villages outside government control. From the standpoint of May 2007, the omen was not good; during the first three months of 2007 1,000 insurgency-related deaths were reported, that is twice as many as during the corresponding period of 2006.[7]

koran, kalashnikov and laptop

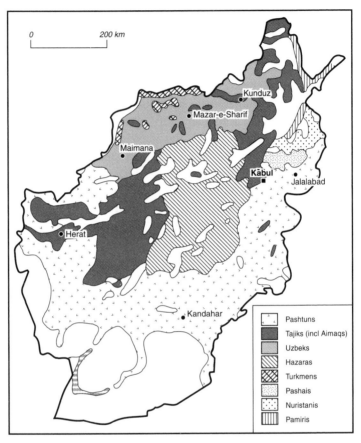

Map 9. Geographical distribution of ethnic groups.

Source: based on maps included in *Le Fait Ethnique en Iran at en Afghanistan*, CNRS 1988.

conclusion

NOTES

1   See, among others, former Indian diplomat M.K. Bhadrakumar, 'The Afghan exit strategy', *Asia Times Online*, 19 January 2006.
2   Several times I took part in discussions concerning this issue when serving in UNAMA in 2003–4.
3   Tom Coghlan, 'Fury as Karzai plans return of Taliban's religious police', *Independent*, 17 July 2006; 'Ulema plan to launch TV in Afghanistan; Ulema Council plans to launch Islamic television channel to balance "immoral and un-Islamic" current programs', *Dawn*, 3 May 2005; Amin Tarzi, 'President orders creation of new Afghan Ulama posts', *Radio Free Europe/Radio Liberty*, 8 July 2006.
4   Mike Blanchfield, 'NATO needs to negotiate with some Taliban', *Ottawa Citizen*, 18 December 2006.
5   Rubin (2007); Middlebrook and Miller (2006).
6   Horton (1998), pp. 121–2.
7   Denis D. Gray, 'NATO pushes to improve Afghan army', *Associated Press*, 25 April 2007.

BIBLIOGRAPHY

Afghan Independent Human Rights Commission (2004), *Annual Report 2003/4*, Kabul.
—— (2005), *Annual Report 2004/5*, Kabul.
Allan, Nigel J.R. (2003), 'Rethinking Governance in Afghanistan', *Journal of International Affairs*, vol. 56, no. 1.
Amnesty International (2003), *Afghanistan: Police Reconstruction Essential for the Protection of Human Rights*, ASA 11/003/2003, London.
Baily, John (2001), *Can You Stop the Birds Singing?*, Copenhagen: Freemuse.
Barno, David W. (2006), 'Challenges in Fighting a Global Insurgency', *Parameters*, summer.
Belasco, Amy (2006), *The Cost of Iraq, Afghanistan, and Other Global War on Terror Operations since 9/11*, Washington, DC: Congressional Research Service.
Cassidy, Robert M. (2003), *Russia in Afghanistan and Chechnya: Military Strategic Culture and the Paradoxes of Asymmetric Conflict*, Carlisle Barracks, PA: Strategic Studies Institute.
Clark, Gen. Wesley (2002), 'An Army of One? In the War on Terrorism, Alliances are not an Obstacle to Victory. They're the Key to it', *Washington Monthly*, September.
Clutterbuck, Richard (1985), *Conflict and Violence in Singapore and Malaysia: 1945–1983*, Boulder, CO: Westview.
Coll, Steve (2004), *Ghost Wars*, New York: Penguin.
Connell, Michael and Alireza Nader (2006), *Iranian Objectives in Afghanistan: Any Basis for Collaboration with the United States?*, A Project Iran Workshop, Alexandria, VA: The CNA Corporation, <http://www.princeton.edu/~lisd/publications/

finn_Iran_Afghanistan.pdf>.

Cordesman, Anthony (2006), 'Press Briefing on Afghanistan', Washington, DC: The Center for Strategic and International Studies.

—— (2007), *Winning in Afghanistan: The Challenges and the Response*, Washington, DC: The Center for Strategic and International Studies.

Davis, Anthony (2002), 'Recent Violence Obscures Deeper Threats for Afghanistan', *Jane's Intelligence Review*, October.

—— (2003), 'Afghan Opposition Gains Coherence', *Jane's Terrorism & Security Monitor*, May.

Dixit, Aabha (n.d.), *Soldiers of Islam: Origins, Ideology and Strategy of the Taliban*, New Delhi: Institute for Defence Studies and Analysis, <http://www.idsa-india.org/an-aug-2.html>.

Dobbins, James (2003), *America's Role in Nation-building: From Germany to Iraq*, Santa Monica, CA: Rand.

Dobbins, James *et al.* (2005), *The UN's Role in Nation-building: From the Congo to Iraq*, Santa Monica, CA: Rand.

Dorronsoro, Gilles (2000), *Pakistan and the Taliban: State Policy, Religious Networks and Political Connections*, Paris: CERI, <http://www.ceri-sciencespo.com/archive/octo00/artgd.pdf>.

—— (2005), *Revolution Unending*, London: Hurst.

Dyke, John R. and John R. Crisafulli (2006), *Unconventional Counter-Insurgency in Afghanistan*, Monterey, CA: Naval Postgraduate School.

Erben, Peter (n.d.), *Election Assessment: 2005 Elections – A Milestone for Afghanistan*, Washington, DC: IFES, <http://www.ifes.org/ctpcg-project.html?projectid=afghanmilestone>.

Gallis, Paul (2006), *NATO in Afghanistan: A Test of the Transatlantic Alliance*, Washington, DC: Congressional Research Service.

Gerges, Fawaz A. (2006), *Journey of the Jihadist*, Orlando, FL: Harcourt.

Ghufran, Nasreen (2006), 'Afghanistan in 2005: The Challenges of Reconstruction', *Asian Survey*, vol. 46, no. 1.

bibliography

Giustozzi, Antonio (2003), 'Military Reform in Afghanistan' in M. Sedra (ed.), *Afghanistan: Assessing the Progress of Security Sector Reforms*, Bonn International Center for Conversion.

—— (2004), *'Good' State vs. 'Bad' Warlords? A Critique of State-Building Strategies in Afghanistan*, Working Paper 51, London: Crisis States Research Centre.

—— (2006), *'Tribes' and Warlords in Southern Afghanistan, 1980–2005*, Working Paper Series 2, no. 7, London: Crisis States Research Centre.

—— (2007a), 'The Privatizing of War and Security in Afghanistan: Future or Dead End?', *The Economics of Peace and Security Journal*, vol. 2, no. 1.

—— (2007b), 'Auxiliary Force or National Army? Afghanistan's "ANA" and the Counter-Insurgency Effort, 2002–2006', *Small Wars and Insurgencies*, vol. 18, no.1 (March).

—— (forthcoming), 'The Inverted Cycle: Kabul and the Strongmen's Competition for Control over Kandahar, 2001–2006', *Central Asian Survey*, forthcoming.

Hammes, Thomas X. (2005), 'Insurgency: Modern Warfare Evolves into a Fourth Generation', *Forum* (National Defense University), no. 214.

—— (2006), *The Sling and the Stone*, St Paul, MN: Zenith.

Harpviken, Kristian Berg *et al.* (2002), *Afghanistan and Civil Society*, Bergen: CMI.

Horton, Lynn (1998), *Peasants in Arms: War and Peace in the Mountains of Nicaragua, 1979–1994*, Athens, OH: Ohio University Centre for International Studies.

Human Rights Watch (2006), *Lessons in Terror Attacks on Education in Afghanistan*, vol. 18, no. 6.

'Increasing Afghan IED Threat Gives Forces Cause for Concern', *Jane's Intelligence Review*, August 2006.

Interagency Assessment of Afghanistan Police Training and Readiness (2006), Washington, DC: Offices of Inspector General of the Departments of State and Defense.

International Crisis Group (2003a), *Afghanistan: Judicial Reform and Transitional Justice*, Asia Report no. 45.

—— (2003b), *Disarmament and Reintegration in Afghanistan*, Asia Report no. 65.

—— (2006a), *Countering Afghanistan's Insurgency: No Quick Fixes*, Asia Report no. 123.

—— (2006b), *Pakistan's Tribal Areas: Appeasing the Militants*, Asia Report no. 125.

Jandora, John J. (2005), 'Factoring Culture', *Joint Force Quarterly*, no. 39, 4th quarter.

Jelsma, Martin *et al.* (2006), *Losing Ground Drug Control and War in Afghanistan*, Debate Papers no. 15 (December), Amsterdam: Transnational Institute.

Johnson, Thomas H. and M. Chris Mason (2007), 'Understanding the Taliban and Insurgency in Afghanistan', *Orbis*, winter.

Jones, Seth G. (2006), 'Averting Failure in Afghanistan', *Survival*, no. 1.

Karimi, Farah (2006), *Slagveld Afghanistan*, Amsterdam: Nieuw Amsterdam.

Katzman, Kenneth (2006), *Afghanistan: Post-War Governance, Security, and U.S. Policy*, Washington, DC: Congressional Research Service.

Kemp, Robert (forthcoming), 'Counterinsurgency in Eastern Afghanistan' in *Countering Insurgency and Promoting Democracy*, Washington, DC: Council for Emerging National Security Affairs.

Lister, Sarah and Hamish Nixon (2006), *Provincial Governance Structures in Afghanistan: From Confusion to Vision?*, Kabul: AREU.

Long, Austin (2006), *On 'Other War': Lessons from Five Decades of RAND Counterinsurgency Research*, Santa Monica, CA: Rand.

Maley, William (1998), 'Interpreting the Taliban' in W. Maley (ed.), *Fundamentalism Reborn?*, London: Hurst.

Marzban, Omid (2006), 'The Foreign Makeup of Afghan Suicide Bombers', *Terrorism Monitor*, vol. 3, no. 7 (21 February).

bibliography

McCaffrey, Barry (2006), *Academic Report: Trip to Afghanistan and Pakistan*, United States Military Academy.

Middlebrook, Peter J. and Sharon M. Miller (2006), *All along the Watch Tower: Bringing Peace to the Afghan–Pakistan Border*, New York: Middlebrook & Miller.

Ministry of Defence of Afghanistan (2002), *Main Principles and Guidelines for the Creation of the New Afghan National Army and for the Collection of Arms*, Kabul.

Naylor, Sean D. (2006), 'A Stronger Taliban Lies Low, Hoping the U.S. Will Leave Afghanistan', *Armed Forces Journal*, no. 2.

Nivat, Anne (2006), *Islamistes: comment ils nous voient*, Paris: Fayard, 2006.

Pirnie, Bruce R. *et al.* (2005), *Beyond Close Air Support: Forging a New Air-Ground Partnership*, Santa Monica, CA: Rand.

Rahmani, Waliullah (2006a), 'Afghan Authorities Apprehend Leaders of Kabul Suicide Cell', *Terrorism Monitor*, vol. 3, no. 39.

—— (2006b), 'Helmand Province and the Afghan Insurgency', *Terrorism Monitor* (Jamestown Foundation), vol. 4, no. 6.

Rashid, Ahmed (1999), 'The Taliban: Exporting Extremism', *Foreign Affairs*, November/December.

—— (2000), *Taliban*, London: IB Tauris.

Rothstein, Hy S. (2006), *Afghanistan and the Troubled Future of Unconventional Warfare*, Annapolis, MD: Naval Institute Press.

Roy, Olivier (1998), 'Has Islamism a Future in Afghanistan?' in W. Maley (ed.), *Fundamentalism Reborn?*, London: Hurst.

—— (2000), *Pakistan and the Taliban*, Paris: CERI, October <http://www.ceri-sciencespo.com/archive/octo00/artor.pdf>.

—— (2002), *Islamic Radicalism in Afghanistan and Pakistan*, Writenet Paper no. 06/2001, Geneva: UNHCR.

Rubin, Barnett R. (2006), *Afghanistan's Uncertain Transition from Turmoil to Normalcy*, CSR no. 12, Washington, DC: The Center For Preventive Action (Council On Foreign Relations).

—— (2007), 'Saving Afghanistan', *Foreign Affairs*, January/February.

Schiewek, Eckart (2006), 'Efforts to Curb Political Violence in Afghanistan' in Pervaiz Iqbal Cheema, Maqsudul Hasan Nuri and Ahmad Rashid Malik (eds), *Political Violence and Terrorism in South Asia*, Islamabad Political Research Institute, pp. 150–71.

Sedra, Mark and Peter Middlebrook (2005), 'Revisioning the International Compact for Afghanistan', *Foreign Policy In Focus*, 2 November.

Senlis Council (2006a), *Afghanistan Five Years Later: The Return of the Taliban*, London.

—— (2006b), *An Assessment of the Hearts and Minds Campaign in Southern Afghanistan*, London.

—— (2006c), *Canada in Kandahar: No Peace to Keep. A Case Study of the Military Coalitions in Southern Afghanistan*, London.

—— (2006d), *Field Notes. Afghanistan Insurgency Assessment. The Signs of an Escalating Crisis. Insurgency in the Provinces of Helmand, Kandahar and Nangarhar*, London.

—— (2006e), *Helmand at War: The Changing Nature of the Insurgency in Southern Afghanistan and its Effects on the Future of the Country*, London.

—— (2007), *Countering the Insurgency in Afghanistan: Losing Friends and Making Enemies*, London.

Shahzad, Syed Saleem (2007), *Pakistan, the Taliban and Dadullah*, Briefing no. 3, Bradford: Pakistan Security Research Unit.

Smith, Ben (2005), *Afghanistan: Where Are We?*, Camberley: Conflict Studies Research Centre, British Defence Academy.

Taber, Robert (1965), *The War of the Flea: A Study of Guerrilla Warfare: Theory and Practice*, New York: L. Stuart.

Tahir, Muhammad (2007), 'Iranian Involvement in Afghanistan', *Terrorism Monitor* (Jamestown Foundation), vol. 5, no. 1 (18 January).

Trives, Sébastien (2006), 'Afghanistan: réduire l'insurrection. Le cas du Sud-Est', *Politique étrangère*, no. 1.

van der Schriek, Daan (2005), 'Recent Developments in Waziristan',

bibliography

Terrorism Monitor (Jamestown Foundation), vol. 3, no. 5.

Weinbaum, Marvin G. (2004), *Nation Building in Afghanistan: Impediments, Lessons, and Prospects*, paper prepared for a conference on 'Nation-Building: Beyond Afghanistan and Iraq', sponsored by The School of Advanced International Studies, 13 April 2004.

Wright, Joanna (2006a), 'Taliban Insurgency Shows Signs of Enduring Strength', *Jane's Intelligence Review*, October.

—— (2006b), 'The Changing Structure of the Afghan Opium Trade', *Jane's Intelligence Review*, 9 September.

INDEX

index

index